A Message in the Sky

The Protoevangelium of James states:

> **21. And behold, Joseph prepared to go forth to Judea. And there took place a great tumult in Bethlehem of Judea. For there came wise men saying "Where is the [new-born] king of the Jews? For we have seen his star in the east and have come to worship him."**

Throughout history—biblical and non-biblical—The Star of Bethlehem has claimed a significant place in astronomical and religious theories. But who wrote the true story of the world's most amazing celestial phenomenon? And what facts authenticate the actual existence of such a star?

One by one, David Hughes ingeniously provides far-reaching and conclusive answers to these questions and many more to bring you the truth of the star of wonder—

THE STAR OF BETHLEHEM

THE STAR
OF BETHLEHEM

An Astronomer's Confirmation

David Hughes

PUBLISHED BY POCKET BOOKS NEW YORK

POCKET BOOKS, a Simon & Schuster division of
GULF & WESTERN CORPORATION
1230 Avenue of the Americas, New York, N.Y. 10020

Published by arrangement with Walker and Company
Library of Congress Catalog Card Number: 79-88870

ISBN: 0-671-83679-X

First Pocket Books printing December, 1980

10 9 8 7 6 5 4 3 2 1

POCKET and colophon are trademarks of Simon & Schuster.

Printed in the U.S.A.

Contents

Illustrations

to Sandra my wife
and in memory of my parents

ACKNOWLEDGMENTS

The author would like to thank David Davies, the editor of *Nature*, and Mary Lindley, on the editorial staff of *Nature*, for kindling the flame of this investigation; and all those friends and relatives who, by their continued inquiries as to the progress of the book, stopped the fire from going out.

The author and publisher are grateful to Lutterworth Press and The Westminster Press for permission to quote from *The New Testament Apocrypha*, volume I, © translation Lutterworth Press, 1963.

Introduction

What was the star of Bethlehem? Did it really exist? What does it tell us about the birth of Jesus? These questions have been asked throughout the ages and numerous answers have been given over the course of many centuries.

Even now the star that was said to herald the birth of the greatest religious leader the world has ever known is the most popular star in the heavens, appearing every year on millions of Christmas cards, twinkling above stables, illuminating shepherds and leading an assortment of wise men on camels across all kinds of desert.

Above all, the star of Bethlehem is a mystery. If it did exist, then it is one of the most amazing phenomena ever witnessed by man. The flow of serious scientific works and popular articles on the star goes on unabated. Theories vary from a nova or supernova to a comet, from a conjunction of Saturn and Jupiter in the constellation Pisces to Venus, quite apart from other explanations such as a fireball, zodiacal light, ball lightning and the variable star Mira. Even the possibility that the star was simply a legend has to be taken seriously. At the other extreme, an explanation in terms of a miracle beyond the scope of science also has its advocates.

This book is an investigation into the astronomical, biblical, historical, religious and astrological evidence about the star. It asks a whole series of questions and works out the answers as far as possible. Why, for example, was the star only mentioned in Matthew's gospel and the Protoevangelium of St. James but not in Luke's gospel? How did the star appear twice? What is the meaning of its rising in the east? Why did Herod the Great and all the other inhabitants of Jerusalem fail to see it?

Numerous other questions arise. Who were the wise men and what sort of people were they? Were they Median priests of Zoroastrianism? Where did they come from—Babylon, Arabia, Persia, or somewhere else? Why did they make the journey? Why has tradition changed the Magi into kings and reduced their number from twelve to three? What was the year, month and date of the birth of Jesus? How can the date of the taxation decree sent out by Caesar Augustus, the death of Herod the Great, the birth of John the Baptist and the time of the ministry and crucifixion of Christ throw light on this problem? Is the fact that the shepherds were in the fields at the time significant? Why does the western church celebrate the birth of Christ on 25 December, the date of the pagan feast of the unconquered Sun? Why did the eastern church pick 6 January?

If, as I shall argue, the triple conjunction of Saturn and Jupiter in the constellation of Pisces is the most probable contender, what are the scientific facts weighing against the rival theories? What are these other celestial manifestations and how do their appearance and characteristics fit in with the evidence? There is also the question of the astrological meaning of the star. How relevant is Babylonian and Jewish astrology?

From the Bible we know a great deal about the life and character of Jesus Christ. Some astrologers have used the events in his life and his character traits to build up a retrospective horoscope, working backwards to deduce the positions of the Sun and planets among the star signs when Christ was born. This gives a different, but unreliable, perspective to the birthday of Jesus.

Many other circumstances surrounding the star need investigation too. What, for instance, was life like in Bethlehem and Jerusalem at the time of Christ, around 8 BC? What kind of ruler was Herod? Why was the flight of the holy family into Egypt not only possible but also probable? How did the Romans come into the picture? How did they collect taxes?

What was the historical sequence of events, from the wise men in their own country, looking at the sky for a sign, to the young Jesus with his family in the carpenter's shop in Nazareth?

When it comes to the idea of the star as just a legend or a miracle, we must ask ourselves how significant were the reported occurrences of other celestial phenomena at the birth and death of kings and gods in ancient times. Did wise men visit other rulers at that time? A great deal of our evidence comes from biblical accounts, but we must ask how accurate they are in terms of science and astronomy. If we are to attach so much weight to what the Bible says about the star of Bethlehem, how do we square this with the presence of midrash or legend elsewhere in the Bible?

These and many other questions will be dealt with in the following chapters. By going along a trail of detection we shall arrive at a definite solution to the star of Bethlehem mystery.

THE STAR
OF BETHLEHEM

1

The sacred star

The Star of Bethlehem is irrevocably linked with the birth of Jesus Christ and it is the Bible itself that can give us the first clues in our attempt to solve the mystery of what the star really was.

The main account of the star is found in the gospel of St. Matthew and in the Authorized Version it begins (Matthew 2:1-2):

> Now when Jesus was born in Bethlehem of Judea in the days of Herod the King, behold there came wise men from the east to Jerusalem, saying, Where is he that is born King of the Jews? For we have seen his star in the east, and are come to worship him.

This passage tells us a great deal. First we are told where Jesus was born—Bethlehem of Judea, a small town in the mountains about 6 miles south of Jerusalem. We are given an important clue as to when Jesus was born—in the days of Herod the King. It is highly probable that King Herod died some time before 11 April 4 BC, so that Jesus must have been born before then. As for the wise men, or Magi, we are not told how many there were, only that the number was more than one, and, we are given the rather vague information that they came from the east. Furthermore, as they did not know that Jesus was born in Bethlehem, they journeyed in search of him to Jerusalem, the capital of Palestine and the city where King Herod resided.

The words "his star" as opposed to, for example, "a star" indicate that the wise men thought one star was important and that this star was associated with the King of the Jews. It is significant that the text speaks of not just the birth of a King of the Jews, but *the* King of the Jews, the king that was awaited not only by Israel but arguably by the whole civilized world at the time. In view of the religious and astronomical leanings of the Magi, this association must have been astrological. The star they saw in the east had a message, a compelling message that was clear enough and urgent enough to make them choose their gifts, organize their caravan of camels and attendants, leave home and travel a distance of well over 500 miles to pay homage to—rather than to "worship," as in the Authorized Version—the newborn king. The homage is reminiscent of Genesis 19:1: "And there came two angels to Sodom at even; and Lot sat in the gate of Sodom and Lot seeing them rose up to meet them; and he bowed himself with his face towards the ground." The worshiping of Christ came a long time after the visit of the Magi.

There is no indication that they followed the star to Jerusalem. The implication is that having seen the rising of the star which they associated with the King of the Jews, they had simply come to the capital city of the Jews for more information.

The term "in the east" has been a topic of much discussion and is generally taken to mean much more than that the wise men were "in the east" when they saw the star. Most scholars regard the Authorized Version translation as incorrect. Originally the phrase "in the east" was written *en te anatole,* which is the Greek singular, whereas "the east" is usually expressed as *anatolai* the Greek plural, so that *anatole* does not refer to the location of the wise men when they saw the star. Furthermore, it is unlikely that the Magi would say "in the east" instead of "in our native country," and it is improbable that the author of

Matthew would use plural and singular in two successive verses to mean substantially the same thing. The phrase in the singular also has a more specific meaning than the translation "in the eastern sky" proposed in a recent paper by Clark, Parkinson and Stephenson. The word *anatole* has a special astronomical significance meaning the acronychal rising. It can also be translated as "rising on high" and was in common use for the Sun. It is most suitable for the acronychal rising. Here the star or planet in question rises in the east just as the sun sets in the west. Astronomically speaking the two bodies are in opposition, and are on opposite sides of the Earth. The star or planet can then be seen throughout the whole night as it moves in an arc from east to west across the sky. Not only is it an astronomically important position, it is also one of the five principal astrological positions that concerned Babylonian astronomers. These positions were carefully calculated for the outer planets Mars, Jupiter and Saturn for many decades into the future and used as a basis for astrological predictions. When a planet was at the acronychal rising position it was regarded as having its maximum influence on worldly events.

The account in the second chapter of St. Matthew's gospel continues, presumably in Herod's palace in Jerusalem:

3. When Herod the king had heard these things, he was troubled, and all Jerusalem with him.
4. And when he had gathered all the chief priests and scribes of the people together, he demanded of them where Christ should be born.
5. And they said unto him, In Bethlehem of Judea: for thus it is written by the prophet,
6. And thou Bethlehem, in the land of Juda, art not the least among the princes of Juda: for out of thee shall come a Governor, that shall rule my people Israel.
7. Then Herod, when he had privily called the

wise men, inquired of them diligently what time
the star appeared.

8. And he sent them to Bethlehem, and said, Go
and search diligently for the young child; and
when ye have found *him*, bring me word again,
that I may come and worship him also.

9. When they had heard the king, they departed;
and lo, the star, which they saw in the east, went
before them, till it came and stood over where the
young child was.

10. When they saw the star, they rejoiced with
exceeding great joy.

11. And when they were come into the house,
they saw the young child with Mary his mother,
and fell down, and worshiped him: and when
they had opened their treasures, they presented
unto him gifts; gold, and frankincense, and myrrh.

12. And being warned of God in a dream that they
should not return to Herod, they departed into
their own country another way.

Herod was well aware of the prophecies in which a
new King was promised to Israel, a King who would
convert the present state of affliction and turmoil into
one of peace. He had lived among the Israelites since
boyhood and had an intimate acquaintance with their
history. Moreover, the rumors of the coming of the
Savior, the Emmanuel, were current not only throughout Israel but also among the neighboring people.
Herod the Great had one burning ambition permeating
his life's work, an ambition he strove to attain without
scruple and without mercy—that of being king. Once
he had obtained kingship he had no other objective in
his later years of rule than to bequeath the kingship
intact to his sons. Earlier in his career he had despised
prophecies, but now they were being brought home to
him forcibly.

It was not so much the report of the Magi that
troubled Herod, it was the stark realization that some

of the old Jewish oracles were about to come true. His position and that of his heirs as Governor of Jerusalem, King of Israel, was being challenged by this new King of the Jews. The probability of war and conflict loomed large. For their part, the people of Jerusalem, even though they were used to trouble and had been hardened by prolonged exposure to Herod's rule, feared that change would simply bring further disasters. They knew only too well the character of Herod and they fully understood what the consequences would be to them or to anyone who might be suspected, however unjustly, of sympathy with any claimant to the royal throne of David.

The "priests and scribes" that Herod consulted were probably the Sanhedrin, the old governing body of the Jewish people. The Sanhedrin drew its members from three groups, the Sadducees (or priests), the Pharisaic scribes and the heads of families (the elders). Herod, however, had long since reduced the Sanhedrin to a mere shadow of its former glory. The priests and scribes were well voiced in Jewish lore, fully conversant with the Old Testament and its prophecies. Why Herod should call together the complete Sanhedrin and not just ask any priest is a mystery. The Sanhedrin then informed Herod of the Old Testament prophecy in Micah 5:2, "But thou, Bethlehem Ephratah, though thou be little among the thousands of Judah, yet out of thee shall he come forth unto me that is to be ruler in Israel." The term "in Judah" is used to distinguish between the other Bethlehem in Zebulun 70 miles to the north in Galilee. Matthew also changes the phrase "though thou be little" into the much less dismissive "not least." Obviously the fact that Jesus had been born there made the evangelist modify the original. At the time, toward the end of the first century, when Matthew was being written it was no longer possible to speak of Bethlehem as being of little account. Of course we read this to mean that the Messiah was to be born in Bethlehem, but this could be an oversimplification. All that the prophet Micah probably meant was that, wherever he might be born, he would come "out" of Bethlehem, i.e. out of the stock of David who was born there.

According to St. Matthew's gospel, Herod then secretly summoned the wise men to establish the exact time at which the star had appeared. The Greek verb *phainesthai* (to appear) used here applies to the heliacal rising of the star that the Magi had seen, though it is also possible to denote this astronomical position by the Greek words *epitole* or *phasis*.

The heliacal rising is the earliest visible rising of a star at daybreak. For any star or planet in the ecliptic—the name for the path across the heavens along which the Sun, Moon and planets appear to move—this only occurs once a year. The star (or planet) is just seen to rise above the eastern horizon at dawn and is then quickly blotted out as its light is swamped by the ever brightening daylight in the east. The heliacal rising, in the popular astrology of the day, was thought to coincide with the birth date of a person. Herod's question to the Magi was equivalent to his asking "When was this king born?"

In considering the tenor of Herod's question there are two possibilities. The first is that neither Herod nor the people of Jerusalem had seen the star and we have a simple inquiry. If someone reports something unusual, it is common for the first reaction to be to ask them when they saw it. Herod received his answer. "What was the star?" would be the second reaction. We do not know if Herod went on to ask the nature of the star, since Matthew does not record an answer. The second possibility is that Herod had seen something astronomical or had at least been told about it. In this case the purpose of his question was to check if the time given by the Magi coincided with the time of the appearance of the phenomenon in Jerusalem. The fact that Herod and all Jerusalem were troubled when they heard the message of the wise men indicates that the first of these two possibilities is the more probable. Herod was not only worried because the birth of a new king had been announced, he was also worried because he had been taken completely unaware and had no knowledge of the sidereal messenger.

The time of the star's heliacal rising is very important as this would be a vital clue to the age and identity of the new king. Herod was anxious to know, not in order to worship him but to kill him and so eradicate a rival to his throne. As we shall see, this time aspect is related to the murder of the innocents, when Herod killed all the children in Bethlehem under the age of two. The time is also important in relation to a Jewish tradition that the star would appear not at the time of the Messiah's birth but two years before it. Obviously we have no idea how long it took the Magi to get from the east to Jerusalem or if they set off soon after they had seen the star or waited around for a time. Herod, with characteristic cunning, did not commit himself in his discussions with the wise men as to whether the Messiah was already born or was only expected, his question to the chief priests and scribes being in the present tense. Knowing now where the Jews looked for the appearance of a rival to his throne, Herod could keep a watch on that place and also on the people generally.

Herod then sent the wise men off to Bethlehem. It is rather unusual, in view of the trouble he went to trying to find Jesus later on, that he did not send one of his close advisers along with the wise men to look into the affair officially and report back. Bethlehem was, after all, not far from Jerusalem—a mere hour and a half's walk away. Instead the Magi went off by themselves with the instruction to report back personally.

Matthew 2:9 contains one of the stumbling blocks of all astronomical "star of Bethlehem" theories. It is said that the star "went before" the wise men. Up to now the story of the Magi is noteworthy for its air of historical probability. There is the expectation of a world redeemer or, in a narrower Palestinian sense, the expectation of a Jewish Messiah. Many elements in the story—the interest of eastern Magi, their presence in the west to pay homage to the new Savior, the fulfillment of the prophet Micah's prediction that the Redeemer was to be born in Bethlehem—are reasonable historical assertions. One detail, however, has a strong legendary and mythical atmosphere: the star which moved before the Magi as they traveled to Bethlehem and then hovered over the house in which the child lay. It is possible that the author of Matthew was exercising poetic licence in his account of the Magi's successful search for the child. It is in any case extremely unlikely that he intended the account to be taken as a bold statement of fact, a literal description of how the star in some strange unnatural manner led the searchers down the Jerusalem-Bethlehem road and enabled them, without other aids, to identify the particular house in Bethlehem in which the holy family were staying. Matthew's text conveys the idea that the star which guided the wise men from Jerusalem to Bethlehem was some ethereal light like the Shekinah (glorious divine presence) resting on the ark in the tabernacle or like the pillar of fire which led the children of Israel through the wilderness. Certainly the wise men referred to the object they saw in the east as a visible star and not some unstarlike manifestation. The star must have been south of Jerusalem when they left the city, pointing out Bethlehem, their destination.

When the Magi arrived the star "stood over" the place where the young child was. In astronomical parlance this means that the star was in the zenith, in other words directly overhead, above the observer. This ties in with a strange legend recounted several decades ago by the astronomer E. W. Maunder. Unfortunately he gives no reference to the origin of the legend and states that he cannot find that it rests on any authority. According to the legend the star had been lost in the daylight by the time the wise men had reached Jerusalem. When they reached Bethlehem, apparently at about midday, one of them went to the well of the inn to draw water. Looking down into the well shaft he saw the star reflected in the water at the bottom of the well. The wise man immediately realized that the star was directly overhead and the re-sighting of the star under such unusual circumstances was to him ample assurance that they had arrived at the place where Jesus Christ was born.

The daytime observation of stars reflected in well water, stars seen by people standing at the bottom of mine shafts and stars seen up tall chimneys and deep foundation shafts is a fine old astronomical chestnut which still awaits a detailed scientific explanation. The phenomenon was known even in Old Testament times and Aristotle wrote that "people in pits and wells sometimes see the stars." This observation was supported by the astronomer Weigel, who had in his house at Jena a deep shaft through which stars could allegedly be seen in the daytime. In a small collection of letters that appeared in the *Observer* newspaper the lock on the Donzère-Modragon dam on the Rhône waterway, reputed to be the deepest in the world, has been put forward as another place where the effect occurs. Stars can be seen shining in the daylight sky as seen from the bottom of the lock chamber.

In interpreting the legend it is worth remembering that the eye has a marvellous capacity for adapting itself to different light levels. When its field of view is restricted by wells and mine shafts the background light from the sky is greatly reduced and the eye has a better chance of picking out the star signals from the background. A scientific account of the effect came from astronomers at the Lick Observatory early in this century. They compared the brightness of the brightest star they could see as they stood outside in the open with the brightest star they could see when inside the observatory dome looking at a small patch of the sky through the dome opening. The eye's sensitivity was found to have increased by a factor of 10, stars that were just visible inside the dome being about 10 times fainter than those visible outside.

What can we now say about the expression "stood over" in Matthew 2:9? The problem here is that any star or planet is an "astronomical" distance away from Earth, so that a star in the zenith standing over the stable at Bethlehem will equally well stand over every object in the neighborhood. For the "star" to pick out an individual building it must hover above the roof-tops, which is something no astronomical star does. The "going before" and "standing over" have led some investigators to suggest that the star was ball lightning, a rather poorly understood atmospheric phenomenon which will be discussed in more detail in Chapter 6.

Another extremely important point in this second passage from Matthew comes in the next verse (2:10). When the wise men saw the star as they left Jerusalem, "they rejoiced with exceeding great joy." This passage can be interpreted as indicating that the star appeared twice. The first sighting would have been when the star induced the wise men to leave the east and set out for Judea. On this journey the star was lost sight of. The second sighting occurred at Jerusalem, when the star pointed the way to Bethlehem, and this sighting made the travellers extremely happy as it indicated that their journeyings were not in vain and that the object of their search was still in reach. Probably the disappearance of the star on their way to Israel was one of the reasons why they went to Jerusalem to seek information about the king. Even though they had vague knowledge of the expectation of a King of the Jews, they did not have the detailed knowledge of the prophecy of Micah telling them where he was to be born. If they had known this prophecy they would presumably have gone directly to Bethlehem. Apart from this, if the star had shone continuously and acted as a guide, it would have made sense for them to go directly to Bethlehem, the place the star eventually stood over. According to Matthew's account, then, the Magi had had their expectation of a king confirmed by the Sanhedrin's reference to a divine oracle, and they had been told the town in which the birth would occur. Furthermore, the star reappeared and pointed out to them the way to Bethlehem. This reappearance of the star is important as it rules out certain astronomical phenomena that occur only once and are never repeated.

How long was the star seen for? The short answer to this is that we do not know, we are not told. Of its first sighting in the east the important facts are that the star had a message and probably rose acronychally. As to its second sighting from Jerusalem, we can have some idea of a lifetime of the phenomenon in that we can at least estimate a lower limit. A normal healthy man, wise or not, could walk from Jerusalem to Bethlehem in about an hour and a half. If the star led the way and stood over the birthplace, it must have lasted for this time at least. This again rules out certain astronomical occurrences that are short-lived: meteors, fleeting flashes of light produced when tiny particles of cosmic dust impinge on the Earth's upper atmosphere with velocities around 60,000 mph, the shooting or falling stars beloved of poets and songwriters. The large majority of these occurrences last for less than a second, to be seen no more. Persistent trains where the luminosity lasts for minutes are rare—the longer the duration the rarer they are.

One very interesting and rather puzzling point about Matthew's description of the star was his omission of the phrase ''that it might be fulfilled which was spoken by the prophets.'' Matthew often used this phrase in his gospel to underline to his readers the fact that the New Testament happenings had been predicted by Old Testament prophecies. Why was this literary device not applied to the star? Balaam, a man from the east with magical powers—in other words a magus—had predicted that a star would rise from Jacob. Balaam, who was counselor to a Pharaoh, said, "I shall see him, but not now: I shall behold him, but not nigh: there shall come a Star out of Jacob, and a Scepter shall rise out of Israel" (Numbers 24:17). If this star was an actual physical star we would expect Matthew to refer to it. Some critics suggest that the historical background for Balaam's prophecy was the emergence of the Davidic monarchy over two centuries after the time of Moses. King David was the star and also the sceptre ruling over the united kingdom of Judah and Israel. Some present-day scholars think the term "star" in the prophecy above applies to the Messiah himself and not to the sidereal phenomenon heralding his appearance. In Judaism long before the advent of Jesus this passage (Numbers 24:17) had been applied to the Messiah, the anointed King of the Jews. And not only before Jesus, for as late as the second century AD the Rabbi Aqiba hailed the revolutionary Simon ben Kosibah as the Messiah. As the leader of the patriots in the second Jewish War of AD 130-135, Bar Kosba changed his nickname, used amongst members of the resistance movement, a name which probably meant "son of a young ram," to Bar Kokhba "son of a star."

Since the words "that it might be fulfilled," which make up a common formula in Matthew, are absent from the passage about the star, some critics argue that the star episode is not historical. These critics also ask why the evangelist did not quote Isaiah 60:3, "And the gentiles shall come to thy light, and the kings to the brightness of thy rising," or 60:6, "The multitude of camels shall cover thee, the dromedaries of Midian and Ephah; all they from Sheba shall come: they shall bring gold and incense; and they shall shew forth the praises of the Lord," or Psalm 72:10, "The kings of Tarshish and of the isles shall bring presents: the kings of Sheba and Seba shall offer gifts."

It is much easier, of course, to explain why people include things in narratives than why they exclude them. Albright and Mann have suggested that the writer of the gospel had a distaste for astrology. The threat of Gnosticism was very soon felt by the early church, as can be seen in the New Testament from the letters of John and from Paul's letter to the Colossians. There is a strong possibility that in the midst of the Gnostic struggle within the church a scribe or editor deliberately removed Matthew's fulfillment formula. Any suggestion that Jesus, through the evangelist's writings, even appeared to acknowledge the legitimacy of astrology would have been avidly seized upon by the Gnostics and used as verbal ammunition against the Christians. Although there is no evidence for this textural doctoring, the view of Albright and Mann does have the merit of preserving the narrative in the second chapter of Matthew as historic. Without it the evidence for the star of Bethlehem would be scant indeed.

Before we go on to descriptions of the star of Bethlehem that do not appear in the Bible, it is helpful to look at the origin of this gospel and to find out who wrote it, for whom and when. There is obviously an interval of time between the star's occurrence and the commitment of the story to paper.

In its present form the gospel of St. Matthew, like the other three gospels of the New Testament, was written in Greek, which is rather unusual in view of the fact that Jesus spoke in Aramaic, a language akin to Hebrew. The language of the gospel is common, as opposed to classical, Greek. This was the international language of the time of Christ and the apostles, and it was spread by the conquests of Alexander the Great in the fourth century BC.

Nearly two millennia have passed since the New Testament books were written and the original manuscripts have long been lost. They were probably written on large papyrus rolls about five inches wide and furnished with a stick at each end for winding and unwinding. As to length, St. Luke's gospel would have needed a roll about thirty feet long. Until the invention of printing in the fifteenth century the texts were handwritten by copyists, who unwittingly but inevitably introduced errors and sometimes tried to correct what they regarded as mistakes by their predecessors. Errors could therefore proliferate all too easily, but biblical scholars are now confident that the large majority of the mistakes have been detected and corrected. After careful comparison with the great Greek manuscripts such as the Codex Vaticanus, Codex Sinaiticus and Codex Bezae, as well as with the early translations of the Greek New Testament into Latin and Syriac, and finally with the quotations from the New Testament that occur in the work of the early Church Fathers (Tatian for example), it is possible to arrive at a satisfactory text. To quote two outstanding scholars of New Testament Greek, Westcott and Hort: "The words in our opinion still subject to doubt can hardly amount to more than a thousandth part of the New Testament."

The third question of interest concerns the canon, which is the list of twenty-seven sacred books that were accepted by the church as authoritative in matters of faith and life and therefore included in the New Testament. How were these books selected? The first obvious point to make is that Jesus Christ wrote no part of the New Testament. The early Christians had as scripture the Old Testament, alongside which were placed "the words of the Lord" as mentioned in Acts 20:35, the story of Christ's ministry which was committed to writing about AD 65 by Mark, and the other three gospels which were written in the next thirty years. Slightly earlier than the gospels were the letters that Paul had written to the churches. These were read publicly, lent to sister churches, copied and eventually collected into book form. In this way the New Testament emerged piece by piece. Apart from the New Testament, of course, there were other devotional books in existence at the time, such as The Shepherd of Hermas, which was rather like an early version of the Pilgrim's Progress, and also a set of highly fanciful gospels and acts which were designed to fill in some of the gaps in the early Christians' knowledge of Jesus Christ and the apostles. These are now collected together and form the Apocryphal New Testament.

The elevation of the twenty-seven books of the present-day New Testament to canonical rank was a gradual process that took nearly three hundred years to complete. By AD 200 the backbone had been assembled, so that only Hebrews, James, Jude, 2 Peter, 2 John, 3 John and Revelation awaited firm acceptance. The job had been completed by Ad 367, the year in which St. Athanasius listed in a famous letter the twenty-seven books of today's New Testament. The selection criteria were public usage—the fact that the book was read regularly in church—and apostolicity, the belief that the book emanated from apostolic circles.

St. Matthew's gospel, which is the only one giving the story of the star of Bethlehem, is one of four gospel books proclaiming the "good news" of Christ. This good news was being broadcast well before anything was committed to paper. In fact the first Christian generation of AD 30-AD 60 existed with no written gospels at all. This was the period of the oral tradition. There was, however, a *kerygma,* a Greek word which means a message that is preached. The New Testament scholar A. M. Hunter sums up the message in this way:

God's promises made to his people in the Old Testament
are now fulfilled.
The long-expected Messiah, born of David's line, has come.
He is Jesus of Nazareth, who
went about doing good and wrought mighty works by God's power:

was crucified according to the purpose of God;
was raised by God from the dead and exalted to
his right hand.
He will come again in glory for judgment.
Therefore let all who hear this message repent
and be baptized for the forgiveness of their sins.

Alongside this *kerygma* were the teachings of Jesus,
his memorable sayings, "the words of the Lord."
These were collected into a document, a so-called
sayings source now sometimes called Q. Q has not
survived, but much of its content can be recovered
from the great sermons which both Matthew and Luke
attribute to Jesus and from the instructions that Jesus
gave to his disciples when he sent them out on their
missions. According to one view, that of T. W. Manson, Q was arranged in four sections, these being
concerned with Jesus and John the Baptist, Jesus and
his disciples, Jesus and his opponents, and finally the
sayings about the last things. It is also possible that Q
was intended as a manual of moral instruction for new
converts to Christianity. In view of its emphasis on the
gentiles, many scholars think that it originated in Antioch, the cradle of gentile Christianity. Its date may be
as early as AD 50.

Before we investigate the origins of the gospel of
Matthew—the gospel of the star—it is necessary to
look at the origin of the earliest gospel, Mark, a book
which provided much of the material for both Matthew's and Luke's gospels. Matthew contains nearly
all of Mark (606 of Mark's 661 verses reappear in
Matthew): many words and phrases are repeated
exactly and the order of events is often the same. St.
Mark's gospel—"the gospel of Jesus Christ the Son of
God"—was completed shortly after the winter of AD
64-65, the time when Rome was devastated by a great
fire during the reign of the Emperor Nero. Christians
were the scapegoats, and persecution and martyrdom
arrived in earnest. Jesus had died and risen thirty years

previously, the people who remembered him when he was alive were getting fewer and fewer. It was important that the facts about Jesus should be committed to writing so that his life, suffering, death and resurrection could act as an example and inspiration to the persecuted. The writing down of these facts, which had not been necessary while the apostles were alive and while Jesus' early return was expected by many, now became a matter of urgency.

The full name of the author of Mark was almost certainly John Mark, a man from Jerusalem, not one of the twelve disciples but someone who knew Jesus during the latter part of his ministry. John Mark may well have been the man who was in the garden of Gethsemane on the night of Jesus' arrest. He escaped from the soldiers' clutches by running off and leaving behind the linen garment he was wearing. Who but the author, it is thought, would include such a trifling detail in the gospel? The basis of the gospel seems to be a series of reminiscences of Jesus told to Mark, by St. Peter, for it was Mark who became closely associated with Peter's preaching. Mark portrays Jesus as man and as the Son of God.

St. Matthew's gospel earns the place as the first gospel in the New Testament mainly because it acts as a bridge between the Old Testament and the New. The author stresses that Christ came in order to fulfill the prophecies in the Old Testament. Furthermore, Matthew sees Christ as the goal of God's purpose and uses arguments based on prophecy. The evangelist is therefore probably a Jewish Christian writing a gospel for his fellow countrymen, a gospel for the Jews.

Modern scholars do not believe that it was the apostle Matthew who wrote the gospel, although he did have strong connections with it. Why should he, one of the apostles, copy the work of Mark, who was not? The apostle Matthew is thought by some to be the compiler of Q. For his gospel the author of Matthew used three sources, Mark, Q and his own recollec-

tions, sometimes referred to as M. The style of Mark
was improved and the text shortened and rearranged.
Mark was enlarged in Matthew with the addition of the
birth story, extra incidents in the passion story, five
great discourses—the sermon on the mount (5-7), the
charge to the twelve (10), the parables of the kingdom
(13), the discourse on true greatness and forgiveness
(18), the discourse on the last things (24-35), plus the
insertion of eleven Old Testament proof texts, the
fulfillment phrases.

These Old Testament fulfillment phrases are of
great importance. Matthew's message was that Jesus
came as the answer to Old Testament prophecy—he
"came not to destroy but to fulfill the law and the
prophets." Jesus was the Son of David, he "appeared
in the fullness of time, in whose life the word of
psalmists and prophets found their fulfillment, who was
the Messiah of whom Jewish history had been one long
prophecy, who came to fulfill the old law by making it
new."

To date the writing of Matthew we have to use the
following facts. He used Mark's gospel and must
therefore have finished the writing of it later than about
AD 65. Matthew 22:7—"But when the king heard
thereof, he was wroth: and he sent forth his armies and
destroyed those murderers and burnt up their city"—
suggests that Jerusalem had already fallen, putting the
date after AD 70. It must have been written before AD
96 because Clement of Rome apparently knew of the
gospel. A. M. Hunter concludes that AD 85 is the best
date and this seems acceptable.

It follows from this that over ninety years elapsed
between the birth of Jesus and Matthew's setting down
of the details, ninety years between the occurrence of
the star of Bethlehem and the recording of it, ninety
years in which the descriptions had been passed on by
word of mouth only. It could be compared to the
present-day case of the Tunguska explosion, an enor-

mously energetic devastating explosion that took place in the wastes of central Siberia on 30 June 1908. Researchers are still puzzling over the event and are rather mystified by the diversity of some of the eye-witness reports. Today, of course, we do not have an oral tradition, whereas in the ancient Near East the memory of words and stories was far better and a ninety-year gap between an event and the written account of it need not have been a serious problem. Matthew might be reporting an event long past, but there is a very high probability that he was reporting it correctly.

There is another interesting aspect in the temporal relationship between Mark, Q and Matthew. The details of Christ's birth seem to have been considered secondary in importance by the early Christians. The important message was Jesus' life, his baptism, his acceptance by John the Baptist, his teaching, his death and resurrection. Preoccupied with their belief in Jesus as man, God and Savior, the early Christians were concerned with his origins almost as an afterthought. Matthew's gospel, steeped in Old Testament traditions, presents one picture of Jesus, while Luke gives another. The gospel stories of the ministry seem to have been molded in the Christian tradition without a knowledge of the infancy narratives. Each of these two evangelists then had to join together two sets of material—the stories connected with the ministry and the infancy narratives.

As the New Testament scholar Raymond Brown emphasizes, Matthew's story of the birth of Jesus seems to have an underlying similarity with the Jewish midrashim that interpret the birth of Moses in Exodus 1 and 2. He points out that in Matthew 2 Jesus relives in miniature some of the main events of the history of Israel such as the exodus and the exile. For example, Joseph the father of Jesus could interpret dreams and went down into Egypt. Joseph of the book of Genesis was also a "man of dreams" and was involved with Pharaoh. This pharaoh was a benevolent figure, but there was a second pharaoh who killed the male infants of the Israelites, with only Moses escaping. This pharaoh later tried to kill Moses. There is a strong similarity here. The following list is given by Brown:

Matthew 2:13-14	Herod was going to search for the child to destroy him, so Joseph took the child and his mother and went away
Exodus 2:15	The Pharaoh sought to do away with Moses, so Moses went away
Matthew 2:16	Herod sent to Bethlehem and massacred all the boys of two years of age and under
Exodus 1:22	The Pharaoh commanded that every male born to the Hebrews be cast into the Nile
Matthew 2:19	Herod died.
Exodus 2:33	The King of Egypt died
Matthew 2:19-20	The angel of the Lord said to Joseph in Egypt: ". . . go back to the land of Israel, for those who were seeking the child's life are dead"
Exodus 4:19	The Lord said to Moses in Midian: ". . . return to Egypt, for all those who were seeking your life are dead"
Matthew 2:21	Joseph took the child and his mother and went back to the land of Israel
Exodus 4:20	Moses took his wife and his children and returned to Egypt

If one goes further and considers the Jewish midrashic

tradition about the infancy of Moses, more parallels come to light. Pharaoh had been warned by one of his sacred scribes of the birth of a Hebrew who would constitute a threat to the Egyptian kingdom. In other stories Pharaoh received the warning in a dream which had to be interpreted by his magicians—rather like the Magi. Pharaoh, like Herod, was also alarmed at this news. In a still later legend about Moses a great light like that of a star or of the Sun and Moon was said to have filled the house at his birth. This is a striking similarity, though it must be stressed that it is difficult to determine the age of some of the midrashic passages and some might easily have been derived from Matthew's gospel. A point of contrast, of course, is that Matthew's Magi come to worship the child Jesus and oppose Herod the wicked king, whereas the magi in the Moses legend are on Pharaoh's side and support his murderous schemes.

By way of summary, then, it must be remembered that the only mention of the star of Bethlehem in the Bible is in the second chapter of Matthew's gospel. Even though this chapter was written about ninety years after the event, this is no reason for doubting the truth of the account. The strong oral tradition of the East worked against erosion and accretion of detail. There are strong similarities between the birth of Christ as told by "Matthew" and the birth of Moses in the book of Exodus and in early Jewish midrashic texts, but the Magi and the star are points of special emphasis in St. Matthew's account. We are left with the strong conviction that Matthew's description of the star is basically correct. We can now list the facts that have emerged:

1. The star was first seen by the wise men when they were in the east.

2. It was observed at its acronychal rising.

3. At this time it had a distinct astrological meaning.

4. It disappeared as they journeyed to Jerusalem.

5. It was so insignificant that Herod and all Jerusalem had overlooked it.

6. The same star appeared again when they were in Jerusalem and then went before them and "stood over" Bethlehem.

2

The great light

The account of the birth of Jesus occurs twice in the Bible, in the gospels of Matthew and Luke, but why is the star only mentioned in Matthew and completely absent from Luke? We seem to be confronted with two different accounts of the birth event. The majority of the material in the gospels has its origin in the recollections and reminiscences of the people who were with Jesus from the time of his baptism until the time of his death and resurrection. But who was at his birth? Obviously Joseph and Mary, who could have told the tale. Unfortunately Joseph seems to have been dead by the time of the ministry—for he was not mentioned in Mark 6:3—and Mary was not a close acquaintance of the disciples before the crucifixion, although she did become a member of the Christian community after the resurrection. Some scholars regard Mary as the source of Luke's infancy material and Joseph as the source of Matthew's material, but the differences between the two are too striking for this to be probable. Raymond Brown concludes that "At most only one of the narratives can stem from family reminiscences with the tacit assumption that most of the other is not historical." Brown opts for Matthew as the "family tradition" gospel and Luke's nativity as the non-historical work, and on this basis he compares and contrasts the two accounts. He finds that the two gospels have the following points in common:

(1) Mary and Joseph are the parents to be, but they are

23

not living together nor have they had sexual relations (Matthew 1:18; Luke 1:27, 34).

(2) Joseph is a descendant of King David (Matthew 1:16, 20; Luke 1:27, 32, 2:4).

(3) Angels announce the birth (Matthew 1:20-23; Luke 1:30-35).

(4) The child is not conceived by intercourse between Mary and Joseph (Matthew 1:20, 23, 25; Luke 1:34).

(5) Conception is through the Holy Spirit (Matthew 1:18, 20; Luke 1:35).

(6) The angel directs that the child should be called Jesus (Matthew 1:21; Luke 1:31).

(7) And also that Jesus is the Savior (Matthew 1:21; Luke 2:11).

(8) The parents are living together when the birth occurs (Matthew 1:24-25; Luke 2:5-6).

(9) Jesus is born in Bethlehem (Matthew 2:1; Luke 2:4-6).

(10) The birth occurs when Herod the Great is king (Matthew 2:1; Luke 1:5).

(11) The child spends his early days in Nazareth (Matthew 2:23; Luke 2:39).

Most of their common points occur in a small section of Matthew (1:18–2:1).

The differences are quite striking. In the first place, the genealogies differ. Furthermore, Luke discusses the birth of John the Baptist to Elizabeth and Zacharias, the census which caused Joseph to travel to Bethlehem, the shepherds, the acclamation and the presentation of Jesus in the temple when he was twelve. Matthew, on the other hand, tells of a completely different set of happenings. He has the star, the Magi, Herod's plot against Jesus, the massacre of the innocent children and the flight to Egypt. In Matthew, Joseph and Mary live in a house in Bethlehem, and there is no discussion as to how they came to be there. In Luke, Jesus is born in a stable, not a house. Luke has the holy family returning peacefully to Nazareth via Jerusalem. In Matthew they return from Egypt. Attempts have been made to combine the two stories into one, but if there was originally one narrative, why should it have become separated into two in the first place? These problems seem to be overlooked by most Christians, who envisage a Christmas scene with stars, shepherds, angels and Magi all happily intermingling around and above the manger in the stable.

We should now turn to a non-biblical text that does mention a star. This occurs in one of the infancy gospels that were omitted from the Bible when the New Testament canon was finalized. The Proto-toevangelium of James states:

21. And behold, Joseph prepared to go forth to Judea. And there took place a great tumult in Bethlehem of Judea. For there came wise men saying: "Where is the [new-born] king of the Jews? For we have seen his star in the east and have come to worship him." When Herod heard this he was troubled and sent officers [to the wise men], and sent for them and they told him about the star.

[And he] questioned them: "How is it written concerning the Messiah? Where is he born?" They said to him: "In Bethlehem of Judea; for so it is written." And he let them go. And he questioned the wise men and said to them: "What sign did you see concerning the new-born king?" And the wise men said: "We saw how an indescribably greater star shone among these stars and dimmed them, so that they no longer shone; and so we knew that a king was born for Israel. And we have come to worship him." And Herod said: "Go and

seek, and when you have found him, tell me, that I
also may come to worship him.'' And the wise
men went forth. And behold, they saw stars (a
star) in the east, and they (it) went before them,
until they came to the cave. And it stood over the
head of the child (the cave). And the wise men
saw the young child with Mary his mother, and
they took out of their bag gifts, gold, and frankincense and myrrh. And being warned by the angel
that they should not go into Judea, they went to
their own country by another way.

22. But when Herod perceived that he had been
tricked by the wise men he was angry and sent his
murderers and commanded them to kill all the
children who were two years old and under. When
Mary heard that the children were to be killed, she
was afraid and took the child and wrapped him in
swaddling clothes and laid him in an ox-manger.

There are some interesting points both here and
elsewhere in the Protoevangelium. There is a possibility of dating the time of the birth from 17:1, which
states that ''Now there went out a decree from the king
Augustus that all [inhabitants] of Bethlehem of Judea
should be enrolled'' [Caesar Augustus was in fact the
Emperor]. The birth seems to have occurred in a cave
which was just outside Bethlehem, ''near to the third
mile [stone].'' According to chapter 18 miraculous
things occurred at the time of the birth: everything—
birds, men, sheep, kids, the heavens—stood still for a
time. Furthermore, when Joseph returned to the cave
with the midwife Salome, ''behold a dark cloud over-
shadowed the cave. And the midwife said: 'My soul is
magnified today, for my eyes have seen wonderful
things; for salvation is born to Israel.' And immediately the cloud disappeared from the cave and a
great light appeared, so that our eyes could not bear
it.'' A short time afterwards the light withdrew until
the child appeared.

One of the passages quoted above shows the wise men first went to Bethlehem (21:1). This could easily be the case if they had prior knowledge of the prophecy in Micah.

The brightness of the star is graphically expressed in James: "An indescribably great star shone among these stars and dimmed them so that they no longer shone." A similar description could be applied to the full Moon, which dims the light of the surrounding stars and leaves only the brightest members of each constellation twinkling in the sky. This enormous brightness, however, is contrary to the impression given by St. Matthew of a star which was so insignificant that Herod and all Jerusalem were surprised when they were told of it. One version of James 22:3 specifically mentions stars in the plural.

According to the scholar Hennecke, in comparison with later non-biblical infancy gospels the Protoevangelium of James "has great merit." Tradition had it that the author was James, the brother of Jesus, who according to the Protoevangelium was Joseph's son by a previous marriage, although this previous marriage is now in doubt. In fact the book could not have been written before AD 150, and it presupposes the canonical infancy stories of Matthew and Luke. The author was probably not Jewish at all, for he exhibits considerable ignorance of Palestinian geography and Jewish customs. The purpose of the work seems to have been the glorification of Mary the mother of Jesus. It vigorously refutes the Jewish mockery of the virgin birth and also the idea spread by the Jews at that time that Jesus was the illegitimate child of a soldier called Panther, which was a common name among Roman soldiers. The miraculous birth of Mary is recorded and the concept of the virgin birth of Jesus is intended to imply Mary's perpetual virginity.

A rather different description of the star of Bethlehem is to be found in the Arabic Gospel of the Savior's Infancy, the first nine chapters of which are a

Syriac compilation of Luke, Matthew and the Protoevangelium of James. Chapter 7 reads:

> And it came to pass, when the Lord Jesus was born at Bethlehem of Judea, in the time of King Herod, behold, magi came from the east to Jerusalem, as Zeraduscht had predicted; and there were with them gifts, gold and frankincense, and myrrh. And they adored him, and presented him their gifts. Then the Lady Mary took one of the swaddling-bands, and, on account of the smallness of her means, gave it to them; and they received it from her with the greatest marks of honor. And in the same hour there appeared to them an angel in the form of that star which had before guided them on their journey; and they went away, following the guidance of its light, until they arrived in their own country.

Here for the first time we have the star guiding them home as well as leading them to Bethlehem.

Another non-biblical reference to the star comes in chapter 19 of the Epistle to the Ephesians written by Ignatius, Bishop of Antioch in Syria:

> A star shone in heaven beyond all stars; its light was beyond description and its newness caused astonishment; all the other stars, with the Sun and the Moon gathered in chorus around the star, but it far exceeded them all in its light.

A second translation reads,

> The virginity of Mary, her child bearing, the death of the Lord—these three mysteries, though destined to be proclaimed aloud, were wrought in the silence of God. The announcement was first made to all the ages by the appearance of a star, which outshone all the celestial lights, and to which Sun

and Moon and stars did obeisance. They were terrified at this strange apparition. Magic vanished before it; ignorance was done away; the ancient kingdom of evil was destroyed, when God appeared in the form of Man. Thus the eternal counsel of God was inaugurated.

This was written when Ignatius was in military custody. He was being taken under guard across Asia Minor to Smyrna and from there up to Troas. He then sailed to Neapolis in Macedonia on his way to martyrdom at Rome. While he was in Smyrna he wrote letters to the nearby churches of the Ephesians, the Magnesians and the Trallians, all of which had sent representatives to greet him. It is not easy to determine the date of the Ignatian letters, but most modern historians think that Ignatius was bishop during the reign of Trajan, who was emperor from AD 98 to AD117.

The account of the star by Ignatius is one of only two passages in his Epistles where he steps outside the canonical gospels. As can easily be seen from the quotation given above, the Epistle is devotional and in its reference to the star it borders on the ecstatic. There are also clear reminiscences of Genesis 37:9, in which Joseph says: "I have dreamed a dream more; and, behold, the Sun and the Moon and the eleven stars made obeisance to me." In the nativity account in Matthew 2, the incident of the star is told very simply. Very early on in the history of the church this simplicity was overlaid by gross exaggerations. We can also quote at this point from the Syriac work called the Cave of Treasures: "For two years before the birth of Christ the star appeared to the Magi; for they beheld the star in a firmament of heaven which shone with a light, the appearance of which was greater than all the stars; and there was a girl in the midst of it holding a boy, and a crown was placed upon his head." A similar account of the appearance of the virgin and child in the star is found in the Ethiopic

"Conflict of Adam and Eve," but this work does not mention the two years. The star is said to have "shone in the heavens in the midst of all other stars."

The star is also mentioned by Ephraem Syrus: "A star shone forth suddenly with preternatural light, less than the Sun and greater than the Sun. It was less than the Sun in manifest light; it was greater than he in secret strength by reason of its mystery. A star in the east darted its rays into the house of darkness." A very similar passage occurs in his first hymn for the feast of Epiphany, written between AD 350 and 360:

> 13. In the Height and the Depth the Son had two heralds. The star of light proclaimed Him from above; John likewise preached Him from beneath: two heralds, the earthly and the heavenly.
> 14. The star of light, contrary to nature, shone forth of a sudden; less than the sun yet greater than the sun. Less was it than he in manifest light: and greater than he in secret might because of its mystery.
> 15. The star of light shed its rays among them that were in darkness, and guided them as though they were blind. . . . The herald from above showed His Nature to be from the Most High . . . the star of light will convince him that He is of Heaven . . . the star of light, lo! it cries out in the air, "Behold the Son of the King!"

All this material contains exaggerations as to the brightness of the star. In early Christian writings it seems that the magnitude of the astronomical event increased as time progressed. Ignatius, the Cave of Treasures and the other writings cannot be used as evidence for the form and brightness of the astronomical event that occurred at the birth of Christ over a hundred years before. In Matthew the star is just a star, a common star with no embellishment. As the theologian Dean Farrar commented, "the Gospels, always truthful and bearing on every page that simplicity which is the stamp of honest narrative, indicate this fact without comment.''

Moving on in time, the third-century writer Origen wrote about the star. Origen was one of the Apologists, a group whose main concern was to assure the Roman authorities that the Christians were not a pernicious and unpatriotic minority group with seditious tendencies and immoral rites, and to present Christianity to the educated classes as an intellectual and respectable religion. To Origen Christianity was a profound philosophy and not an irrational credulity. Celsus the Epicurean wrote a work entitled The True Doctrine, which was an assault upon Christianity. In about AD 248 Origen wrote a point by point refutation of this well-informed opponent's work entitled *Contra Celsum*. The passage about the star of Bethlehem occurs in Book 1, section 58:

> After this instead of the Magi of the gospel Celsus' Jew speaks of Chaldaeans, saying that according to the account of Jesus they were moved to come to his birth to worship him as God, although he was still an infant; and they informed Herod the tetrarch of this: but he sent men to kill those born just at that time, thinking that he would destroy him also with them, lest somehow, after he had lived for the time sufficient for him to grow up, he should become king. See here the blunder of the man who does not distinguish Magi from Chaldeans, and fails to notice their different professions, and who on this account corrupts what is written in the gospel. For some unknown reason he has omitted to mention that which influenced the Magi and does not say that it was a star seen by them in the east according to the biblical record. Let us see then what may be our reply to this. We think that the star which appeared in the east was a new star and not like any of the ordinary ones, neither of those in the fixed sphere

nor of those in the lower spheres, but it is to be classed with the comets which occasionally occur, or meteors, or bearded or jar-shaped stars, or any other such name by which the Greeks may like to describe their different forms.

A minor point in this quotation is that Celsus confuses Herod the tetrarch with Herod the Great, his father. A more important point is that Origen seems to be the earliest writer to speculate on the real physical nature of the star. He states that it was not like ordinary stars, which he divides into two types. First, there are the stars in the fixed sphere: these would be the constellations of stars in the sky which in those days were thought to be fixed on the inner surface of a large celestial sphere revolving daily about the Earth at its center. The second type consists of the stars in the lower spheres. Here Origen is referring to the planets, members of our solar system, which in those days were thought of as wandering stars moving among the constellations of the zodiac. This statement contains strong shades of the Eudoxian theory of planetary motion. According to this Greek mathematician, in the solar system the Moon and Sun each possessed a nest of three spheres, while the planets had nests of four. The outermost sphere of each nest moved in the same way as the sphere of the stars. Inner spheres were attached to outer ones by short axes extending from their poles. The polar axes of the various spheres were not parallel to each other. Judicious choice of the attachment points for these axes and the spin periods of the spheres enabled the complex motions of the innermost spheres to be produced. Planets were thought to be attached to the innermost spheres. The whole system was like a set of interacting compass gimbles.

Aristotle, who was a supporter and embellisher of the system, ended up with the fantastic total of fifty-five spheres. Origen obviously thought that the star of

Bethlehem was one of the celestial interlopers—the "comets" that appear from time to time or "bearded or jar-shaped stars." These terms probably all refer to comets, the differentiation being between the size of the luminous halo around the comet and the length and shape of the tails that curve and streak away from the coma across the sky. In Origen's context the word "meteor" would not just mean a shooting star as it does today. The Greek word "meteor" meant "raised above" or "things up in the air" and could be applied to such upper atmospheric effects as the aurora borealis (the northern lights) as well as to a whole host of lower atmospheric phenomena like lightning, rain, snow, hail, cloud formations and rainbows, in fact most of the phenomena that come under the wing of the present-day science of meteorology.

A final reference to the birth of Christ which contains no mention of any star of Bethlehem or of any wise men occurs in the Koran, the Holy Book of the Moslems, Sourat Mariam, 19, verses 21-31. This will be discussed in Chapter 4 when we consider the problem of the date of Christ's birth.

We conclude this chapter by stating again that the description of the star of Bethlehem in the book of Matthew is the only biblical description and is the description most likely to be correct. It is the soberest and also the earliest. As time passed and the new religion of Christianity spread around the shores of the Mediterranean the descriptions of the star became more and more exaggerated and fanciful. The almost mundane star of Matthew later came to be described as the star that "out-shone all the celestial lights." This transformation probably came about because of the desire on the part of the bishops and apologists to give the birth of Jesus a certain status—any king of significance was born to the accompaniment of some celestial manifestation. It was felt to be difficult to reconcile the birth of Jesus, King of Kings, Lord of Lords, with the advent of an average star.

3

Men from the east

Apart from Jesus, the people traditionally most associated with the star are the Magi. According to the commonest version, three kings brought gifts which they presented to Jesus separately. This tradition can now be shown to contain several errors. In the first place there were not necessarily three people involved, for Matthew 2 does not state any number. Furthermore, they were not kings but simply wise men. The number is now almost exclusively set at three mainly because of the threefold nature of the gifts, but there is no indication in Matthew that the gold, frankincense and myrrh were individual presents from individual Magi. If anything, Matthew suggests that the gifts were given jointly.

In the Roman catacombs of St. Peter and St. Marcellinus, some fourth-century frescoes only show two kings. The third-century catacomb frescoes at St. Domitilla have four kings, while a vase in the Kircher Museum has eight. Some medieval Eastern lists have twelve Magi, complete with names. The early Christian writer John Chrysostom, who wrote a commentary on Matthew, says that there were fourteen. This number perhaps came down from patristic tradition but is in itself unreliable. Chrysostom in any case is drawing upon the apocryphal Book of Seth and a great deal of what he writes about the Magi is clearly legendary, including the statement that when they returned home they were baptized by St. Thomas and "wrought much for the spread of the faith in Christ." Despite all the legends, the only thing we know for certain is that we do not know how many Magi there were.

They were elevated to royalty very early on in Christian tradition, and this could be an example of early midrashic tendencies—midrash being a popular and imaginative exposition of the scriptures for faith and piety. Matthew's common use of the formula, "that it might be fulfilled which was spoken by the prophets," might have made Christian authors mindful of several Old Testament passages which foretold the coming of kings to worship the new Messiah:

Psalm 68:29: "Because of thy temple at Jerusalem shall kings bring presents unto thee."

31. "Princes shall come out of Egypt; Ethiopia shall soon stretch out her hands unto God."

Psalm 72:10: "The kings of Tarshish and of the isles shall bring presents: the kings of Sheba and Seba shall offer gifts."

Isaiah 49:7: ". . . kings shall see and arise, princes also shall worship . . ."

Isaiah 60:3: "And the gentiles shall come to thy light and kings to the brightness of thy rising."

Isaiah 60:10: "And the sons of strangers shall build up thy walls and their kings shall minister unto thee."

In view of these six quotations it is surprising that Matthew, steeped in Old Testament theology as he was, did not make the Magi into kings when he first wrote his gospel. The fact that he did not is another good reason for regarding the whole of Matthew's second chapter as historically true. Furthermore, the absence of any mention of kings from Matthew shows that the whole chapter cannot be dismissed as a midrash, or simply as a story to fulfil Old Testament prophecies and to convince people that Jesus truly was the long-awaited Messiah.

By the end of the second century the Christian writer Tertullian was the first to say that "the Orient for the most part held the Magi for kings." This was written about AD 207 or 208. The first names given to them in the east were Hormizdah, king of Persia, Yazdegerd, king of Saba, and Perozadh, king of Sheba. These have been attributed to the fourth-century Syrian writer Ephraem and also to the Syriac work entitled The Cave of Treasures, which was produced sometime in the sixth century. The Syrian writer of the Book of Adam and Eve called them "Hor, king of Persia, Basantor, king of Saba, and Karsudas, king of the East." The Egyptian Barbaro names them Gathaspe, Melchior and Bithisarea. In an Armenian Infancy Gospel of about AD 500 they were named Melkon, king of Persia, Gaspar, king of India, and Balthasar, king of Arabia. In western Christianity these kings are better known as Balthasar, Melchior and Gaspar, the first reference to these names being in a Latin translation of a sixth-century Greek chronicle. In the famous sixth-century mosaic (Plate 1) in the church of S. Apollinare Nuovo at Ravenna, the Magi are shown in Persian dress, wearing trousers, a fact which is said to have saved the church from the Persian onslaught of AD 614. The legend over the heads of the Magi gives their names and so supports the western tradition, but it is of uncertain date. It reads SCS BALTHASSAR + SCS MELCHIOR + SCS GASPAR, the slight difference in spelling perhaps being introduced if and when the names were given to the Byzantine artist orally.

Another interesting passage about the Magi was written by the Anglo-Saxon historian the Venerable Bede, who lived at Jarrow in Northumbria around AD 700:

The Magi were the ones who gave gifts to the Lord. The first is said to have been Melchior, an old man with white hair and a long beard . . . who offered gold to the Lord as to a king. The second, Gaspar by name, young and beardless and ruddy complexioned . . . honored him as God by his gift of incense, an oblation worthy of divinity. The

third, black-skinned and heavily bearded, named
Balthasar . . . by his gift of myrrh testified to the
Son of Man who was to die.

This is the first known reference to the ethnic
backgrounds of the Magi.

Tradition informs us that Melchior was a descendent
of Shem, Gaspar of Ham and Balthasar of Japheth; not
only were the three made to represent the three
periods of life, but their origins were based on the
three divisions of the globe. The tradition making one
an Ethiopian comes from Isaiah 45:14, "Before him
the Ethiopians shall fall down," and Psalm 68:31,
"Princes shall come out of Egypt, Ethiopia shall soon
stretch out her hands unto God."

In Cologne Cathedral, traditionally the final resting
place of the earthly remains of the three kings, there is
a calendar of saints which contains the following
highly unlikely and anachronistic obituary notice:

Having undergone many trials and fatigues for the
gospel, the three wise men met at Sewa [Sebaste
in Armenia] in AD 54 to celebrate the feast of
Christmas. Thereupon, after the celebration of
Mass, they died: St. Melchior on 1 January aged
116; St. Balthasar on 6 January, aged 112; and St.
Gaspar on 11 January, aged 109.

AD 54 is about 300 years before the advent of the
church's policy of celebrating Christmas in December
and the idea that they celebrated Mass at such an early
date is another anachronism. The relics of the Magi
seem to have traveled on a grander scale than did their
original living owners. Their bodies were "discovered" in the East in the fourth century and were
brought from Persia to Constantinople in AD 490 by
the Emperor Zeno or, according to another tradition,
by St. Helena.

These relics, or others, traveled to Milan on the

consecration of Eustorgius. They were taken there by
St. Asacius who built the Basilica of the Three Kings
in their honor. From Milan they went to Cologne in
Germany in 1164 as part of the booty dispersed by the
Emperor Frederick Barbarossa, who had ravaged Italy
and conquered Milan. Barbarossa gave them to
Rainald von Dussel, Chancellor and Archbishop elect
of Cologne, as a reward for the support he and the
people of Cologne had given him in his conflict with
Pope Alexander III. The bodies had been hidden in
San Georgio during the sack of Milan. Nevertheless,
the remains seemed to be none the worse for travel and
reports tell of the uncorrupted bodies "whole even
unto the hair and skin." The majority of these relics
remain in Cologne Cathedral in a magnificent golden
shrine behind the high altar, though some of the relics
traveled further. In 1903 the Cardinal of Cologne sent
some of the relics back to Milan as a gift to the cardinal
of that city.

The religious festival of the Magi occurs at Epiphany
on 6 January and is combined with a commemoration
of Christ's baptism, his first miracle—the turning of
water into wine at the marriage of Cana of Galilee—
and the feeding of the five thousand. The appearance
of the Magi at Epiphany started in the fourth century
and has reflected a gradually increasing importance in
the solemnities of Epiphany over the centuries. With
the passage of time the lives and attributes of the Magi
have continually been colored by the later churches to
fit in with the concept of the new converts and the
gentiles paying homage to a Jewish messiah.

This elaboration of the story is also evident in the
way the church has given each of the gifts a mystical
significance and symbolism. This is shown well in the
quotation from the Venerable Bede, given above,
though the tradition dates right back to the second-
century work of Irenaeus entitled Against the Here-
tics, as well as to a fourth-century Epiphany hymn by
Prudentius. The symbolism of the gifts—gold for a

king, incense for a God, and myrrh for a man who will redeem the world by his suffering—probably stems from the influence of two Old Testament passages, Isaiah 60:6 and Psalm 72:10, 11, 15. Justin Martyr seems to have been the first writer to see the connection between these Old Testament quotations and the gifts mentioned by Matthew. The symbolism has even developed to cover certain aspects of the Christian response to life and has now led to the symbolical association of gold with virtue, incense with prayer, and myrrh with suffering.

Myrrh, which is a mixture of several aromatic resins, was certainly suitable for a king and was used at a royal anointing. It was also used as a perfume, as can be seen in Psalm 45:8, "All thy garments smell of myrrh," and in Exodus 30:23, "Take thou also unto thee principal spices of pure myrrh five hundred shekels, and of sweet cinnamon half so much, even two hundred and fifty shekels and of sweet calamus two hundred and fifty shekels. And of cassia five hundred shekels after the shekel of the sanctuary, and of oil olive an hin: And thou shalt make it an oil of holy ointment, an ointment compound after the art of the apothecary it shall be a holy anointing oil." (A shekel is a weight of about 19 grams and a hin a liquid volume of about one and a third gallons.) Myrrh was also used for embalming, as in John 19:39, "And there came also Nicodemus which at the first came to Jesus by night and brought a mixture of myrrh and aloes about a hundred pound weight. Then took they the body of Jesus and wound it in linen clothes with the spices, as the manner of the Jews is to bury." Jesus encountered myrrh a third time as an additive to wine to form a narcotic, usually administered to condemned criminals before crucifixion. Jesus refused it: "And they gave Him to drink wine mingled with myrrh: but he received it not" (Mark 15:23).

Frankincense is a bitter-tasting resinous gum obtained by collecting the milky sap which exuded from various trees of the Boswellia family, such as *arbor thuris*. It burns with a steady flame and for a long time and derives its name from the freeness with which it gives off its delightful smell. According to Herodotus it was only found in Arabia. It was used as a constituent of incense, a typical recipe being given in Exodus 30:34: "Take unto thee sweet spices, stacte and onycha, and galbanum, these sweet spices with pure frankincense of each shall there be a like weight. And thou shall make it a perfume, a confection after the art of the apothecary, tempered together, pure and holy." It also seemed to be a common import into Israel: "The Gentiles shall come unto thee. The multitude of camels shall cover thee, the dromedaries of Midian and Ephah; all they from Sheba shall come: they shall bring gold and incense; and they shall show forth the praises of the Lord" (Isaiah 60:6). Sacrificial fumigation was another of its uses, when myrrh was mixed with it to form a perfume (Song of Solomon 3:6), and it was also used to garnish shew bread (Leviticus 24:7).

Gold, then as today, was held in high esteem. It was used in the time of Abraham as a medium of exchange but was not actually coined until the time of Ezra about 450 BC. There is no indication in the Bible of it being mined in Palestine, but some may have come from Egypt or Midian. The Jews were mainly dependent on supplies from Arabia (the Sheba mentioned above), Africa, and Ophir on the west coast of India. There is a slight possibility that some may have come through Tarshish in Spain.

The three gifts can also be considered as part of the common stock in trade of magi. We know, for instance, that magical charms were written with myrrh ink. If the gifts are simply thought of as the tools of the trade of any self-respecting magi, then the gifts may be regarded not so much as gifts of homage but more as a rejection of former astrological and magical practices. This brings us directly to the question as to who the wise men were.

The word magi comes from the Greek *magoi,* which the Authorized Version of the Bible translates as "wise men," the New English Bible as "astrologers" and Moffatt as "magicians." We must note straight away that the modern church and also an enormous weight of Christian tradition regard them as gentiles, in fact the first gentiles to recognize that Jesus was the new Messiah and to bow down before him. It seems that the words "King of the Jews" and the exact terms of the question put to Herod led some biblical commentators to conclude that they were not Jews, who would not use this phrase. Some scholars argue against this idea and say that it shows an ignorance of first-century usage. The phrase was certainly used by the orthodox king Aristobulus I (104-103 BC) and in any case the terms "Hebrews" and "Israel" were largely used for Samaritan and Jewish sectarians respectively. Others, however, contend that any Jew would have known the Messiah was not to be born in Jerusalem, would not have needed to ask Herod the question anyway, and would have simply gone to Bethlehem in the first place. We can only conclude that we do not know whether the wise men were Jews or gentiles, although opinion, however informed or uninformed it may be, favors the latter.

Who were they? Long before the time of Matthew Herodotus in his Histories had intrigued his Greek readers by describing a priestly caste of magi who lived among the Medes six centuries before Christ. He told of their special powers, particularly in interpreting dreams. The magi also had a talent for survival and seemed to exist with the minimum of disturbance through the transfer of power from the Medes to the Persians that occurred around 550 BC as well as through the emergence of Zoroastrianism as the dominant religion. Jeremiah (39:3, 13) gave the head of the caste during his time, one Nergal Sharezar, the title of Rab-Mag, "Chief Magus." The magi's religion still held sway after the downfall of Assyrian and Babylo-

nian power, even though Cyrus completely conquered
the sacred caste and his son Cambyses severely re-
pressed it. The Magians revolted and set up Gaumata,
their chief, as king of Persia under the name of Smer-
dis. He was unfortunately murdered in 521 BC and
Darius became king, this downfall being celebrated
throughout Persia by an annual holiday called
magophonia.

By the time of Herodotus, about 450 BC, the magi
were firmly entrenched as Zoroastrian priests. As time
progressed, their functions became diversified and the
term magus became applicable to any man who was
adept in various forms of secret lore and magic. The
book of Daniel in the Old Testament describes how
magi were flourishing in every corner of the Babylonian kingdom of Nebuchadnezzar around the second
century BC. Along with the enchanters and astronomers they were thought to have the power of interpreting
dreams and visionary messages. When Nebuchadnezzar interrogated David, Hananial, Mishael and Azariah
"in all matter of wisdom and understanding . . . he
found them ten times better than all the magicians and
astrologers that were in all his realm" (Daniel 1:19-20).
"Then the king commanded to call the magicians and
the astrologers and the sorcerers, and the Chaldeans
for to show the king his dreams" (Daniel 2:2). "I saw a
dream which made me afraid, and the thoughts upon
my bed and the visions of my head troubled me.
Therefore made I a decree to bring in all the wise men
of Babylon before me, that they might make known
unto me the interpretation of the dream" (Daniel
4:5-6). "The king cried aloud to bring in the astrologers, the Chaldeans and the soothsayers. And the king
spake, and said to the wise men of Babylon,
Whosoever shall read this writing, and shew me the
interpretation thereof, shall be clothed with scarlet,
and have a chain of gold about his neck, and shall be
the third ruler in the kingdom" (Daniel 5:7).

The religious influence of the Magian priestly caste

that had continued throughout the rule of the
Achaemenian dynasty in Persia was probably still
strong at the time of the birth of Christ under the
Parthian domination. The ancient historian Strabo
says that the Magian priests formed one of the two
councils of the Parthian empire. One of the devotional
exercises of the Zoroastrian priesthood used to be the
worship of fire. Another writer to mention the Magi
was Philo of Alexandria, a contemporary of Jesus. He
discusses both the scientific magi and the other sort,
magi who are simply charlatans and magicians. Indeed, the charlatans and astrologers seem to have
come to the fore in the first century AD. Tacitus tells
us that the senate ordered the expulsion of astrologers,
and a similar state of affairs was reported by
Suetonius, who records how the Emperor Tiberius
banished all the astrologers around the year AD 19. St.
Luke recounts in Acts 8:9-24 how Simon, a magus in
Samaria who lived around AD 30, had used sorcery
and bewitched the people of Samaria, claiming to have
special powers. St. Luke also tells in Acts 13:6 of how
Barnabas and Saul met Elymas or Bar-Jesus, a Jewish
magus—"a sorcerer, a false prophet," according to
Acts—at Paphos in Cyprus, where he was associated
with the court of Sergius Paulus. Josephus, a contemporary of St. Luke, writes of a Cypriot magus called
Atomas who worked at Caesarea Maritima in Palestine
in the 50s and was attached to the court of Governor
Felix. It seems therefore that around the time of Christ
the term magus referred to anyone engaged in the
occult arts, to astronomers and astrologers, fortune
tellers, priestly augurs and magicians of varying
plausibility.

We can also see that the title of "magus" was
applied to different people and professions as time
progressed:

(1) In early times, Herodotus regarded them as a
priestly caste of the Medes, similar to the medicine

men and shaman groups of various early people and somewhat akin to the Brahmans of India in their earlier period.

(2) Herodotus also indicates that they were Zoroastrian priests who adopted the religion of their Aryan conquerors and eventually assumed considerable power.

(3) They were the scholars of the Mediterranean world. Elymas, Simon Magus and Atomas were all Jews, so that the profession was by no means limited to those of Persian nationality. Some magi in the Mediterranean area had established a sound reputation for both character and learning. Matthew indicates no value judgment as to the characters of the wise men that visited Jesus. Others, however, such as Simon and Elymas, are presented in the New Testament as vile men without true understanding or moral principles.

(4) The title "magus" indicated someone adept at magic. Daniel uses the word to mean a conjurer or necromancer. In many Old Testament contexts the word magus is used to designate magicians of foreign cultures, such as Egyptians, Persians and Babylonians, or to designate outlawed magical practitioners among the Hebrews. Sometimes magus means the spirit that a medium possesses and uses to cast out demons, and in this context Jesus was a magus (see John 7:20).

(5) The title was finally adopted by some Christian bishops. Cyprian, Bishop of Carthage in the third century, refers to himself as a *magos philosophos*.

Why did the Magi come to Jesus? Matthew simply states that they came to pay homage, the Christian church expanding this so that the wise men became the three kings, the first gentiles to recognize Jesus as the Messiah and Savior, the first gentiles to worship him. In Calvin's words, "The Magi were led to Judea to be witnesses and heralds of the new King." Popular Christian fancy was much keener on the mysterious wise men from the east than on the rather pedestrian shepherds of Luke's nativity. It may well be that the shepherds have been catching up in the last few centuries as the mainstay of Christmas carols, mainly as a result of the Protestant Reformation, the shepherds "being free from all taint of the Popish superstition of relic adoration." But what was in the minds of the wise men? There is a possibility that they simply intended to salute Christ in Persian fashion as a future great king. They probably implied no more than that he was to be a man endowed with exceptional power and dignity. It is likely that they regarded him as a possible future ruler and not as a spiritual Messiah and that they paid homage to him in anticipation, hoping that he might be well disposed toward them if he should happen to conquer the east and rule over them.

The scholar C. S. Mann wonders if the Magi were as "respectable" as Christian tradition has made them. He says that far from being "kings of the Orient" or "wise men," the Magi were dabblers in the black arts rather like Simon and Elymas mentioned above. The tradition of the benevolent wise men had taken too great a hold in the western world for the correct translation of *magos* as professional magician to be used in the Bible. The early Christian writer Justin states that the Magi came to Christ and adored him to show that they had "gone away from that power which had taken them captive." Mann concludes that the Magi narrative is Matthew's way of telling us that the Christ event heralded the end and rout of the fatalism and astrological speculation that was current at that time. In Matthew 2, the sorcerers are driven to acknowledge that they have met their match, that the reign of their superstition is over, and that in token of their submission to the Conqueror they bring to him gold, the ill gotten gains of their trade, together with the incense and myrrh of their frantic divinations.

Why does the evangelist not mention Psalm 72 or Isaiah 60? The reason seems to be that the wise men were not gentile kings coming to pay homage to a God-king, but magicians casting away both trappings and gain. There is not a shred of evidence that the Magi were gentiles, so that they may have been Babylonian Jews, "fallen, as were so many more, into astrology and the magic arts." Either way, just as the sorcerers of Egypt were vanquished by Moses, so the power of the astrologers was broken by the advent of Christ.

All these cases are just variations on an ancient theme. Ignatius stated in his Epistle to the Ephesians (19): "The announcement was first made to all the ages by the appearance of a star. . . . They were terrified at this strange apparition. Magic vanished before it, ignorance was done away; the ancient kingdom of evil was destroyed, when God appeared in the form of Man." Origen in his *Contra Celsum* went even further and asserted that the Magi were in communion with evil spirits. In his view, their sorcery was confuted and their power overthrown by the advent of Jesus, and they were traveling to Israel to find out why their charms and trickery no longer worked. This and other denunciations by the Christian Fathers shows the large hold which magic, witchcraft, astrology and the like occupied in the popular non-Christian religions of the time. Raymond Brown introduces a cautionary note here: "My own opinion is that such references reflect a Christian use of Matthew in an apologetic against magic rather than a true exegesis of Matthew. There is not the slightest hint of conversion or of false practice in Matthew's description of the Magi: they are wholly admirable. They represent the best of pagan lore and religious perceptivity which has come to seek Jesus through revelation in nature." The revelation is, of course, the star which we shall discuss in Chapter 6.

There is another important question relating to the Magi who visited Jesus. Was it just the Jews who were expecting a Messiah at that time or had this expectation of a great new leader spread to most of the Mediterranean cultures? Jewish expectations are well-known and the Old Testament has many passages in which the coming of the anointed one to rescue and redeem Israel was foretold by the prophets. According to the main tradition the new ruler of the world was expected to come from Judea. These expectations carried on into the New Testament writings and there is an example in the Song of Simeon in Luke 2. In the non-Jewish world the evidence about messianic expectation is considerably less clear. Josephus, Tacitus and Suetonius all report this expectation and all apply it to Vespasian. Obviously this is a form of political propaganda to support the purposes of the Flavian dynasty (AD 79). In view of such instances many biblical scholars conclude that the spread of the expectations among the gentiles has been somewhat exaggerated.

Virgil's Fourth Eclogue is often quoted as a witness for the widespread expectation of a world ruler who would bring peace. Virgil talks of a time when "a golden race [will] spring up throughout the world." The poem also mentions a virgin (Lady Justice), daughter of Jupiter and Themis, who was driven from the Earth by the wickedness of men during the long wars. Her return was the signal for peace and for the advent of a divinely descended child, to whom the Earth would pay homage during the age of peace when the remaining traces of guilt would disappear. Virgil lived between 70 and 19 BC, the poem being composed in 40 BC, just after the Peace of Brundisium ended a hundred years of Italian civil war. The Fourth Eclogue, the author confesses, is derived from the Cumaean Sibyl and based on book three of the Sibylline Oracles, a book of Jewish authorship and dating from 160 BC. The Christian messianic interpretation of the poem came after AD 300, Lactantius and Constantine being the main instigators. St. Jerome (c. 342-420) brought people back to Earth and dismissed the prophetic interpretation as a product of ignorance.

On balance we can say that in both Jewish and gentile writings a guilty and weary world was dimly expecting the advent of its deliverer. Rabban Simeon, the son of Gamaliel, said, "The dew of blessing falls not on us and our fruits have no taste," an expression which might sum up much of the literature of the age. In a sense therefore the Fourth Eclogue of Virgil is one of the great unconscious prophecies of paganism, so that when the gentile audience first heard of the nativities of Matthew and Luke they would not have regarded the details as all that strange.

What about the country of origin of the Magi in Matthew? The major clue is the phrase "the east" in Matthew 2:1. Now it is much too naive simply to take Jerusalem and draw a line on the globe extending due east, and conclude that the starting-point of their journey lies on that line. In the language of the Old Testament, and most probably St. Matthew as well, the term "the east" was very vague and included countries considerably to the north as well as to the east of Palestine. Origen thought that "the east" meant all of the countries known to Josephus by that name, this being an area which stretched roughly from Aleppo in the north-west to the modern city of Mosul in Iraq on the Parthian border. In the first century AD this was an important region with a vast Jewish population, in fact probably the most important and influential branch of post-exile Judaism. It seems that east of Palestine only the ancient countries of Media, Persia, Assyria and Babylonia had a Magian priesthood at the time of the birth of Christ.

Which country can it have been? Persia and Parthia were favored by Clement of Alexandria and Cyril of Alexandria. This location is also favored by one of the definitions of the term magi which associates it closely with the Medes and the Persians. Between 250 BC and AD 225 the Arsacid dynasty ruled the Persian empire, the region to the east of the Zagros mountains in present-day Iran. At this point early Christian art comes to our aid. In the basilica at Bethlehem, built by Constantine and rebuilt by Justinian, there was a mosaic showing the Magi in Persian dress—belted tunics with full sleeves ending in close cuffs and tibiales or tight-fitting trousers. Ample cloaks hang from their shoulders and on their heads they wear pointed Phrygian caps. Recognizing their own countrymen, the armies of Chosroes who were busily sweeping over Palestine wreaking havoc and burning churches spared the Bethlehem church.

Clement of Alexandria suggested that the magi had a Zoroastrian background. In fact there was a belief at that time that Zoroaster himself was a prophet. Paul the apostle is quoted by Clement as saying that a clear reference to the coming of a Son of God is made in the book called the Oracle of Hystapes, a mixture of Persian apocalyptic and Jewish lore dated some time between 100 BC and AD 100. A later book entitled the Arabic Gospel of the Infancy stated that "some magi came to Jerusalem according to the prediction of Zoroaster" (7:1). Ephraem Syrus, writing between AD 350 and 360, was also a firm supporter of Persia.

Commagene is another location favored as a starting-point for the Magi's journey. This was a region in the border area between north-east Syria and Parthia, and on the fringe of the Roman Empire. It lay between Cappadocia and Syria, in the valley of the River Euphrates around Somsat in Turkey. This area was very close to the region where Matthew's gospel was written. The New Testament commentator Bacon concluded that although Matthew's gospel was "hebraic to the core," its distinctive material—the parts which did not come from Q or Mark—suggests that it was written somewhere that was not in close touch with Jerusalem and was outside "the range of control which apostles and other eye-witnesses would have exercised." Bacon looked to the Greek-speaking

Jewish-Christian communities of northern and north-eastern Syria as the birthplace of Matthew's gospel. A great Christian center arose at Edessa some fifty miles south-east of the Commagene border. The writing of the gospel would have taken place sometime around AD 85. The Magi were supposed, according to this theory, to have come from Commagene nearby, a city in which astrology flourished. This is proved by the fact that a horoscope of the Roman king Antiochus I (69-31 BC) was found at an archeological dig at Nemrud Dagh, a famous excavation site in Commagene. We therefore have evidence that the magi of this area applied their astrological knowledge to the casting of horoscopes at the time of royal births.

There existed at Commagene a community which was interested in the stars and in predicting the future by studying the movement of the planets among them. The author of Matthew also had very close links with this community. Nevertheless, there is still some doubt as to whether this community at Commagene was expecting a Jewish Messiah and therefore whether it would have associated the star event with his coming.

Another possible place of origin is Babylon. Jerusalem fell to the Babylonians during the time of Nebuchadnezzar (about 587 BC) and the Jews were taken captive to Babylon. The fall of Babylon to Cyrus the Persian led to the return of most of the Jewish exiles to their homeland. The decree allowing the exiles to return to Jerusalem was published in the first year of the reign of Cyrus, some time around 538-537 BC. The Babylonians had developed a considerable interest in astronomy and astrology, and at the time they were the world leaders in such knowledge. This makes Babylon the most likely origin of the Magi's journey for all those who consider mainly the astronomical implications of the star of Bethlehem and its acronychal rising. Even though many (42,360 of them, according to Ezra 2:64!) of the Israelites did go back across the desert to Jerusalem, a large colony of Jews remained behind. The Babylonian magi would therefore not only be steeped in astrology but would also know about the Jewish messianic expectations. As we shall see, they would have had every reason to associate a particular planetary conjunction with the birth of the King of the Jews, and we know in any case that magi were important members of the Babylonian royal court. Babylon has therefore had its advocates, including the early Christian writers St. Maximus and Theodotus of Ancyra. Babylon is also linked tradition-ally with Balaam, the son of Beor. He lived on Pethor, "which is by the river of the land of the children of his people" (Numbers 22:5).

Arabia or the Syrian Desert has also been put for-ward, especially by those who regard the gifts as clues. Gold and frankincense are associated with the desert camel trains from Midian, in north-west Arabia, and from Sheba in south-west Arabia. In Old Testament parlance the terms "people of the east" often was applied to the Qedemites, the desert Arabs. In 1 Kings 4:30 we read of "the wisdom of all the children of the east," even though it was inferior to that of Solomon. The Qedemites had a reputation for wisdom and it would be most surprising if there were no magi among their number. The Arabs were famous for their study of astronomy and astrology, and four Arabian tribes took their names from stars. Arabia also had strong Jewish contacts. From about 120 BC when Dhu Nowas, the Arabian king of the Yemen, turned to the Jewish faith, up to about AD 600, that part of Arabia embraced Judaism. There were strong trade links be-tween Israel and South Arabia that went back to the times of Solomon. Furthermore, there were Jewish colonies around Medina.

If we consider the works of the early Christian fathers we see that Arabia was their first choice as the starting-point of the Magi's journey, even though Per-sia seemed to take over later on. Justin in his Dialogue

wrote: "Magi from Arabia came to him [Herod]." This
was written around AD 160. About AD 210 the Christian writer Tertullian deduced from the nature of the
gifts that the Magi were associated with Damascus and
Arabia. Epiphanius also supported the Arabian view.
The background to this belief seems to stem simply
from the honors paid by the kings in Psalm 72:10: "The
kings of Tarshish and of the isles shall bring presents:
the kings of Sheba and Seba shall offer gifts." Once
the parallels between this verse and the visit of the
Magi had gained currency, the floodgates of loose
exegesis were flung wide open, leading right up to the
elaborations of later devotional texts.

How long did the journey of the Magi take? When
the Magi arrived in Jerusalem they saw the star again,
and it is important to get an idea of the interval
between these two sightings. Figure 1, which is a
large-scale map of the Middle East around the time of
Christ's birth, shows eight probable starting-places as
well as the possible routes taken. Figure 2 shows a
more detailed map of the principal roads of the time.
The route from Babylon is the one favored by the
astrological implications of the star and it had been
covered by the returning Israelites about 500 years
previously. There is an account of this journey in the
Old Testament (Ezra 7). Ezra left Babylon during the
reign of King Artaxerxes. According to verse 9, "upon
the first day of the first month began he to go up from
Babylon, and on the first day of the fifth month came
he to Jerusalem according to the good hand of his God
upon him." Finegan, who is an authority on biblical
chronology, calculates that Ezra left on 8 April 458 BC
and arrived in Jerusalem on 4 August of that year after
a journey taking about four months. This timing can be
compared with an incident in Ezekiel 33. Jerusalem fell
to Nebuchadnezzar on 29 July 587 BC. Ezekiel tells
how a man escaped from Jerusalem and came to him in
Babylon to tell him that the city had fallen. He arrived
in Babylon on 19 January 586 BC after taking a little

Fig. 1 Eight possible routes taken by the Magi as they journeyed to Jerusalem and Bethlehem

less than six months for the journey. In view of the difficult conditions in the early sixth century BC, this time compares favorably with the four months taken by Ezra.

Which route did Ezra and the man mentioned in Ezekiel take? The shortest route, as the crow flies, was straight across the Syrian desert, but it is most unlikely they took it. This route is number 1 in Figure 1 and is 550 miles long. A much more probable route is round the "fertile crescent"—number 2. Instead of setting out across a barren and inhospitable desert, the

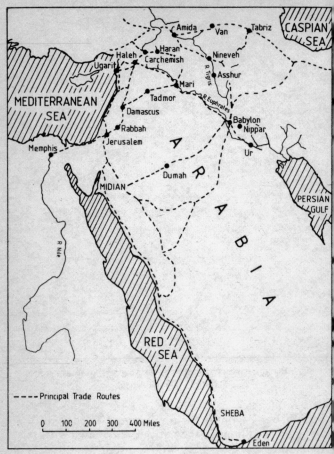

Fig. 2 The principal roads in the Middle East at the time of the
birth of Jesus

Magi probably went from oasis to oasis, taking a much easier but longer trade route through Mari, Haleb, Hameth, Kadesh, and Damascus to Jerusalem. The latter part of this route from Damascus to the south would be by what is now the great Mecca route (darb el-haj, the pilgrim's way), with the Sea of Galilee and the Jordan to the west, until the ford of the Jordan is reached near Jericho. While the short route in Figure 1 is about 550 miles long, the two fertile crescent routes numbered 2 and 3 are respectively 750 and 900 miles in length.

Another possibility, the journey from Commagene to Jerusalem (route 4), is only about 570 miles long. If it took Ezra four months to complete the Babylon-Jerusalem journey, we can crudely estimate that the average speed of a camel train in those days would have had to be about six miles a day. This seems to be a gross underestimate, since a fit man can walk easily at about three and a half miles an hour. Ezra and those traveling with him must therefore have gone slowly or made longer stops. In the time of Herod the Great traveling in the east seems to have been a very slow and leisurely affair, especially when there was political strife.

A more up-to-date estimate of journey time comes from T. E. Lawrence, writing of the Arab Revolt in *The Seven Pillars of Wisdom*. Lawrence recorded that a fully loaded camel, under an experienced rider, could, if hard pressed, cover 80 to 100 miles in a 24-hour period, depending on the country, and that 50 miles ridden in the same period was considered a holiday by comparison. Even the most inexperienced and clumsy riders, who positively hindered their animals, could travel 30 miles a day. The length of stages undertaken in the crossing of a desert is limited, of course, by the distance between wells, but even so the Magi could have completed their journey from Babylonia in two weeks at the outside, or in ten days with less comfort. Allowing two weeks for preparation (gathering of stores, hiring of men and beasts, and so on), the whole enterprise would have taken a month at the most. Ultimately, however, we just do not know how long it took the Magi to travel, and it is probably safest to assume that it might well have taken three to four months.

If the Magi came from Parthia (route 5), the region just to the south of the Caspian Sea near Tehran, or Persia, the region between Isfahan and Shiraz in present-day Iran (route 6), the journey could easily have taken twice as long. Ephraem Syrus, who was convinced that the Magi were Persians, even goes so far as to give the route they followed. According to him they traveled down the southern branch of the old Royal Road of Persia to Tigranacerta in the foothills of the mountains of Armenia. They then crossed the Euphrates to Antioch and Damascus, finally arriving in Jerusalem.

The journey from the kingdom of Sheba (route 7), around the city of Marib which now lies in the Yemen, was over 1250 miles long. Midian is the mountainous region to the east of the Gulf of Aqabah, a region rich in mineral wealth, especially copper, and connected with the Kenite tribe. The journey from Midian (route 8) to Jerusalem is about 200 miles long.

The conclusion we can draw is that the journey time of the Magi from their homeland to Jerusalem was at least three or four months and probably considerably longer. The Magi gave no impression of being in a hurry and Ezra's journey times give a more realistic estimate of the time taken. We do not know how long it took them to prepare for the journey, but two weeks seems reasonable. Also we have no idea as to how long it took them to decide to make the journey after the star had been seen in the sky. They must have needed time to make up their minds that the star heralded the birth of the King of the Jews. In total, we therefore seem to be dealing with a period between five months and a year and this is the interval we must consider when trying to decide what the star was. The astronomical phenomenon must appear in the east, disappear, then reappear at Jerusalem, with the appearance and reappearance separated by this time interval.

When it came to their return journey, according to Matthew 2:12 the Magi did not go back through Jerusalem, where Herod's palace was: "And being warned of God in a dream that they should not return to Herod they departed into their own country another way." It seems safe to suppose that they spent more than a few hours in Bethlehem. The verse above indicates that they spent at least one night and it seems highly unlikely that the Magi would spend months traveling and then simply stay for an extremely short time. Presumably, however, the warning about Herod made them leave quickly.

Of the two other ways back from Bethlehem (Figure 3), one went around the south of the Dead Sea, leaving Bethlehem on the main road for Hebron or going through the wilderness of Judea past Beit Sahur, Za-tara and then on to Mizpe Shalem. The route then continued round the Dead Sea through Sodom, to Petra and the Great Highway, the Mecca route in the land of Moab. The other route was past Beit Sahur, St. Theodosius, Mar Saba and Nabi Musa to the ford across the Jordan north of the Dead Sea. This second route is supported by an old legend that the imposing monastery of St. Theodosius (Arabic names Deir Dosi and Deir Ibn 'Ubaid) was built on the site of the cave or shelter *(ma'wa)* where the Magi stayed on their way back to their own country. The fact that St. Theodosius is only six miles away from Bethlehem seems to go against this theory, for surely the Magi would have traveled faster than six miles a day.

It is important to bear in mind that magi were mobile people and the journey to Bethlehem would not have been unusual. Magi moved around the Middle East visiting kings and emperors on numerous occasions. In fact Herod had at least two visitations in one decade.

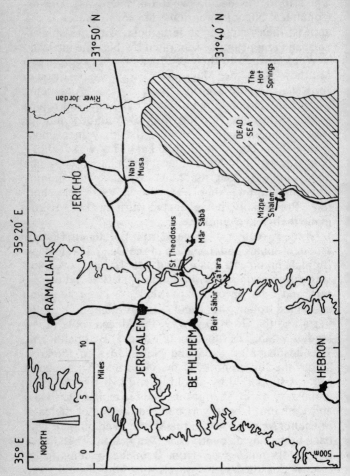

Fig. 3 A large-scale map of the Bethlehem district showing two of the
possible return routes of the Magi

Josephus in his Antiquities tells how King Herod was visited by envoys from many nations with gifts after he had completed the building of Caesarea Maritima in 10-9 BC. A visit by magi to Jesus would not have struck the readers of Matthew's gospel as all that unusual or as naively romantic.

To take an example, Jerusalem was visited in AD 44 by Queen Helen of Adiakene, a kingdom that paid tribute to the Parthians. The Queen was a recent convert to Judaism and came to Jerusalem with gifts for those who were suffering from the famine that was raging in Palestine at the time. Reading Dio Cassius, Suetonius and Pliny we learn of an amazing procession of magi that came to pay homage to Nero in AD 66. This procession was led by Tiridates the king of Armenia, a country to the north-east of Commagene, and he was accompanied to Rome by the sons of three of the neighboring Parthian rulers. Their journey from the northern Euphrates was like a triumphal procession. The delegation most probably passed through Edessa and Aleppo on the way to Rome, right through the Jewish-Christian regions in which St. Matthew's gospel first came to light. The authors mentioned above tell how the length and breadth of the city of Rome was festooned with lights and garlands, and all the people turned out to see Tiridates as he payed homage to Nero. Tiridates announced himself as a descendant of Arsaces, the founder of the Parthian empire, and then said to Nero, "I have come to you, my god, to pay homage as I do to Mithras." Nero then confirmed Tiridates as the king of Armenia. Then a rather interesting parallel to Matthew's nativity story occurred: "the king did not return by the route he had followed in coming," but sailed back to Armenia by a different way.

Cicero reports the story that on the night when the temple of Diana at Ephesus was burned down, Alexander the Great was born to Olympias. According to Egyptian legend this was a supernatural birth by divine generation. Be that as it may, the important point is that magi were present there too and when daylight broke ''the magians cried out that the plague and bane of Asia had been born that night.'' There is also a story attributed to Aristotle in which a Syrian magus foretells the life of Socrates and informs him that he will die a violent death. Seneca also informs us that magi who happened to be in Athens had visited the tomb of Plato and had offered incense to him in recognition of his divinity.

In conclusion, the journey and visit of the Magi is entirely plausible, as long as we keep in mind all the necessary qualifications about their role and status, as well as their number.

4

The birthday star

If we are to discover which star it was that heralded the birth of Christ, it is important to search through the astronomical records of the time and through some of the recent ephemerides or astronomical tables prepared for that time for evidence of an astronomical happening. This search is greatly simplified if the approximate time of the birth of Christ is known. The first clue comes from the nativity story in the second chapter of St. Luke's gospel:

1. And it came to pass in those days, that there went out a decree from Caesar Augustus, that all the world should be taxed.
2. (And this taxing was first made when Cyrenius [Quirinius] was governor of Syria.)
3. And all went to be taxed, every one into his own city.
4. And Joseph also went up from Galilee, out of the city of Nazareth, into Judea, unto the city of David, which is called Bethlehem; (because he was of the house and lineage of David:)
5. To be taxed with Mary his espoused wife, being great with child.
6. And so it was, that, while they were there, the days were accomplished that she should be delivered.
7. And she brought forth her firstborn son, and wrapped him in swaddling clothes, and laid him in

a manger; because there was no room for them in the inn.

8. And there were in the same country shepherds abiding in the field, keeping watch over their flock by night.

9. And, lo, the angel of the Lord came upon them, and the glory of the Lord shone round about them: and they were sore afraid.

10. And the angel said unto them, Fear not: for, behold, I bring you good tidings of great joy, which shall be to all people.

11. For unto you is born this day in the city of David a Savior, which is Christ the Lord.

12. And this shall be a sign unto you; Ye shall find the babe wrapped in swaddling clothes, lying in a manger.

13. And suddenly there was with the angel a multitude of the heavenly host praising God, and saying,

14. Glory to God in the highest and on earth peace, good will toward men.

15. And it came to pass, as the angels were gone away from them into heaven, the shepherds said one to another, let us now go even unto Bethlehem, and see this thing which is come to pass, which the Lord hath made known unto us.

16. And they came with haste, and found Mary, and Joseph, and the babe lying in a manger.

17. And when they had seen it, they made known abroad the saying which was told them concerning this child.

18. And all they that heard it wondered at those things which were told them by the shepherds.

19. But Mary kept all these things, and pondered them in her heart.

20. And the shepherds returned, glorifying and praising God for all the things that they had heard and seen, as it was told unto them.

21. And when eight days were accomplished for

the circumcising of the child, his name was called
JESUS, which was so named of the angel before
he was conceived in the womb.

22. And when the days of her purification according to the law of Moses were accomplished,
they brought him to Jerusalem, to present him to
the Lord.

The first two verses of this passage are particularly
important in any attempt to obtain an accurate date for
the birth of Christ. The term "in those days" brings us
back to the context of the first chapter and refers
probably to the period of John the Baptist's conception
and birth. The obvious reference is to Luke 1:5: "In
the days of Herod, the king of Judea, there was a priest
named Zacharias." We shall look at this later in the
present chapter, but first we should discuss Caesar
Augustus and the decree.

The first emperor of the Roman Empire was Octavian and he ruled from 31 BC to AD 14. He was known
as Caesar Augustus. He took the name "Caesar" from
his adoptive father Julius Caesar although Octavian
was actually the great nephew of Julius Caesar. Augustus was a title conferred on him and meant "one
who is revered." The word decree *(dogma)* means an
"edict of a recognized authority" and this was published by the Emperor Augustus in order that "all the
inhabited world" should be taxed. The phrase "all the
world" refers to the Roman Empire, "orbis ter-
rarum," for at that time the inhabited world and the
Roman Empire were practically synonymous terms. In
a rather loose way this expression might be used to
mean only the provinces, but in no way could it be
interpreted to mean only Palestine. The word *apog-
raphe* is translated rather misleadingly in the Authorized Version as "taxed," whereas a more accurate
translation would be "enrolled." It refers to the in-
serting in an official public register of the names, ages,
professions and fortune of each head of a family with a

view to the assessment of a tax. The fiscal taxation which followed was more particularly indicated by the term *apotimesis*.

Taxation was then, as it is now, a two-part process. The first stage would have started with the instruction and training of personnel in the taking of a census and in assessing income and ability to pay on the "rateable" values of the properties. This would be an "on the spot" operation from which the statistics would have to be compiled centrally. It would not be a speedy process and might take up to two years to complete. (In order to make a rough comparison for census timespans, the Domesday Survey of England, which followed the Norman Conquest and took place in AD 1086, occurred within a year and was perhaps the most remarkable administrative achievement of the Middle Ages.) Once the assessment of incomes and the evaluation of properties had been completed it would be possible to arrive at the rate of tax to be levied to yield the required revenue. This collection of taxes would have been the second stage of the process.

Now the first verse of Luke's second chapter is not without its critics and several objections have been put forward as to its truth. In the first place, no historian of the period mentioned such a decree of Augustus. Secondly, even if Augustus had issued such an edict some critics point out that it would not be applicable to the states that Herod ruled over in general nor to Judea in particular, simply because this country was not reduced to the status of a Roman province until ten or eleven years later—in AD 6. Thirdly, a Roman edict executed within Herod's kingdom would have been executed according to the Roman rules. Under this system there was no need for Joseph to put in an appearance at Bethlehem. According to Roman law the registration was made at the place of birth or residence and not at the place where the family originated. The critics point out fourthly that even if it was necessary for Joseph to travel from Nazareth to

Bethlehem this obligation did not extend to Mary his wife. Under Roman law women were not liable to registration.

These objections have to be answered if the historic truth of Luke's second chapter is to be established. Let us start by considering Augustus. From the beginning of his reign he had aimed at a stronger centralization of the empire. Julius Caesar produced a complete survey of the empire in order to make an exact tax assessment. This work took thirty-two years to complete and was only finished under Augustus. Augustus followed in his father's footsteps and his *Breviarium totius imperii,* which he had written by hand and which was read in the Senate after his death, was a detailed statistical document which applied to the empire proper and to the allied kingdoms, including that of Herod. This gave the number of citizens and the number of allies under arms and fleets and their ability to pay tributes and taxes. It is probable that such a document was based on a previous compilation of statistics, which encompassed not only the empire proper but also the allied states. And if Augustus had ordered this work, Herod, whose kingdom was ultimately answerable to Rome, could not have refused to take part in it. The silence of historians in regard to this fact proves simply nothing against its reality, though of course this only applies to the silence of contemporary historians.

Later writers often refer to the enrollment. Tertullian mentions "the census taken in Judea under Augustus by Sentius Saturninus," the detail about Sentius Saturninus proving that his source of information was independent of Luke's. The historian Suidas states that "Caesar Augustus having chosen twenty men of the greatest ability sent them into all the countries of the subject nations and caused them to make a registration of men and property." Unfortunately our knowledge of the affairs of the Roman Empire about the time of the birth of Christ is very limited, and far more meager than for some earlier as well as some later periods.

The second point raised by the critics was that Herod's kingdom would not have been "taxed" by the Romans. This overlooks the fact that Herod's independence was distinctly limited. No money was coined in his name, the silver coins circulating in his dominion being Roman. Furthermore, when Herod went to war with Arabia without the permission of Augustus, he was sharply reprimanded and demoted from "friend" to "subject." From the time when Jerusalem was taken by Pompey in 63 BC the Jews paid the Romans a double tribute, a poll tax and a land tax. Tacitus tells how the people of Syria and Judea complained about the taxes which burdened them. Also at about this time the Jews had been obliged individually to take an oath of obedience to the emperor. Herod was therefore simply a vassal of Augustus and the application of a taxation decree presents no problems. The interesting point is that Augustus would respect the sovereignty of King Herod and he would ensure that the decree was administered by Herod and in the Jewish manner. This means that Joseph would not have to obey the Roman custom and present himself for taxation at his place of residence, but he would be subject to the Jewish custom of going to the place where his family originated—a tradition that probably reflects the fact that Israelite organization is based on tribes and families. This made the census that took place under Quirinius ten years later in AD 6 all the more controversial because it was conducted by the Romans without the intervention of the national power of Jewish custom. This caused considerably more resentment than the previous one and the Jews, now having their subjection really brought home to them, broke into revolt.

The fourth point concerns Mary. Why did she accompany Joseph? Several possibilities have been put forward. It seems, according to the ancient writer

Ulpian, that in Syria—including Palestine in this context—men were liable to the capitation from their fourteenth year, women from their twelfth to their sixtieth. Perhaps Mary was summoned to appear in person so that her age might be assessed. The fact that Mary was an heiress—the sole representative of one of the branches of her tribe—might again have obliged her to appear in person. The most probable reason stems from the fact that the baby Jesus was born only six months after her marriage to Joseph. Even though Mary did not have to travel to Bethlehem she might have been eager to leave Nazareth. Evil tongues might have spared her so far, but the birth would probably have made her the topic of gossip. The circumstances which removed them from Nazareth at the time of the birth might have been regarded as providential.

The next verse of Luke, "And this taxing was made when Cyrenius [Quirinius] was governor of Syria," does cause problems. The translation given by Godet, "The census, which was the first, took place when Quirinius governed Syria," does little to help us out of our difficulty. The problem is simple. The historical sources indicate that Quirinius did not definitely become governor of Syria until AD 6. The sequence of governors of Syria taken from Schürer is shown in Table 4.1. Even though the date (3-2 BC) of the first governorship of Quirinius is doubtful, he must have begun as governor some months after the death of Herod the Great. This is not compatible with what we read in Matthew 2:1, "in the days of Herod the king,"

Table 4.1 Governors of Syria

10-9 BC	M. Titius
9-6 BC	C. Sentius Saturninus
6-4 BC	P. Quinctilius Varus
3-2(?) BC	P. Sulpicius Quirinius
1 BC-AD4	C. Caesar
AD4-5	L. Volusius Saturninus
AD6-7	P. Sulpicius Quirinius

and Luke 2:1, "and it came to pass in those days."
Two main attempts have been made to solve this
difficulty. The first involves "correcting" the text. The
philological approach is summarized excellently by
Godet, who mentions such interpretations as "This
enumeration took place before that which Quirinius
executed," "This enumeration took place before
Quirinius was governor," and "As to the taxation
itself (which followed the registration) it took place
only when Quirinius was governor." In the third interpretation the implication is that Caesar Augustus
published the decree, although the taxation following
this was not immediately enforced and was only re-
sumed and completely carried out under Quirinius.

None of these renderings is very satisfactory, although all three have their advocates. The New Testament scholar F. F. Bruce points out that the Greek
word *protos*, which is translated as "first" in the
Authorized Version, strictly speaking means the first
of at least three. The word *protos* is the superlative
derived from *pro* meaning before, the comparative
being *proteros*, meaning former or sooner. By way of
contrast, the scholar E. V. Hulse points out that the
Hellenistic Greek used in New Testament times was as
flexible as English is now and that "first" is often used
when "former" or "prior" would be more grammati-
tical. The view put forward by N. Turner, that the
words should be translated "This enrollment was
before that made when Quirinius was governor of
Syria," would put the enrollment some time in 8 BC
and so solve the problem at a stroke.

The second approach is the historical one. Quirinius
was consul in 12 BC and at some time between 12 BC
and AD 1 he conducted the Homanadensian War. It
is highly probable that the resistance of the
Homanadensians, a tribe in the Cilician Taurus country in Asia Minor, was broken by the time the net of
Roman roads was laid out in the province of Galatia in
6 BC. This probably terminated at least the major part

of the war. It is certain that Quirinius, a person honored with the emperor's entire confidence, took a
considerable part in the affairs of the east, especially in
Syria during the years following 6 BC. For example, in
AD 2-3 he was adviser to Gaius Caesar in Armenia.
One suggestion is that while Varus was the political
and military governor of Syria, Quirinius administered
the financial affairs. It was in this capacity as quaestor
that he presided over the census which took place
among the Jews at this time. In this case Quirinius
presided over the first enrollment that took place
under Herod the Great, and subsequently under
Herod's son he directed the second census, which
provoked the revolt of Judas the Galilean. This second
census was reported by Luke in Acts 5:37 and took
place "in the thirty-seventh year of Caesar's victory
over Antony at Actium," in other words AD 6.

From Egypt there are dated census returns for AD
34, 48, 62 and other years too, suggesting that a regular
census took place every fourteen years. In about 1924
an ancient inscription was unearthed in Ankara, Turkey, giving a list of years in which orders were issued
for tax collection and the most feasible date on this list
for the Caesar Augustus decree was 8 BC. All this
information, which can be summed up in diagramatic
form (Figure 4), seems to point to the year 8 BC for the
census. Slow travel and communications, however,
could have delayed the collection of taxes by up to a
year or two. In any case, 8 BC seems to be the earliest
year for the birth of Christ and we can now concen-
trate on the other end of the time period, the latest
possible date for his birth.

Here we have one very important clue. Matthew
states quite specifically that Herod the Great was on
the throne at the time of Christ's birth. The latest
possible time for this birth must therefore be the day
on which Herod died. To find this date we turn again to
the Jewish historian Flavius Josephus. Herod died
within a few days of an eclipse of the Moon visible

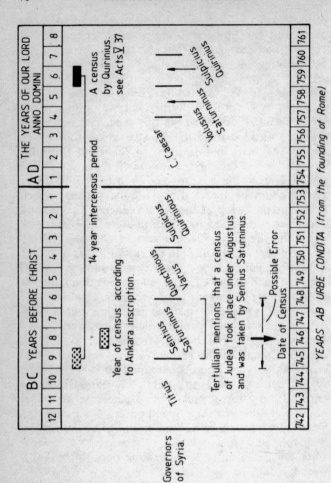

Fig. 4 The governors of Syria and the times of census

from Jericho. Josephus writes: "As for the other Matthias, who had stirred up the sedition, [Herod] burnt him alive along with some of his companions. And on that same night there was an eclipse of the Moon." This is the only eclipse mentioned by Josephus. Lunar eclipses are fairly common, occurring every time the Moon enters the Earth's shadow. This happens whenever the Moon is in opposition—in other words on the opposite side of the Earth to the Sun, the Moon then being "full"—and close to an "orbital node," the technical term for each of the two points on the lunar orbit where it intersects the ecliptic plane, the plane of the Earth's orbit around the Sun. If the Moon travels through the center of the Earth's shadow cone, the totality of the eclipse can last for up to 100 minutes. During totality the Moon is a dull red color, an effect caused by sunlight refracted through the Earth's dusty and light-scattering atmosphere. The redness is brought about in the same way as the redness sometimes seen at dawn and dusk.

All lunar eclipses can be seen from all points on the Earth's surface for which the Moon is above the horizon and in ancient times they were looked on with great fear, superstition and interest. It is not surprising therefore that Josephus recorded this natural spectacle. In some old mythologies it was suggested that the Moon was swallowed by a dragon during the eclipse and this has led to the nodal points in the lunar orbit being known as the draconitic points. Eclipses of the Moon are visible from a specific place on the Earth's surface only every few years and this makes eclipse records very valuable for dating certain ancient events. If we consider the time from 8 BC to 1 AD, astronomical records show that only four lunar eclipses were visible from Palestine. The dates of these eclipses are shown in Table 4.2.

At this time Herod was suffering from a serious illness, as Josephus reports in his Jewish Antiquities:

Table 4.2 Lunar eclipses visible in Jerusalem near the time of the birth of Christ

Date	Time	Comments	Time between eclipse and passover
5 BC 15/16 September			6 months
4 BC 13 March	01.28	4/10th of disc covered	1 month
3 BC	none		
2 BC	none		
1 BC 10 January	00.03	total	3 months
1 BC 29 December		Midpoint occurred shortly before Moonrise in Jerusalem—visible in early evening	3 months

Herod's illness became more and more acute, for God was inflicting just punishment upon him for his lawless deeds. The fever that he had was a light one and did not so much indicate symptoms of inflammation to the touch as it produced internal damage. He also had a terrible desire to scratch himself because of this, for it was impossible not to seek relief. There was also an ulceration of the bowels and intestinal pains that were particularly terrible, and a moist, transparent suppuration of the feet. And he suffered similarly from an abdominal ailment, as well as from a gangrene of his privy parts that produced worms. His breathing was marked by extreme tension, and it was unpleasant because of the disagreeable exhalation of his breath and his constant gasping. He also had convulsions in every limb that took on unendurable severity.

Would this condition have prevented Herod the Great from seeing the star of Bethlehem?

It has been suggested that he was at this time an old man suffering from arteriosclerosis, and therefore increasingly prone to mood changes, delusions of persecution, uncontrolled outbursts of hypertensive cerebral attacks and even attempted suicide. If this is so, his heart and kidney functions would have deteriorated and dropsy would have developed, affecting the lungs and causing breathlessness. Poisons, no longer excreted, would have accumulated in the blood. The mouth would have become ulcerated with foul breath, and there would have been a burning pain in the stomach, ulceration of the bowel wall and diarrhoea. A low-grade fever normally accompanies this condition and convulsions might have occurred at any time. The dropsy steadily increases, the liver becomes enlarged and painful and the abdomen fills with fluid. At this stage the scrotum may be enormously distended and any dependent part gangrenous. Such a lesion would quickly become infested with maggots.

In view of his state of health Herod might well not have seen the star over Jerusalem when it first appeared. For the last ten years of his life and even at times before that period Herod was not of sound mind. And yet even if Herod did miss the star of Bethlehem, it must still be borne in mind that anyone trying to usurp his kingdom would be at the forefront of his interest, and stars heralding their appearance would be considered important and not taken lightly. After trying a health cure at the warm springs at Callirrhoe near the north-east end of the Dead Sea, a "cure" which proved to be of no help at all, Herod returned to Jericho. Here a black mood seized him and made him so bitter toward everyone that, even though he was at the point of death, he devised the following plan. The notable Jews were commanded to come from all parts of the nation and were shut up in the hippodrome. At his death they were to be murdered by his soldiers. This would give Herod considerable pleasure, albeit posthumous, first because his soldiers had obeyed him and carried out his instructions, and second because the nation would then mourn at his death, if not for him at least for their own departed, instead of mocking and ridiculing him. Fortunately his sister Salome frustrated this scheme.

When Herod's suicide attempt was foiled by his cousin Achiab the resulting tumult led Antipater, his imprisoned son, into thinking that the king was dead. Antipater then urged his jailer to release him so that he might assume authority. When Herod heard of this, he ordered his guards to kill Antipater at once and to send his body for burial hugger-mugger at Hyrcania. Herod then remade his will and died four days later at the comparatively old age (for those days) of sixty-nine. The feast of the Passover occurred shortly after (according to Josephus) amidst the tumult of the acclamation of Herod's son Archelaus as king. At the same time there was considerable unrest fermented by the Jews who were concerned that Matthias had been deprived of the honor of being properly mourned. Passover started on 11 April that year, so we have a narrow time slot for the possible date of Herod's death. It probably occurred between the night of 12-13 March 4 BC and 11 April 4 BC.

Most of our knowledge of Herod's rule comes from the writings of Josephus. Herod received his kingship from Antony and Octavian "in the hundred and eight-fourth Olympiad, the consuls being Gnaeus Domitius Calvinus, for the second time, and Gaius Asinius Pollio." It was the custom in Rome to designate a year by the mention of the two consular officials in office that year. The consular date for Calvinus and Pollio is 40 BC. Herod took Jerusalem and began his reign there after Antigonus had been slain, which was in 37 BC. Josephus states that Herod died thirty-four years after that. The fact that thirty-seven minus thirty-four gives 3 BC as the year of Herod's death underlines one of the problems of biblical chronology which is still being hotly debated. The Jewish new year for kings started on the first of the month Nisan (approximately equivalent to April). With the Jewish "inclusive system" of measurement both the initial and terminal fractions of a year in a king's reign would be counted as full years so that the inclusive reckoning of the length of a reign would exceed the actual length by a year or so. This explains the discrepancy of one year in the account of Josephus. Modern opinion is virtually unanimous that Herod died at the end of March or the beginning of April 4 BC. The scholar Ormond Edwards does not agree and he puts forward his argument in a fascinating small book entitled *A New Chronology of the Gospels,* published in 1972. There are two main points to his argument. Modern opinion rests on the assumption that Josephus added up years of rule in an "inclusive" manner. Ormond Edwards turns to the Jewish Antiquities and finds that between February 135 BC and October 63 BC Jerusalem had six rulers in 72 years 8 months. The lengths of reigns as given by Josephus add up to a total of 71 years 6 months. In Edwards' words, "This is very exact and is certainly evidence that Josephus did not reckon 'inclusively.' "

Herod's reign actually began with the death of his predecessor Antigonus, who had been captured in autumn 37 BC and dispatched in chains to Antony in Rome. Antony intended keeping Antigonus alive until his triumphal return to Rome after subduing the Parthians, but as the Jews would not recognize Herod as king as long as Antigonus lived Antony executed him in Nisan 36 BC just before he went on the expedition against the Parthians and just before he gave Arabia to Cleopatra. Taking thirty-four years, which is the length of Herod's reign according to Josephus, from 36 BC takes us well past the spring of 4 BC, the widely held date of Herod's death. The eclipse before Herod's death immediately slips in time to become the one on 10 January 1 BC. The second point raised by Edwards relies on the work of the theologian Florian Riess. The interval between eclipse and Passover in 4 BC was 30 days, in 1 BC it was 88 days. Riess contends that the events crowding the pages of Josephus between these times—the condemning of Matthias and the ringleaders of the temple revolt, the trip with the doctors to Callirrhoe, taking the waters, the oil bath, the rounding up of the heads of the Jewish families in the hippodrome at Jericho, the death of Antipater and then Herod, the funeral, Archelaus' week of mourning, the return of the court to Jerusalem and the beginning of Passover—would take 86 days. Both authors contend that Herod died between 10 January and about 8 April 1 BC.

Majority opinion says that Jesus was born between 8 BC and March/April 4 BC, the first date being fixed by the enrollment decree of Caesar Augustus, the second by the death of Herod. There is, however, a vociferous minority that would move the latter date to January/April 1 BC. This view is, in turn, opposed by Timothy D. Barnes, who introduces some very telling historical points which we shall list briefly. Barnes starts by looking at synchronisms between events in the life of Herod's successors and events datable in the wide context of Roman history.

(1) Archelaus was deposed from the throne of Judea and banished to Gaul when he was in the tenth year of his reign. This occurred in AD 6. Herod the Great therefore died in 5 or 4 BC.

(2) Herod Antipas ruled for forty-three years and lost his tetrarchy during the second year of the reign of Emperor Gaius (March AD 38 to March AD 39).

(3) Philip reigned for 37 years, the reign ending in the twentieth year of Tiberius, AD 33/34. Both these lead to the same conclusion about the date of Herod's death. All three reckoned their reigns from either Herod's death or from Augustus' confirmation of his last will.

(4) When Philip was tetrarch he refounded the city of Julias. This was named after Augustus' daughter and must have occurred before 2 BC.

(5) Josephus said Varus was governor of Syria just after Herod's death. He held that post from 6 to 4 BC.

(6) Gaius Caesar was at the imperial consilium when Archelaus and Antipas pressed their rival claims to the throne of Judea before Augustus. Barnes concludes that this was the first occasion on which Gaius sat on his father's consilium. The date would have to be 5 BC or early 4 BC.

(7) Gaius left Rome at the end of 2 BC and so could not have been present at a consilium in 1 BC.

Another interesting point has come to light. The Megillat Taanit, a Jewish list of days on which, because of notable events associated with them, Jews were not allowed to fast, was compiled shortly before the destruction of the temple in AD 70. Reasons for the holidays are given for every case except two, these occuring on 7 Kislev and 2 Shebat. Jewish tradition has it that these holidays commemorate the death of Herod and the death of Jannai. Barnes concludes his paper by stating that the only precise evidence which exists for the day of Herod's death gives 7 Kislev 5 BC.

This changes the time period of Herod's death from 13 March-11 April 4 BC, with a preference for the first week of this period, to 16 September 5 BC-11 April 4 BC, with a strong preference for the 7th of the Jewish month Kislev. On the basis of Tuckerman's tables I calculate that this date is equivalent to 6 December 5 BC.

Before we consider exactly when the "star" appeared in this period we must look at three other points which relate, in time, the occurrence of the star to the birth of Jesus. These are the age of Jesus when the

Magi visited him, the murder of the innocents, and the ancient Jewish legends about the star which would herald the Messiah. Unfortunately, while we know that the star occurred twice—once when the wise men were in their own country and a second time as they journeyed from Jerusalem to Bethlehem—we do not know the time interval between these two occurrences, even though it must be somewhere in the region of four months to a year.

How old was Jesus when the Magi arrived at the house in Bethlehem? The answer is that we do not know for certain and what follows is obviously open to some conjecture. The main events of the early infancy of Jesus are as follows:

(1) His parents travel from Nazareth to Bethlehem to be enrolled, a journey of some eighty miles (Luke 2:1).

(2) While they were in Bethlehem Jesus was born. The mother Mary and the child stayed in a cave or cattle-enclosure because the town was full of other people of the house of David being enrolled and there was no room at the inn. Mary wrapped Jesus in swaddling clothes, long strips of cloth, as was customary in Palestine. That Mary herself wrapped the child points to the fact that it was a lonely birth and they were poor. That he was laid in a manger has traditionally been taken to mean that Jesus was born in a stable. He may have been, but it is possible that the birth took place in a very poor home where the animals shared the same roof as the family. It could have been a khan, a public stopping place covered with a roof and having in its one room a number of stalls ranged one beside the other along the walls. The travellers could lodge and rest in the stable, while in the middle of the room some space was provided for the beasts of burden and mangers were installed for them. As Jesus was born soon or immediately after Mary and Joseph had arrived at Bethlehem, we can imagine the town throng-

ing with strangers, the khan crowded, and Mary and Joseph having to lodge in the open space in the middle, under the stars. Justin Martyr says Jesus was born in a cave (as does the Protoevangelium of James 21:3). The khan could easily be situated partly in a cave. The grotto under the altar of the Church of the Nativity which is said to contain the exact spot of the birth event may owe its distinction to an authentic tradition. The manger might have been a movable trough placed on the ground or a cavity in a low rock shelf. The newborn baby was visited by shepherds who had been guided there by the angel of the Lord (Luke 2:6-16).

(3) They were enrolled, a process that could not have taken more than a few days. After this they would normally have been free to return to Nazareth, but restrictions on travel were imposed on mothers with newborn babies by Levitical Law (see Leviticus 12).

(4) Eight days after his birth the baby boy was circumcised (Luke 2:21). To the Jewish infant this represents the voluntary subjection to the conditions of the Law and the acceptance of the obligations and privileges of the covenant between God and Abraham and his seed. At this time the child received the angel-given name of Jeshua, the Semitic equivalent of Jesus (Luke 2:21).

(5) According to the Law the firstborn of every household should be "redeemed" a month after birth (Numbers 18:6). The earliest period of presentation was thirty-one days after birth, so as to make the legal month quite complete. The child had to be his mother's firstborn, and had to be free from "all such bodily blemishes as would have disqualified him from the priesthood." The price of redemption was five shekels and could be given to any priest. The original idea was that the firstborn should spend his life serving the Lord in a special way, but he could be bought back from this service for five shekels. Attendance at the temple was not necessary. The account of this redemption of Jesus is not given in the Bible.

(6) The purification is definitely mentioned (Luke 2:22-24) and was made forty-one days after the birth of a son. Purification is not equivalent to the modern "churching" of women, which is a service of thanksgiving, but is rather a sin offering for the Levitical defilement symbolically attached to the beginning of life, and a burnt offering that marked the restoration of communion with God. The sin offering was a turtle dove or young pigeon. The burnt offering could be a young lamb, if you were wealthy. Mary and Joseph were poor and substituted for the lamb another turtle dove or a pigeon, we are not told which. Jewish mothers did not need to attend the temple, but those who found themselves within a convenient distance and especially the more devout would attend personally. In these cases the redemption of the firstborn and the purification were combined, and this is most probably what happened with Mary and Jesus. The very moving meeting between Simeon and Jesus and that between Anna and Jesus, as well as their recognition of him as the Savior, followed this service. Mary and Joseph "marvelled at those things that were spoken of him" (Luke 2:33), this being yet another confirmation that Jesus was the Messiah, angels and shepherds and possibly the Magi by that time also having confirmed the fact.

(7) "And when they had performed all things according to the law of the Lord they returned into Galilee to their own city Nazareth" (Luke 2:39).

All the events in sections (1) to (7) are from Luke's account of the nativity. We now have to fit in the parts from Matthew: the visit of the Magi and the flight to Egypt. There is no contradiction between the two narratives and even though both are probably fragmentary we may fairly regard them as supplementing each other.

(8) The Magi visited Jesus and presented him with

gifts. The second appearance of the star guided them to Bethlehem. When they arrived Jesus was (according to the Authorized Version) "a young child" (Matthew 2:11, 13). In the Greek the word is *paidion,* which is translated as "a very young child" or "infant." Matthew 2:1 states that the Magi came "when Jesus was born," intimating that he was a newborn baby on their arrival. This is a view supported by Justin Martyr, who speaks of "the Magi from Arabia who, as soon as the child was born, came to worship him."

(9) And being warned of God in a dream that they should not return to Herod they departed into their own country another way.

(10) After the Magi left, the holy family ran away from the impending wrath of Herod, to Egypt.

Matthew 2,

> 13. And when they [the Magi] were departed, behold, the angel of the Lord appeareth to Joseph in a dream, saying, Arise, and take the young child and his mother, and flee into Egypt, and be thou there until I bring thee word: for Herod will seek the young child to destroy him.
> 14. When he arose, he took the young child and his mother by night, and departed into Egypt:
> 15. And was there until the death of Herod: that it might be fulfilled which was spoken of the Lord by the prophet, saying, Out of Egypt have I called my son.

(11) Realizing that the Magi were not coming back to Jerusalem to report to him, Herod ordered the "massacre of the innocents."

How can we fit these two sets of facts together to form a unified picture (Figure 5)? Luke implies strongly that the holy family did not leave the Bethlehem-Jerusalem area for the forty-one days following the birth of Jesus.

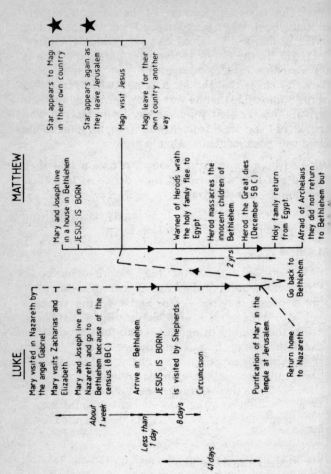

Fig. 5 One of the ways of integrating the nativity stories in the gospels of Matthew and Luke

Even so, it seems completely impossible to sandwich the visit of the Magi and the journey to and from Egypt, the murder of the innocents and the death of Herod the Great between the birth of Jesus and the purification forty-one days after. This is only possible if we have a very long postponement of the purification, but apart from the fact that this would go against Levitical law it also seems to be completely contradicted by Luke, who repeats the expression twice (2:22, 39).

How do we tie the two stories together, assuming both stories are correct in all parts? There are difficulties. One easy way out is to have the holy family return to Bethlehem after their visit to the temple, which was only a two-hour walk away. Luke's narrative is against this, for he says they immediately returned from Jerusalem to Nazareth. Matthew 2:11 implies that Mary and Joseph lived in a house in Bethlehem: there is no mention of their living in Nazareth before the birth of Jesus, nor is there any mention of the Augustan census as a mechanism for moving the holy family from Nazareth to Bethlehem—they just lived in Bethlehem all the time. They would go from the temple in Jerusalem back to their house in Bethlehem simply because they were going home. Then they were visited by the Magi and after that fled to Egypt. They returned from Egypt after Herod's death, so it is important that we get some idea of how long they were there. This would tell us the time interval between the second appearance of the star and the death of Herod.

Some of Matthew's critics dismiss his account of the flight to Egypt simply as a midrash based on the elaborate tradition of the birth of Moses (Exodus 1-2 and Josephus) or as a prelude to Matthew's prophecy fulfillment formulae tied in with Hosea 11:1: "When Israel was a child then I loved him, and called my son out of Egypt." What are the facts?

Egypt was a classic refuge for those trying to flee the tyranny of Palestine. Rhinokalura (now Wady el-

Areesh) could be reached from Bethlehem in three days and once people had reached its further bank they were beyond the reach of Herod. Egypt had been under Roman control since 30 BC and Herod had no power there. The Old Testament is full of flights to Egypt: Jeroboam fled there from King Solomon (1 Kings 11:40), the prophet Uriah did likewise when pursued by King Jehoiakim (Jeremiah 26:21), and the high priest Onias IV fled to Egypt in 172 BC to escape King Antiochus Epiphanes.

The apocryphal gospels abound with stories of the visit by the holy family. The Gospel of Pseudo-Matthew (18-20), written some time between the fourth and eighth century AD, says that they were protected from dragons, revered by lions and leopards which wagged their tails in homage, and that the roses of Jericho blossomed wherever the holy family had put their feet. They were fed by palm trees which miraculously bent down before them. There are many spots in Egypt that claim to be the resting place of the family during their stay. Matariyal to the north-east of Cairo is favored by the Arabic Infancy Gospel (24). The church of Abu Serghis, near the ancient Qaraite Jewish synagogue of Cairo, purports to be over the site of the home of the holy family. The pagan idols of Hermopolis Magna (El Ashmunein), some 175 miles south of Cairo on the Nile, apparently fell to the ground as the holy family passed through (Pseudo-Matthew 22-24). The family were supposed to have lived for six months at the site of the monastery Deir el Muharraq, near El Qusiya, fifty miles south of Hermopolis Magna (Arabic Infancy Gospel 23), and legend reports that they heard of the massacre of the innocents here. One of the subsequent Jewish explanations of the miracle-working power of Jesus was that he learned sorcery in Egypt.

Both Origen and Eusebius state that Jesus and the holy family were in Egypt for two years and they returned in the first year of Archelaus, one of Herod's

successors. This fact is extremely useful in dating the
second occurrence of the star. Presumably the Magi
departed for their own country shortly before Mary
and Joseph left for Egypt, a reasonable assumption
considering how touchy Herod the Great would have
been about the possible usurper of his throne and
remembering also how quickly his suspicions would be
aroused by the delay in the Magi's return to him to tell
him about the new Messiah. If we also assume that
Origen and Eusebius were right and the two years is
exact, then the second appearance of the star took
place two years before Herod's death. The first
difficulty is that Origen and Eusebius would have
meant "about two years," and unfortunately their
opinion about the length of stay in Egypt is only one
among several, though it does conform to ancient
legends. Other opinions exist, St. Bonaventura in his
book *De vita Christi* going as far as saying that they
stayed there seven years.

We are again assuming that the holy family came
back from Egypt soon after the death of Herod. They
were informed of the death in a dream. Matthew
2:19-23 has this to say:

19. But when Herod was dead, behold, an angel
of the Lord appeareth in a dream to Joseph in
Egypt,
20. Saying, Arise, and take the young child and
his mother, and go into the land of Israel: for they
are dead which sought the young child's life.
21. And he arose, and took the young child and
his mother, and came into the land of Israel.
22. But when he heard that Archelaus did reign in
Judea in the room of his father Herod, he was
afraid to go thither: notwithstanding being warned
of God in a dream, he turned aside into the parts
of Galilee:
23. And he came and dwelt in a city called
Nazareth: that it might be fulfilled which was

spoken by the prophets, He shall be called a Nazarene.

Origen and Eusebius also state that Jesus was two years old when the Magi came, an opinion which is not shared by Justin Martyr and gets little support from Matthew's gospel. It does add a grain of support to the supposition that Mary and Joseph lived in Bethlehem and only went to Nazareth after the return from Egypt. This two year interval occurs again in the massacre of the innocents, which we shall consider next.

In Matthew 2:16 we find this statement:

16. Then Herod, when he saw that he was mocked of the wise men, was exceeding wroth, and sent forth, and slew all the children that were in Bethlehem, and in all the coasts therof, from two years old and under, according to the time which he had diligently inquired of the wise men.

When Herod realized that the wise men were not coming back to report to him, his anger and jealousy led to tragic consequences. He sent his murderers to Bethlehem (Protoevangelium of James 22) and in what is generally supposed to have been one single hour of dreadful butchery put to death all the children under the age of two. All the children in "Bethlehem and the coasts therof" might seem a large number, but it was probably quite small. In those days Bethlehem and its surroundings had a population of about one thousand, the annual birthrate being about thirty. In view of the high infant mortality the number of boys under two would have been around twenty. This of course did not stop later Christian writers from exaggerating. Justin Martyr ignored the age limit and had Herod slaughtering *all* the boys. The number of "holy innocents," as they are known, is 14,000 in the Byzantine liturgy, 64,000 in some Syrian calendars of saints, and subsequently as much as 144,000 to fit in with Revelation 14:1-5.

A second report of this incident comes in the less reliable and apocryphal Gospel of Pseudo-Matthew (17):

> And when Herod saw that he had been made sport of by the Magi, his heart swelled with rage, and he sent through all the roads, wishing to seize them and put them to death. But when he could not find them at all, he sent anew to Bethlehem and all its borders, and slew all the male children whom he found of two years old and under, according to the time that he had ascertained from the Magi.
>
> Now the day before this was done Joseph was warned in his sleep by the angel of the Lord, who said to him: Take Mary and this child, and go into Egypt by the way of the desert.

According to Alex Walker, one early manuscript starts this chapter with "And when Herod, coming back from Rome the year after, saw . . ." This is a clue as to the time interval between the visit of the Magi to Herod and the massacre of the innocents. It is also interesting to note that this apocryphal gospel states that the interval between the flight of the holy family and the massacre was only one day.

Some people doubt the historicity of the account of the massacre, mainly because Josephus does not mention it in his Histories. It has been argued, for instance, that Herod would hardly have had to slaughter all the children, since Jesus would have been well known in Bethlehem after the public recognition he was given by the Magi. In the 1950s C. S. Mann noted the "quite arresting parallel with a legend of Abraham's birth" and also with Pharaoh's attempt to kill Moses, and he went on to dismiss the whole story as myth. He argued that Josephus is hardly likely to have kept silent on "anything so notorious as we must imagine such a massacre to have been." But was it notorious? It can just as well be argued that the murder of a few un-

weaned infants in an insignificant little village seemed
scarcely worthy of mention in a reign stained by so
much blood. In any case, Josephus' history of Herod
contains other omissions and inconsistencies too, and
he seems to suppress systematically any mention of
Christ. This may be because it did not fit in with his
religious views, or else mention of Christ may have
seemed to him inconvenient or dangerous in the Rome
of the time. Josephus, who seemed to be somewhat of
an opportunist, was writing for Emperor Titus, whose
Jewish mistress Berenice was descended from the
priestly enemies of Herod, the Hasmoneans. It was in
Josephus' interest to blacken Herod's character. If he
had known about the massacre he would most probably have written about it.

The massacre was completely in keeping with
Herod's character. At about this time two eloquent
Jewish teachers, Judas and Matthias, incited their
students to pull down the large golden eagle which
Herod had placed above the great gate of the temple.
The attempt was defeated and Herod had Judas and
Matthias, together with forty of the students, burned
alive. Herod had murdered priests and nobles, he had
decimated the Sanhedrin, and he had had his
brother-in-law Aristobulus drowned before his eyes in
pretended sport. He had also strangled the only
woman whom he loved passionately, Mariamme the
Maccabean princess, who actually had far more right
to the sovereignty of his kingdom than he did. Deaths
by strangulation, burning, and being cleft asunder;
secret assassination, confessions under torture, acts of
incredible debauchery, all these were notorious in a
reign which was so cruel that some Jewish ambas-
sadors to the Emperor Augustus spoke of how the
survivors during Herod's lifetime were even more
miserable than the sufferers.

There are those who think that Josephus painted too
black a picture and argue that there was much to praise
in Herod, especially his concept of the responsibilities,

privileges and destiny of Jewry. We must also remember that Herod lived in a brutal and violent age. Acts like this were by no means uncommon and in pagan antiquity the life of a newborn child was at the mercy of its father or the state. A few months before the birth of Augustus a prophet foretold the birth of a king for the Roman people. The senate was so frightened that it decreed that none of the children born that year should be brought up. Later on Nero, worried by the appearance of a comet, ordered the execution of the leading Roman aristocrats. Their children were driven from Rome and died of hunger and poison. Human life was of little more account than that of cattle, crucifixions were ordered by the score as a commonplace sentence of a court of law, torture was a recognized legal procedure, the destruction of man by man was a popular amusement. Twenty babies would therefore have been of little account.

What is the significance of the words "from two years old and under according to the time which he had diligently inquired of the wise men"? The time referred to is that of the first appearance of the star, the one which encouraged the wise men to make the journey to Jerusalem. Let us consider four possibilities:

(1) The first appearance of the star preceded the birth by a specific time period.

(2) It coincided with the conception.

(3) It coincided with the birth.

(4) It did not coincide with anything exactly and just had a loose temporal relationship with the birth.

Herod obviously tried to relate the occurrence of the star to the day on which Jesus was born and he, like us, must have realized that there was some confusion. He did not know for sure how old the baby Jesus would be, so he played safe and sent his murderers to murder all the boys from nought up to two years of age. The people of Bethlehem would presumably not have helped Herod's men, since he was a despised and hated ruler, and they would hardly have led his men to Jesus. Herod's men would therefore have had no means of identifying the royal infant. The last place they would have looked for the new Messiah was in the cavern stable of the village khan. It may well be that the term "young child," used for example in Matthew 2:8, means a babe at the breast and that since eastern mothers usually suckle their children for two years Herod decided to kill all those younger than two. It has also been pointed out that the expression in Matthew 2:16 usually translated "from two years old and younger" may mean "just beyond the age of one year." In any case a Jewish child who had completed one month of his second year seems to have been reckoned as two years old, in which case thirteen months would have been the upper age limit of the murdered children.

What about ancient Jewish tradition? Like most others from the Mediterranean region it is tinged with astrology. The Messiah Haggadah (Aggadoth Mashiach) opens as follows:

A star shall come out of Jacob. There is a Boraita in the name of the Rabbis: the heptad in which the Son of David cometh—in the first year, there will not be sufficient nourishment; in the second year the arrows of famine are launched; in the third, a great famine; in the fourth, neither famine or plenty; in the fifth, great abundance, and the Star shall shine forth from the East, and this is the Star of the Messiah. And it will shine from the East for fifteen days, and if it be prolonged, it will be for the good of Israel; in the sixth, sayings [voices], and announcements [hearings]; in the seventh, wars, and at the close of the seventh, the Messiah is to be expected.

Of course very little credence should be given to this astrological seven-year cycle. It has no foundation in fact and one reads of no famine or war occurring in Israel about the time of Christ's birth. The myth is persistent, though, and from the same source we read at the end of a collection of three midrashim entitled "The Book of Elijah," "Chapters about the Messiah" and "The Mysteries of R. Simon" that a Star in the east was to appear two years before the birth of the Messiah. We are not sure whether this tradition preceded the birth of Christ or originated after the event.

Another view was expressed by the well-known Jewish commentator Abarbanel (born 1437, died 1508). In his Commentary on Daniel, Abarbanel wrote that conjunctions of Jupiter and Saturn in the constellation of Pisces signified not only the most important events but also events which referred especially to Israel. The Rabbi argued that as the conjunction had taken place three years before the birth of Moses, an event which heralded the first deliverance of Israel, so it would also precede the birth of the Messiah and the final deliverance of Israel. The Messiah mentioned here is not Jesus but the one that Abarbanel's Jewish contemporaries were still awaiting.

The biblical picture of the two occurrences of the star of Bethlehem is summarized in Figure 6. The two-year stay in Egypt, the two-year upper age limit for the massacred children and the two-year precedence of the heralding star are obviously not exact periods and could be very wide of the mark. Furthermore, all references to two years could derive from one source (Matthew 2:16) and are therefore probably not independent.

When it comes to estimating the date of Christ's birth, there is a rather remarkable divergence of opinion (Figure 7). Ancient writers tend to favor 3 BC (Table 4.3), while more modern opinion favors 6 BC. Of course the most famous dating of the birth of Christ was by Dionysius Exiguus, a prominent scholar and

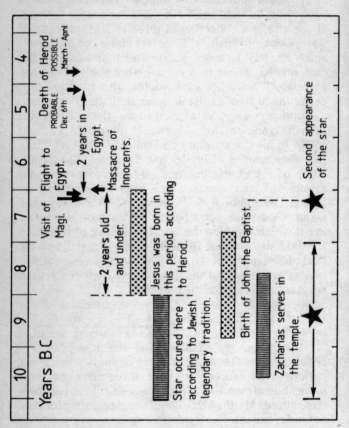

Fig. 6 An integration of the times of birth of Jesus and
John the Baptist.

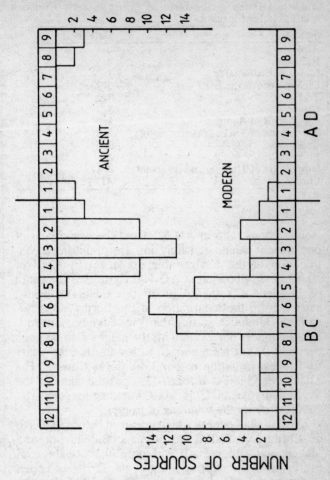

Fig. 7 The numbers of sources that pick specific birth years for Jesus in ancient and modern literature

Table 4.3 Dates of the birth of Christ in early Christian sources (after Finegan)

Source	Date (BC)
Alogi	4
Iranaeus	4/3
Caesiodorus Senator	3
Clement of Alexandria	3/2
Tertullian	3/2
Origen	3/2
Hippolytus of Rome	3/2
Hippolytus of Thebes (1st fragment)	3/2
Eusebius	3/2
Epiphanius	2
Hippolytus of Thebes (2nd fragment)	2/1
Chronographer of AD 354	AD 1

Roman monk who in AD 525 fixed the origin year of our present calendar. Dionysius was preparing a continuation of the Easter-table drawn up by Cyril of Alexandria, who died in AD 444. Cyril used the death of Diocletian as the origin of this table. Dionysius started from the incarnation of the Lord (''ab incarnatione Domini''), stating that ''we have been unwilling to connect our cycle with the name of an impious persecutor, but have chosen rather to note the years from the incarnation of our Lord Jesus Christ.'' His calculations indicated that AD 1 was the same as the Varronian year AUC754, AUC standing for ''ab urbe condita'' (from the founding of Rome).

The dating of events which occurred before the birth of Christ was based on Roman, Babylonian and Macedonian schemes. It was only in the eighteenth century that the starting-point of the Christian epoch was used for prior reckoning, and from that time the BC (before Christ) system was used. There was no year zero in this reckoning, the year AD 1 being preceded immediately by the year 1 BC. Mathematically speaking this is wrong and the year zero should not have been omitted from the sequence. The astronomical method of reckoning gets over this problem by using the following equivalents:

Historical	AD 4	AD 3	AD 2	AD 1	1 BC	2 BC	3 BC
Astronomical	+4	+3	+2	+1	0	−1	−2

The omission of the year zero cannot be blamed on Dionysius, who was not using his system to date events before the birth of Christ. Unfortunately, however, he omitted the four years during which Emperor Augustus ruled under his own name of Octavian and this seriously upset his reckoning.

Does the date of the crucifixion and the ministry of Jesus give us a clue? If we knew how old Jesus was when he was crucified and the year in which this occurred it would be a simple matter to work our way backward and find his birth date. Unfortunately in biblical studies nothing is that simple. First there is a considerable controversy as to the year of the crucifixion. The gospels all agree that it occurred on a Friday. In St. John's Gospel it is stated that the day of Jesus' trial and execution was "the day of preparation for the passover," the day on which people prepared for the feast and on which the passover lamb was slain. In the Jewish calendar this day is 14 Nisan and a careful perusal of the years AD 27 to AD 34 indicates that 14 Nisan falls on a Friday only twice. The two dates which are thus astronomically and calendrically possible for the crucifixion are Friday 7 April AD 30 and Friday 3 April AD 33.

Scholars also cannot agree as to the length of the ministry of Jesus. By considering the number of times the feasts and fasts of the Jewish religious year are mentioned in the four gospels one concludes that there are two chief possibilities. According to Matthew, Mark and Luke the duration could have been a year and a few months, Jesus being baptized in the autumn and crucified in the next but one spring. The gospel of

St. John indicates that the total ministry lasted for three years and a few months. Luke 3:1-2 says: "Now in the fifteenth year of the reign of Tiberius Caesar, Pontius Pilate being governor of Judea, and Herod being tetrarch of Galilee, and his brother Philip tetrarch of Ituraea and of the region of Trachonitis, and Lysanias the tetrarch of Abilene, Annas and Caiaphas being the high priests, the word of God came unto John the son of Zacharias in the wilderness." It is clear that Luke is anxious to give a precise date here for the appearance of John the Baptist and the date of the baptism of Jesus and the beginning of his ministry. Tradition—for example the early writer Epiphanius—puts the baptism in autumn. Unfortunately, depending on whether the Roman or Jewish method of reckoning is used, the year in question could be AD 29 or AD 28.

If we start reckoning from the time when Tiberius was a joint ruler of the province with Augustus, the baptism could even have occurred in AD 26. We are told that at this time Jesus was about thirty years of age (Luke 3:23), an expression which has been variously reported to mean anything from Jesus being exactly thirty to being somewhere in the region between twenty and forty. Thirty was the age when Levites began their service of the ministry, and it was also regarded in those days as the age at which a man was fully mature. There are three other clues as to the age of Jesus and the time of his ministry. In John 8:57 the Jews say to Jesus: "You are not yet fifty years old." The early Christian writer Irenaeus insists that this means that Jesus was between forty and fifty. Jesus was definitely not more than fifty, as the half shekel tax collected from Jesus and Peter in Matthew 17:24-27 was payable by men between the age of twenty and fifty. The temple reference is a more difficult one to interpret. This occurs in John 2:20, in which the Jews informed Jesus during one of his discussions in Jerusalem: "Forty and six years was this temple in building." It may be that the word "temple" in this passage refers to the inner temple and not the whole area of open and public outer courts. This inner temple was completed by the priests in 17 BC. Counting forty-six years from then brings us to AD 29. If we assume that the forty-six refers to the number of years the inner temple had stood after it was built, we are brought to AD 30.

All these chronological points are summarized in Figure 8. If we take Luke 3:23 as being a statement about the exact age of Jesus, i.e. thirty, then moving backward in time from the possible dates of baptism gives a time range for his birth between autumn 5 BC and autumn 2 BC. As Herod probably died in December 5 BC, this leaves no time for the flight to Egypt or the massacre of the innocents. If we simply assume Luke indicated that at baptism Jesus was about thirty years old, say twenty-six to thirty-four, the possible birth range falls well around our previous calculations but gives no unambiguous hint as to the exact year of birth. The time period in which the ministry must have taken place has been obtained by simply adding the length of the shortest possible ministry (one year and a few months) to the earliest baptismal date and the length of the longest possible ministry to the latest date. The forty-six years after the inner temple, given in John 2:20, falls easily in this range but does favor the later date, 3 April AD 33, for the crucifixion. Obviously "you are not yet fifty" must be taken in a broad sense, Jesus being in his late thirties at that time.

On the basis of biblical references, therefore, the most likely date for the birth of Christ was during the years 8 BC to 6 BC, with the year 7 BC falling in the center. This is in any case close to the majority opinion of modern scholars (Figure 7). We shall approach this problem from an astronomical standpoint later and this will give us another estimate for the nativity year.

The search for the month and day of Christ's birth may seem all the harder in view of the difficulty about even the year. One possible approach is that used in

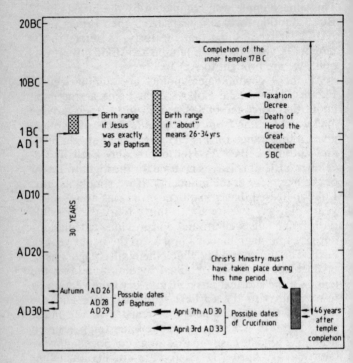

Fig. 8 An integration of the date of the crucifixion with the time
of birth of Jesus

the Koran. This is a much later book than the Bible
and many of the legends told in the Koran originate
from the apocryphal Arab Infancy Gospel. This gospel
combined three main topics, the birth of Jesus, the
miracles in Egypt during the stay of the holy family
immediately after the birth (Mary plays a dominant
role in these), and finally the miracles of the child
Jesus, most of which have been borrowed from the
Gospel of Thomas. As the Arab Infancy Gospel was
written in Arabic its contents were well known to
Mohammed and to many other Moslems. The tale of
the birth of Jesus in the Koran is very moving and it
comes in Sourat 19, the Chapter of Miriam (or Mary). I
shall quote verses 22 to 26 from the Adulla Yusuf Ali
translation:

22. So she conceived him,
And she retired with him
To a remote place.
23. And the pains of childbirth
Drove her to the trunk
Of a palm-tree:
She cried [in her anguish]:
"Ah! would that I had
Died before this! would that
I had been a thing
Forgotten and out of sight!"
24. But [a voice] cried to her
From beneath the [palm-tree]
"Grieve not! for thy Lord
Hath provided a rivulet
Beneath thee;
25. "And shake towards thyself
The trunk of the palm-tree:
It will let fall
Fresh ripe dates upon thee.
26. "So eat and drink
And cool [thine] eye."

I would like to thank Professor Ahmed K. Helmy for pointing out to me the significance of the more correct alternative to "fresh ripe dates" in verse 25. It should read "will fall about you readily collectable rutab." The word rutab is a horticultural term for fully matured dates. Dates are at first green in color and then as they ripen become red or yellow according to the variety. Then they turn dark brown or black and it is in this state that they are called rutab. It is the rutab dates that are dried and exported to Europe to become, among other things, a Christmas speciality. Now rutab dates fall from the palms between the end of August and the beginning of October, the exact time of maturation varying slightly from place to place. If we regard this story of the birth of Jesus as a true record, the date of birth must be before November, and December is completely ruled out. The Koran intimates that September is the most reasonable month. The historicity of this report, however, must be in some doubt. Its similarity to a "miracle" told of the holy family on their way to Egypt (Gospel of Pseudo-Matthew 20) is striking.

Another approach to this problem is to search for a relationship in time between the lives of Christ and John the Baptist. "There was in the days of Herod, the king of Judea, a certain priest named Zacharias, of the course of Abia: and his wife was of the daughters of Aaron and her name was Elizabeth" (Luke 1:5). Zacharias and Elizabeth were the parents of John the Baptist. "A certain priest" eliminates the possibility that Zacharias was the high priest. The course of Abia or Abijah is one of the twenty-four divisions of the priesthood set out in I Chronicles 24:1-19. As only four divisions returned from the Babylonian exile it is inferred that these four were redivided into twenty-four and given the old names (see Nehemiah 12:1-7). The course of Abijah was the eighth division. Beginning at noon on the Sabbath of the first week of the Jewish year each course served in the temple, in order, for one week. When the twenty-four courses were completed the system started again. Added to these forty-eight weeks there were three weeks during which all the priestly courses served, these being Passover, Pentecost and Tabernacles. The first course therefore begins on the first Sabbath of the Hebrew month Nisan, in the early spring. Zacharias was eighth in order and began his course in the ninth week because Passover always occurred during the third week, when all the courses served. The week following would have been Pentecost and all the priests served during that week as well.

We are told that both Zacharias and Elizabeth were highly honored, pious people who lived in the hill country at some distance from Jerusalem. Unfortunately they were both well into middle age and at the time of Luke 1:5-13 still without children. This was a matter of considerable concern to Zacharias who continually asked God to grant him a son. The most sacred service that the priests performed was that of burning incense in the holy place. Lots were cast to see who should be privileged to make this offering. Zacharias won, and whilst in the sanctuary of the Lord the angel Gabriel visited him and told him that his wife would have a son who was to be called John. This John was John the Baptist. At the end of this course of service in the temple—and according to Luke 1:8 it was one of the usual courses of service and not one of the special Passover, Pentecost or Tabernacle weeks—Zacharias returned home and his wife Elizabeth conceived. We assume that John was born forty weeks later, for a common Jewish reckoning was that pregnancy lasted ten lunar months, 280 days. Elizabeth apparently hid herself away for the first five months (20 weeks) of her pregnancy. Luke 1:26 continues the story. In the sixth month after the miraculous conception by Elizabeth the angel Gabriel was sent again by God on a special mission, this time to Nazareth, a city of Galilee, to a virgin who was living in that town and who was engaged to be married to a carpenter by the name of Joseph.

"And the angel said unto her, Fear not, Mary: for thou hast found favor with God. And behold, thou shalt conceive in thy womb, and bring forth a son, and shalt call his name Jesus" (Luke 1:30-31). Mary, being a virgin at this time, was obviously worried by what Gabriel had told her and he comforted her saying "thy cousin Elizabeth she hath also conceived a son in her old age: and this is the sixth month with her, who was called barren" (Luke 1:36). Mary then visited Elizabeth, stayed with her for twelve weeks and left before Elizabeth's baby was born. We can conclude from the above that John the Baptist was six months, or twenty-four weeks, older than Jesus. If we can date the conception of John then the birth date of Jesus is easily found by adding on sixty-four weeks.

But can we date the conception of John? According to one body of opinion we know too little about the details of the priestly arrangements of those days to derive any certain chronology from the statements made by Luke. By way of contrast, according to a much bolder view the temple in Jerusalem was destroyed on 4 August AD 70 and according to the Talmud the first course of priests were on duty on that day. Calculating backward from this date and assuming that the year which preceded the birth of Jesus was 6 BC, it is possible that the course of Abia was on duty in that year from 17 to 23 April and from 3 to 9 October. John the Baptist would be born nine months after one of these two dates and Jesus six months later, that is in either July 5 BC or January 4 BC. This calcuation can be made for any assumed year of Christ's birth and the two dates given above are just one example. Dates for nearby years will not be more than a week or so either side of the above.

The scholar William Simmons calculates the days of the temple service of Zacharias by starting with the 1st day of Nisan, which in 5 BC was a sabbath. On our

Roman calendar this day is 6 April. The ninth week, the one in which Zacharias served was between 27 Iyyar and 5 Sivan (1-8 June). Pentecost week was 12-19 Sivan (8-15 June) and according to Simmons, Elizabeth must have conceived immediately after this. The birth of John the Baptist would have occurred about the end of March 4 BC, in the very early spring. Jesus, being six months younger than John, would have been born in mid September, the early autumn. Now these calculations by Simmons simply rely on the date of 1 Nisan. This varies from year to year in an analogous way to the variation of the Christian festival of Easter. This means that even if we discount the 5 BC date put forward by Simmons and move this backward in time to the period 10BC to 8 BC, which according to Figure 4 we must do, the calculation can still be made and gives Jesus a birth month around September. It must also be stressed that St. Luke does not tell us on which of two possible weeks of the year Zacharias was actually serving. Simmons assumes that it was the one preceding Pentecost. It could have been the one that occurred about twenty-six weeks later on. With this six month ambiguity we can only conclude that Jesus was born either in September or March.

Another approach to the problem of finding the month of Christ's birth from biblical sources comes from a consideration of the sheep farming practices of Jewish shepherds around the time of Herod the Great. We turn to Luke 2 and read his beautiful account of the adoration of the shepherds:

8. And there were in the same country shepherds abiding in the fields, keeping watch over their flock by night.
9. And lo the angel of the Lord came upon them, and the glory of the Lord shone round about them: and they were sore afraid.
10. And the angel said unto them, Fear not: for

behold I bring you good tidings of great joy, which shall be to all people.

11. For unto you is born this day in the city of David a Savior, which is Christ the Lord.

12. And this shall be a sign unto you: Ye shall find the babe wrapped in swaddling clothes, lying in a manger.

13. And suddenly there was with the angel a multitude of the heavenly host praising God, and saying,

14. Glory to God in the highest, and on earth peace, good will toward men.

15. And it came to pass, as the angels were gone away from them into heaven, the shepherds said one to another, Let us now go even unto Bethlehem, and see this thing which is come to pass, which the Lord hath made known unto us.

16. And they came with haste, and found Mary, and Joseph, and the babe lying in a manger.

The small village of Beit Sahur about a mile to the east of Bethlehem (see Figure 3) is close to the spot where the shepherds were traditionally keeping watch over their flock. The actual field is purported to be a mile further on toward the Dead Sea and below the snow line. The problem that confronts us is the following. Would the shepherds be out in the fields on the birthday of Christ if he was born in December, in the middle of winter? The fields of Bethlehem in winter are rather inhospitable, mean rainfall being high and temperature low. Typical values are given in Figure 9: the night time average temperature was in the forties Fahrenheit for four months and snow was not uncommon. January and February on the hills were severe, often being cold enough to make a fire a real necessity. Some researchers regard the existence of the shepherds and their sheep on the hills at the time of the birth of Christ as an indication that he was not born in the winter, though this idea is probably wrong. Two opinions are ex-

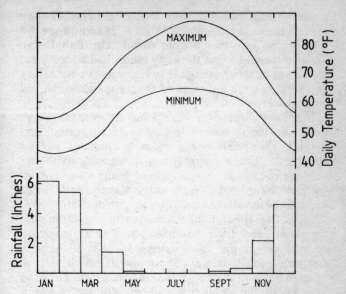

Fig. 9 The temperature and rainfall in the Jerusalem area
throughout the year

pressed in the Talmud as to whether the flocks of
sheep should lie out in the winter months. According
to one, the "midbariyoth" or animals of the wilderness
are those which go out into the open at the time of the
Passover and return at the first rains, about November. Elsewhere, however, it is said that "the wilderness flocks remain in the open alike in the hottest
days and in the rainy season," in other words they
stay there all the year round. It seems probable that
the shepherds mentioned in Luke were pasturing
flocks destined for the temple sacrifices. In the Mish-
nah Shekalim we are told that animals found between
Jerusalem and Migdal Eder (near Bethlehem) were
used for that purpose.

As a class, shepherds had a bad name. Their work
kept them from the observance of Jewish ceremonial
law, which of course meant a great deal to religious

people. They had the reputation of stealing as they moved about the country and they frequently grazed their flocks on other people's land. The Babylonian Talmud mentions that the early rabbis had added them to the list of those ineligible to be judges or witnesses and so they were not allowed to give testimony in law courts.

Since the sheep they were watching over may have been sacrificial sheep, it has been suggested that Luke's shepherds were from a class of sacred shepherds, but we simply do not know. With the passage of time the romantic and gentle shepherds in the field have replaced the rather luxurious Magi as symbols of the common man at the crib of the newborn Christ. The apocryphal gospels, with their fondness for detail and their readiness to invent imaginary names, called the four shepherds Misael, Acheel, Cyriacus and Stephanus. According to legend they all came from Beit Sahur. Since, however, we know so little about the shepherds and the practice of sheep farming in those days, it is impossible to draw any firm conclusions as to what time of year it was. Flocks would have been watched over because they were valuable and also as a means of guarding them from attacks from wild animals. Special care would obviously have been needed in the lambing season in the early spring, but the possibility that they were sheep for the temple sacrifices means that all months are equally probable.

The early church fathers had their own ideas as to which time of year Jesus was born. Clement of Alexandria, writing about AD 194, calculated that the interval between the birth of Christ and the death of Commodus was 194 years, 1 month and 13 days, which gives 18 November as the birth date. Unfortunately the year was 3 BC, two years after the death of Herod the Great. Clement recounts that according to others, described as the followers of Basilides, the birth occurred in the same year (the twenty-eighth year of Augustus, 3-2 BC), on 20 May. He also reports that 19 or 20 April has been favored by other calculations as the nativity day. It is interesting to note that even though Clement calculated an exact date, he spoke disapprovingly of others who carried out the same calculations and accused them of "profane curiosity."

The early writer Epiphanius (AD 315-403) reported in his Panarion that the Alogi, a religious group in Asia Minor around AD 180, put the birth of Jesus in the year AD 9, at a date equivalent to either 20 June or 21 May. Although according to Clement the followers of Basilides favored 20 May, Epiphanius thought that this was the date of conception and that "Christ was born on the eighth day before the ides of January, thirteen days after the winter solstice and the beginning of the increase of the light and day." This is 6 January, the winter solstice in those days being on 25 December. Epiphanius was convinced as to the date of birth but uncertain about the date of conception, wavering between 20 June with a seven-month pregnancy and 20 March with a pregnancy of nine months, fourteen days and eight hours. In the latter case the month and day were consistent with his calculation for the date of Jesus' death.

Apart from the details, all these dates seem to agree with an old tradition that Christ was conceived in the spring and born around midwinter. As time has progressed, there has been a greater divergence of opinion. The date of Christ's birth has been thought to become both less exactly known and more so. From one point of view, what was unknown in the time of Clement of Alexandria is unlikely to have been discovered afterward. On the other hand, some very specific dates have been put forward, and in recent decades at least one writer has argued that the birth of Christ took place on 21 August 7 BC and that the Magi came from Ur in Babylonia, the home of Abraham's family.

In the Arabic Infancy Gospel we are told how Joseph and Mary were nearing Bethlehem on their journey, "And having come to a cave, Mary told Joseph that the time of birth was at hand and that she could not go into the city; but said she, 'Let us go into this cave.' This took place at sunset."

In the 1950s John Addey, using a traditional astrological approach which we shall discuss in more detail in Chapter 9, concluded that the birth date is 22 August 7 BC. He mentioned an early Christian tradition that Jesus was born on the day after the Jewish Sabbath, though in fact there is also a tradition that he was born on Wednesday. 22 August 7 BC was a Saturday. According to Addey, Jesus was born in the evening and we must remember that the Jewish day does not change at midnight like ours, but at sunset. The Christian tradition referred to by Addey is therefore consistent with the birth on the evening of Saturday 22 August 7 BC. The precision of this date is certainly based on flimsy evidence. According to G. Mackinlay, who again went beyond the evidence, the birth took place in autumn 8 BC—on the Feast of Tabernacles (20 September).

Mackinlay, however, does put forward a very interesting point. All male Jews were ordered to be present in Jerusalem three times a year to worship in the temple, at Passover, Pentecost and Tabernacles, in spring, early summer and autumn. Jerusalem and its neighborhood would be regularly crowded at these times and Bethlehem being only six miles away would be crowded too. Now the enrollment that brought Mary and Joseph to Bethlehem would probably not fill the town as much as a feast crowd would. Furthermore, at enrollment many of the visitors belonged to the town and would have lodged with relatives. Under these circumstances it is difficult to understand why the inn was full, unless the enrollment took place at the same time as a feast. In any case, a feast was an ideal

time for Herod to organize the enrollment. It would
not have interfered with agricultural operations, since
Jewish men had to travel to Jerusalem at that time
anyway. If enrollment day coincided with one of the
festivals there would not be a fourth interruption of the
home routine. Linking the census edict with a religious
feast therefore had much in its favor. On the first day
of Tabernacles the populace will have had little chance
of meeting beforehand and grumbling at the command.
Apart from this, Tabernacles was a joyful occasion,
the harvest and vintage had been gathered in, and
praise was being given to God for this. Any unrest
should soon vanish in the general festivities.

Mackinlay also stressed that caravan journeys to
Palestine were not made in the hot season of the year
and this rules out the height of summer for the Magi's
journey.

In concluding this chapter we can say with considerable certainty that we know to a month or so the date
of the death of King Herod the Great. Majority opinion
favors March/April 4 BC. I tend to favor the more
recent result put forward by Timothy Barnes, December 5 BC. Either way, the two dates are refresh-
ingly close. If we bear in mind the time the holy family
spent in Egypt and the phrase "aged two years and
under" used in connection with Herod's slaughter of
young children, we move the birth date of Jesus back
in time to the period January 8 BC to December 7 BC
(Figure 6). This moving back of the date can be stopped abruptly if we consider Luke's census, the reason
he gives for the journey of Mary and Joseph from
Nazareth to Bethlehem. As can be seen from Figure 4,
the most probable date for this census is 8 BC. From
this we can be sure that Christ was born some time
between January 8 BC and December 6 BC, the year 7
BC being the most probable date. This is the biblical,
historical date of the birth of Christ. In later chapters
we shall consider the astronomical happenings,

strange or otherwise, that occurred in this period to see if we can unambiguously pick out the star which heralded the birth of Jesus and "stood over" Bethlehem when he was a very young child. We then have the possibility of confirming the year and perhaps even the month of his nativity.

5

The feast of the star

One of the greatest shocks to the people who read the reports of my first article on the star of Bethlehem seemed to be the revelation that Jesus was not born on 25 December. What real evidence is there for this traditional date?

The first reference we have to 25 December as the date of Christ's nativity comes in a Roman city calendar for the year AD 354, at least 360 years after the original event being celebrated. This Chronographus Anni CCCLIIII (Chronograph of 354), as it later became entitled, was edited by Furius Dionysius Filocalus, who later became calligrapher to Pope Damasus (AD 366-384). Among other things the calendar contains a list of the burial places of martyrs, with the days on which they were remembered and on which festivals were held in their honor. This "depositio martyrum," as it is called, contains material from around AD 336 and makes the statement "VIII Kal. Ian. natus Christus in Betleem Iudeae," which means that Christ was born in Bethlehem of Judea on the eighth day before the Kalends of January—in other words 25 December.

The originator of our modern Christmas celebration has always been thought to be John Chrysostom. He was born in Antioch about AD 345, later preached there, subsequently became Bishop of Constantinople, and died in AD 407. In AD 386 he delivered two famous sermons on the subject of Christmas. In the first, given on 20 December, he looked forward eagerly—and urged his congregation to do the same—to the Christmas festival which was to be celebrated in five days time. Chrysostom says that the festival of the nativity must take its rightful place with the other great festivals of the Christian year because without the birth of Christ there would be no reason to celebrate his baptism at Epiphany, his crucifixion and resurrection at Easter, or the sending down of the Spirit at Pentecost.

The second sermon was given on 25 December AD 386 and was reported by Theodoret, Bishop of Cyprus. Chrysostom reminded the congregation that they had only known the festival for ten years, but he also stressed that it had long been very well known to those who lived in the west as well as to the people who lived between Thrace and Gades. How did Chrysostom justify 25 December as the date of the festival? He was probably relying on the incorrect assumption that Zacharias was high priest and would have entered the temple to burn incense (Luke 1:9) on the Day of Atonement, the one and only day of the year when the high priest entered the holy of holies. According to Leviticus 16:29 this occurred on the tenth day of the seventh month (10 Tishri). It was followed shortly afterward by the Feast of Tabernacles, which started on 15 Tishri and went on for a week. Tishri falls normally in September/October (Appendix 1 gives a list of the Jewish months and their Roman-western equivalents).

In AD 386 there was a new Moon on 10 September, and the Day of Atonement fell on 20 September. The Feast of Tabernacles occurred between 25 September and 1 October. Chrysostom assumes that John the Baptist was conceived in September and he counts six months forward to arrive at April as the month of the conception of Jesus. From here he counts nine months to December, the birth month of Jesus. This of course assumes that Jesus was a nine months baby, but this is not certain. The early writer Epiphanius, for example, was convinced that Jesus was only in the womb for seven months. The Egyptians held the same view, Jesus being in this respect similar to Osiris, who was also said to have been born seven months after conception.

When we go back in time to the oldest work of Christianity apart from the Bible, we find the conception of Jesus put in the spring, and the birth in the midwinter at a time in line with many of the old traditions.

One extremely fanciful approach to this problem, with its origins in deep antiquity, relies on a "plan of the ages." According to this the seven days of creation represent seven periods of a thousand years. The sabbath, or the seventh millennium which it becomes, represents the time in which the Messiah will reign. It was argued that the first coming of the Messiah was in the middle of the sixth day, leaving five hundred years to run before the end. The theory has now already been falsified by the passage of time.

In the words of Cyprian, written about AD 243, there is an account of the lost research work by Hippolytus in which a very complicated proof was given that the nativity occurred on 28 March. This was based on the idea that the first day of creation was the vernal equinox, Sunday 25 March, the Sun and Moon being created on Wednesday 28 March. Hippolytus concluded that the day of the nativity was the same day as that of the creation of the Sun. Christian tradition follows him here and often places Christ's birth on a Wednesday. Another equally dubious argument simply puts Christ's birthday on the feast of the passover, which in AD 225 fell on 25 March. According to a rather cyclical argument it is concluded that as the paschal lamb was a type of Christ, he must be born at the time of the passover. 25 and 28 March are obviously nowhere near the traditional midwinter Christmas and so the suggestion that the nativity occurred in March was freely taken to mean that this was the day

of conception, so making 25 December the date of
birth. Another tradition in favor of the March conception can be traced as far back as Tertullian, according
to whom there is an exact number of years in a divine
life, so that Jesus must have been conceived at the
same time of the year as his crucifixion.

The Christmas feast was instituted in a rather complex way. Before the fourth century the celebration of
the nativity, if it occurred at all, was on 6 January,
which is the Epiphany or Feast of the Baptism. It is
also the feast day on which the visit of the Magi and
the miracle at the wedding of Cana are celebrated. The
nativity was displaced from this date in Rome in AD
353/354 by Pope Liberius, being on 6 January in AD
353 and 25 December in AD 354. The minor point as to
the date of the intervening Christmas is uncertain. It is
possible that the institution of Christmas on 25 December is associated with the foundation of the Church
of S. Maria Maggiore, which was the center of the
Roman celebration of the feast. Christmas services in
Rome are now centered on the Church of Liberius while
those of Epiphany are in the older basilica of St. Peter.
From Rome the celebration on 25 December spread
throughout Christendom. In Constantinople it was introduced by Gregory Nazianzen in about AD 379.
Before then, in the time of Theodosius, Constantinople
was Aryan and 6 January was the favored day.

The two sermons of Chrysostom that we have discussed previously were given in Antioch at Christmas
time AD 386. It is thought that these were delivered at
the first December celebration of the nativity at that
church. In Cappadocia the December Christmas was
definitely celebrated by Gregory of Nyssa in AD 383.
By AD 394 the feast on 25 December had become
general in Europe and Asia Minor. It arrived in
Alexandria rather later, somewhere between AD 400
and 432. Juvenalis (AD 425-458) introduced the observance of the Feast of the Nativity in Jerusalem. In an
interesting but probably unauthentic letter from Cyril

of Jerusalem to Julius the Bishop of Rome (AD 337-352), Cyril asks Julius to go through the books brought from Jerusalem to Rome by the Jews at the time of Titus to see if he can find out what the real date of the nativity was. The reason was simply that he was finding it very difficult to be in two places at the same time and, because of the difficulties of travel, on the same day. These two places were Bethlehem for the celebration of the nativity and the banks of the Jordan near Jericho for the celebration of the baptism.

In Armenia the observance of 25 December is still unknown and the nativity and baptism are both celebrated on 6 January.

The main point, however, is that Christmas is a relatively new feast in the Christian calendar and only started about 350 years after the birth of Jesus. It is obvious that the birth of Jesus was a much less important event for celebration in the early church than for example his baptism, ministry, crucifixion and resurrection. The seemingly impenetrable uncertainty as to the actual date and time of year of the nativity is ample evidence of this.

Most of the Christmas customs which now prevail in the world are not genuine Christian customs at all, but are relics of old heathen ones which have been absorbed or tolerated by the Church. Saturnalia is a good starting-point here. Many people think that Christmas was moved to 25 December simply to replace the Roman feast of Saturnalia. There is doubt about this, however, especially since the dates do not coincide exactly. Originally the day of Saturnalia, in the strict religious sense, was 17 December, and even though the popular holiday associated with this was extended according to common usage by as much as seven days, it still did not coincide with 25 December. Furthermore, there seems to be very little evidence that the early Christian writers connected the two feasts. Nevertheless, we cannot dismiss the possibility completely as there is evidence of other Christian feasts being moved to replace Roman ones. For example, the procession with lights on the Feast of the Purification on 2 February at Candlemas, forty days after the nativity, marks the end of the Christmas season and was possibly introduced to Christianize an obscure Roman procession known as the Amburbale.

As another example, the Litania major or greater litany on St. Mark's Day, 25 April, took the place of the Robigalia, a pagan Roman festival in which puppies of a red or reddish color were sacrificed in a rite of sympathetic magic. Similarly the Litania minor or Rogation day occurred on the three days before Ascension Day and so took the place of the Ambarvalia, a rite with a procession of the sacrificial victims—a bull, a sheep and a pig—all around the fields, driven by a garlanded crowd carrying olive branches and chanting.

Since Christmas incorporated many elements of the feast of Saturnalia, could this pagan festival have been the immediate predecessor of the Christian celebration? Saturn was an ancient Greek agricultural god and in his Roman form he became connected with all things that are put into the earth—seeds, treasure and perhaps even stores of produce. In Rome he was closely associated with the market, and market days were sacred to him. Even though the god was somewhat obscure, his feast was not. As a popular holiday it was extended from the one-day religious observance to about a week. Augustus, the emperor of Luke 2, limited it to three days in respect of legal business, but later on this was increased to five. Seneca tells us that in his day all Rome seemed to go mad on this holiday.

The popularity of Saturnalia was probably based on the human need to rest and enjoy oneself in midwinter. A widespread celebration took place among the northern tribes at about the time of the longest night, when the evenings ceased to draw in and the Sun began its return to the northern skies to warm the land. Saturnalia started on 17 December with a public sacrifice at the temple of Saturn followed by feasting, and 18 and

19 December were general holidays. During the feast the day began with an early bath. Later, sucking pigs were sacrificed and cooked, friends were visited, and it was a time for happiness and merry making, games and the presentation of gifts. Noticeable among the many gifts were wax candles which rather like the traditional yule log were thought to commemorate the returning power of the Sun's light after the solstice. During the festival the schools were closed, and no punishments were inflicted. The toga was replaced by a more informal garment.

The best-known feature of Saturnalia was the part played in it by the slaves. Distinctions of rank were laid aside, slaves sat at table with their masters, and in many cases the roles were completely reversed, the slaves actually being waited on by the masters. Slaves were allowed for once in the year to say exactly what they liked. They were allowed to gamble with dice, something which at other times was completely illegal.

What of our present Christmas customs? The adoration of the cradle of Christ which takes place on Christmas Eve seems to have been taken over from the cult of Adonis. The Empress Helena took over the cave where the child Adonis was born and this cave was richly decorated by the Emperor Constantine in AD 335. Christmas obviously inherited the general merriment of Saturnalia, the excessive eating and drinking, the games, the gifts, the abundance of sweatmeats. It also inherited some of the ceremonial elements, especially the burning of candles. Centuries later at the English Court a Lord of Misrule was appointed to organize the revels, while in Scotland the function was in the hands of the Abbot of Unreason.

Houses and churches were decked with evergreens, and mistletoe was especially important, being a definite remnant of early Celtic, druidic religions. The Christmas tree is an old German custom which can be traced back to the seventeenth century, but its popularity in England owes a lot to Prince Albert, Queen

Victoria's Consort. It was introduced to France by Princess Helena of Mecklenburg. The yule log is a survivor from the calend fires. In England a tenant had the right to feed at his lord's expense so long as the log would burn. Gervase of Tilbury told how grain was exposed on Christmas night to gain fertility from the dew which falls in response to the sacred text "Rorate coeli." A tenth-century Arab geographer related the tradition that trees and flowers blossomed on Christmas night. In England Joseph of Arimathea's rod was supposed to flower at Glastonbury, a phenomenon which was carefully investigated in 1752. This was the year in which the calendar was changed and the third day of September became the fourteenth. Apparently two thousand people watched to see if the thorn bush would flower on the new style Christmas. As it did not, they refused to accept the calendar change.

The day became a favorite for court ceremonial. On Christmas Day AD 800 Pope Leo III inaugurated the Holy Roman Empire by crowning Charlemagne. William the Conqueror was crowned on Christmas Day at Westminster. Woden and his wife Berchta descended from the Home of the Gods between 25 December and 6 January. Other figures traditionally associated with Christmas are Knecht Ruprecht, Petzmärtel mounted on a wooden horse, St. Martin on a white charger, St. Nicholas and his modern equivalent, who in a sense has elements from these, Father Christmas. Things apparently got so far out of hand that under Cromwell in 1644 the Dissenters banned Christmas by Act of Parliament. The day was to be a fast and a market day, with shops compelled to be open and plum puddings and mince pies condemned as heathen. Ironically, Christmas seems now to have more in common with the Roman Saturnalia than it has had for nearly two millennia.

Following the Saturnalia, which lasted from 17 to 24 December, was the festival described as "dies natalis solis invicti" or "sol novus" which occurred on 25

A sixth-century mosaic of the three kings in the church of S. Apollinare Nuovo, Ravenna

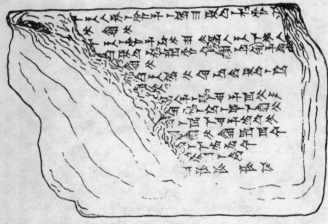

The star almanac of Sippar (7/8 BC) that refers to the triple conjunction

Conjunction of August 12, 3 BC

Conjunction of June 17, 2 BC

The conjunctions between Venus and Jupiter that occurred in the constellation Leo, 3 and 2 BC

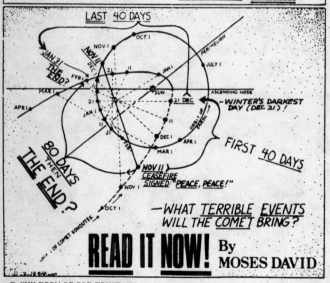

Alarm at the approach of Comet Kohoutek

December. This was the feast of the unconquered Sun, on which the victory of light over darkness was celebrated. It took place when the lengthening of daylight became apparent. This day, consecrated to the Sun, was naturally ripe for conversion into a Christian festival. It stems from the supposition that Jesus is equated to the Sun in the "plan of ages" creation myth. It is possible that the coincidence was accidental, with the calculations of 25 December coming first, the adoption of the "sol invictus" trappings coming soon after.

At the end of the twelve days of Christmas we have the feast of Epiphany and it is clear that this day, 6 January, was an older feast day than the one on 25 December. Originally it was probably a pagan feast associated with the winter season and the Sun god. It is also clear that before the middle of the fourth century many churches celebrated both the baptism of Jesus and his nativity on the same day, 6 January. Records show that the Epiphany was in general observance by AD 311. After the separation of the nativity from the Epiphany the eastern church concentrated on its significance as the feast of baptism, whereas in the west it became chiefly associated with the visit of the Magi to Bethlehem. The twelve day interval between the feast of the nativity on 25 December and that of the Magi on 6 January is not significant. There is no indication or implication that twelve actual days elapsed between these two occasions.

Why was 6 January chosen for the ceremony? Nobody knows for sure. Epiphanius tells of the feast which used to be held in Alexandria at the Temple of Kore on 6 January. The night preceding this day was spent in singing and in attending to the images of the gods. At dawn the worshippers descended into the crypt and brought up a wooden image which had the sign of a cross and a star of gold marked on the hands, knees and head. This was carried around and then returned to the crypt to celebrate "the Maiden giving birth to the Aeon."

6 January was also associated with pagan water ceremonies. Water drawn and stored on that day had special powers and was supposed to improve with age like wine. Epiphanius goes further and says that the water actually became wine and he linked the pagan ritual with the marriage at Cana in which Jesus actually turned the water into wine. An ancient belief was that water was especially dangerous at the turn of the year and it became propitious once more when the days started to lengthen and the Sun returned to the sky. Epiphany used to be the time for blessing the water for baptism and was the feast of the two incidents in the life of Jesus connected with water, his baptism by John and the Cana marriage, though both of these elements were secondary to the main element of the Christian feast—the coming of Christ. In view of the importance of this coming and the manifestation of Christ's divine nature, by John and at Cana, it was natural that the visit of the Magi, the third manifestation, should also be celebrated at the same time.

We can conclude that 25 December, although it is one of the days calculated to be the birthday of Jesus, has no special merit over any of the others. Furthermore, the calculation relies on the assumption that Zacharias was the high priest, but he was not. The Epiphany celebration of the Magi's visit again produces absolutely no proof that 6 January was the actual date on which they paid homage. We must therefore regard Christmas Day, 25 December, as the official rather than the actual birthday of Jesus. The date of the real event is still shrouded in mystery. Can the star of Bethlehem help?

6

Star or planet?

Many celestial objects have been put forward as possible candidates for the role of star of Bethlehem. These include a triple conjunction of the giant planets Saturn and Jupiter, and a nova, but Venus, Halley's comet, other comets, fireballs and the variable star Mira have all had their supporters. Before we explain in detail the astronomical features of each of these objects, let us briefly list the conditions they have to satisfy.

(1) The star had to appear first to the wise men while they were in their own country.

(2) They saw it rising "acronychally." This only occurs once a year for any specific star or for an external planet in the ecliptic. The star is just seen to rise in the east as the Sun sets in the west. It then stays in the sky all through the night as it moves in an arc across the heavens from east to west.

(3) The star had a message, probably astrological in nature, which told the wise men that the King of the Jews had been born. The Magi had been expecting this birth. Even so, the message must have been clear enough and unambiguous enough to make them plan and carry out a long and difficult journey to Jerusalem.

(4) The "star" probably appeared twice: first when the Magi were at home and secondly when they left Jerusalem after the audience with Herod. There is a

distinct probability that it became unobservable or "went out" between the two appearances.

(5) The first appearance was rather insignificant, something that the general public would miss. Herod had not seen it and it had not been brought to his notice.

(6) The "star" went before them and "stood over" Bethlehem.

(7) According to the Protoevangelium of James the star was very bright, and sufficiently so to dim the surrounding stars. It must be remembered, however, that in a much earlier account St. Matthew indicated that there was nothing particularly special about the star. Matthew's account is much more likely to be correct.

(8) From our historical investigation of the time of the birth of Christ we can conclude that the second appearance of the star, which led the Magi from Jerusalem to the newborn baby Jesus at Bethlehem, occurred in 7 BC. If we consider all the possible errors inherent in this calculation we must extend the possible birth period to one between early 8 BC and late 6 BC. The first appearance of the star, the one seen by the Magi in their own country, preceded the second appearance by as little as four months, which corresponds with our calculation for the minimum journey time of the Magi, or by as much as two years, which fits the longer possible journey times and the ancient Jewish legend.

These are the conditions that have to be satisfied, assuming of course that Matthew's account is correct. We now have to search the astronomical records for the years 10 BC to 6 BC to see if anything resembling the star of Bethlehem was seen and recorded. If nothing can be found in the records, we shall need to look for some astronomical phenomenon which is well known today and which could account for the eight points listed above. Unfortunately not one of the phenomena mentioned at the beginning of the chapter satisfies all the conditions, though some are much better candidates than others. It is also important to remember that there are very few actual new suggestions as to what the star of Bethlehem was. Recent research has tended to take old suggestions and re-examine their significance in the light of modern knowledge.

One suggestion is that the star of Bethlehem was a triple conjunction of Saturn and Jupiter. These two planets, which are members of the Sun's solar system just as our planet Earth is, occasionally appear to come together in the sky. This is a slow process: they approach each other, usually stay together for a time and then separate. When they are together they are said to be in conjunction. On more rare occasions Saturn and Jupiter come together not just once but three times, in about a year, to make a "triple conjunction." One of these occurred in 7 BC, between May and December, which is exactly the time when we think Jesus was born.

The list of supporters for the conjunction theory is long and stretches back far in time. In the chronicles of Worcester Priory (1377) it is recorded that a conjunction of Jupiter and Saturn occurred in the constellation of Aquarius in AD 1285. The unknown author adds a note that "it had not happened since the incarnation." This may well mean that the star had already been interpreted as a conjunction by the year AD 1285.

An important advocate of the conjunction theory was Johannes Kepler. He was a mathematical astronomer who succeeded Tycho Brahe in 1601 as Imperial Astronomer to Emperor Rudolph of Bohemia, an enlightened ruler with a great interest in science. Shortly before Christmas 1603, on 17 December, Kepler was observing a conjunction of Saturn and Jupiter from his observatory in the Hradcyn in

Prague. This coming together of the planets (Figure 10) is always a rather slow process and the planets are close together in the sky for a reasonable time, in this case at least ten days. It has been suggested that on very rare occasions two planets move so close to each other that they appear as a single larger and more brilliant star. This was clearly not the case with Kepler's conjunction, for the two planets at their closest were one degree apart, the space between them—the "angular distance"—appearing to an observer as twice the diameter of the full Moon or twice the diameter of the Sun.

Kepler seems to have been fascinated by the conjunction, but he apparently thought that the constellation in the sky in which it took place, Pisces, was important too. He may have remembered the work of Rabbi Abarbanel, the fourteenth-century Jewish commentator who stated in his commentary on the book of Daniel that not only does a conjunction of Jupiter and Saturn in the constellation of Pisces foretell important occurrences but it also has a special significance for Israel. Mindful of this, Kepler worked back to see if a similar conjunction to the one that he had seen just before Christmas in 1603 had occurred around the time of the birth of Christ. His calculations revealed the triple conjunction that we shall discuss later on. His astronomical calculations also showed that this occurred in 7 BC, so in true Keplerian fashion he put the conception of Mary in 7 BC and the birth of Jesus in the year 6 BC. Kepler published his work in a book entitled *De anno natali Christi*, but because of the aura of mystery which surrounded much of Kepler's work theologians rejected and finally disregarded it.

What was Kepler's real interest in all this? It is possible—as Jack Finegan suggested some years ago—that it was not so much the actual conjunction of 17 December 1603 that fascinated Kepler as the massing of planets that occurred shortly afterward when

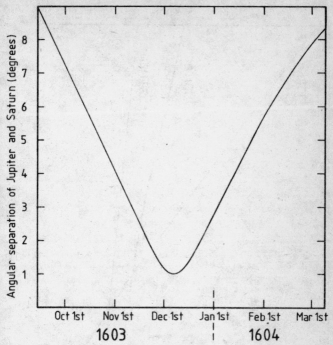

Fig. 10 The separation between Saturn and Jupiter during the
AD 1603 conjunction

Mars joined Jupiter and Saturn in the sky. It can be
seen from Figure 11 that in September and early October 1604 the three planets were very close together
(within about 8 degrees), the whole group being at the
edge of Scorpio and Sagittarius, and not in Pisces.
Finegan goes on to say that Kepler calculated that
similar massings of Saturn, Jupiter and Mars occurred
every 805 years and an extrapolation back from the
observed massing in 1604 indicated to Kepler that a
similar massing occurred in 7 BC, which he took to be
the star of Bethlehem. Apparently Kepler went on to
deduce that similar planetary massings coincided with

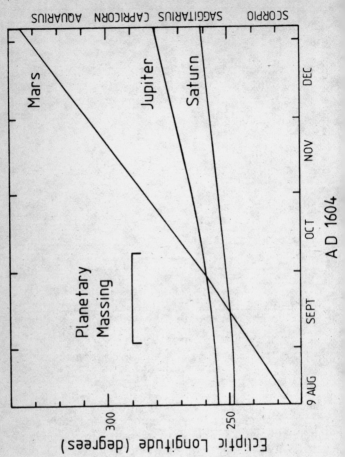

Fig. 11 The massing of Mars, Jupiter and Saturn that took place in AD 1604

seven other great climacteric epochs in the history of civilization. Here we see Kepler the astrologer and mystic in top form. His epochs are as follows:

Adam	4032 BC
Enoch	3227 BC
the Deluge	2422 BC
Moses	1617 BC
Isaiah (about the beginning of the Greek, Roman and Babylonian eras)	812 BC
Christ	7 BC
Charlemagne	AD 799
the Reformation	AD 1604

According to this view the next great event would be in AD 2409.

The frequency of planetary massings depends to a large extent on how close they have to be before they are counted as one. In the case of Mars, Jupiter and Saturn their angular speed across the celestial sphere decreases progressively. Jupiter and Saturn are slow, Mars rather fast. Mars in fact has a sidereal period of 687 days—in other words it moves completely around its orbit in this time—but its mean daily motion across the sky is 0.524 degrees per day, so that on average it takes 697 days to move completely round the ecliptic and return to the same constellation. Since conjunctions of Jupiter and Saturn occur fairly slowly, the faster movement of Mars enables it often to come close to them while they are in conjunction. In the long triple conjunction that occurred in 7 BC, Mars came close to Jupiter and Saturn before and after the conjunction. The first massing (Figure 12) was a loose one. In January 8 BC Jupiter and Saturn were separated by thirty degrees and Mars lay between them. The angular distance between Jupiter and Saturn decreased as time progressed, and the conjunction between them occurred in 7 BC. After 7 BC the planets are shown in Figure 13 getting further and further apart as time progressed and again Mars swept through the picture.

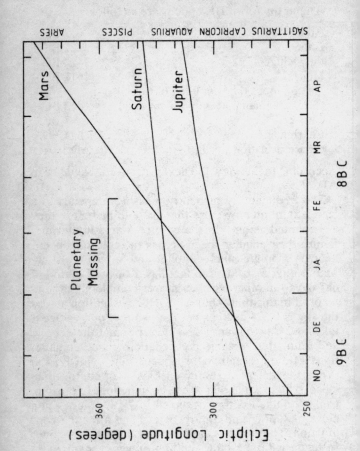

Fig. 12 The 9 BC massing of Mars, Jupiter and Saturn

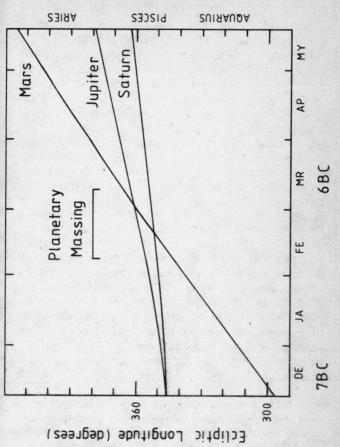

Fig. 13 The 6 BC massing of Mars, Jupiter and Saturn

In February 6 BC another massing occurred, this time a much closer one with a separation of about eight degrees.

Now in October 1604 a most unusual astronomical event took place. A supernova exploded. This is a star which suddenly increases its light output enormously and appears, to the Earthbound observer, to spring out of nowhere. It was discovered on 9 October at a time when it was three degrees to the northwest of Mars and Jupiter (both then near conjunction) and about four degrees to the east of Saturn, in an area of the sky which, on account of the conjunction, was under constant surveillance. This supernova remained visible for almost exactly a year and is the most recent supernova to be discovered in our Galaxy. It is an interesting coincidence that the sequence of the Jupiter-Saturn conjunction followed by a new star occurring in the years 1603-1604 repeated almost exactly the events of the years 7 BC-5 BC. It is possible that in Kepler's view the conjunction had caused the development of the nova and it is even possible that he thought the conjunction at the time of Christ's birth caused the nova of 5 BC.

We move next to the middle of the nineteenth century and the works of two scholars who made a special study of the star of Bethlehem, Dr. Ideler and the Reverend C. Pritchard. Dr. Ideler in his *Handbuch der Mathematischen und Technischen Chronologie,* which was published in 1825 and held in great respect, attempted to calculate the true date of the birth of Jesus by considering that the conjunction of Jupiter and Saturn wholly fulfilled the conditions and phenomena recorded in connection with the star of the Magi. Ideler held that of the three conjunctions which occurred in the year 7 BC the first would have aroused the attention of the Magi and provided the motive for their journey to Jerusalem. Furthermore, he regarded the last of the three conjunctions as so close that to weak eyes the discs of the two planets might have appeared fused into one, and might also satisfy the condition of being in a proper position at sunset to lead the Magi from Jerusalem to Bethlehem.

This idea of the two stars coming so close together that they fused was taken up eagerly, but the "weak eye" qualification was soon dropped and it became a common view that even an ordinary eye would regard the conjunction as one star of surpassing brightness. As to Ideler's dates, while Pritchard agreed that three conjunctions did take place in 7 BC, he thought that Ideler had been mistaken about their timing. According to Pritchard the third conjunction occurred in the very early morning of 5 December when the planets had a difference in geocentric latitude of 1° 2′ 40″. We shall see later that the time of this conjunction is not critical and that the two planets were in close proximity for a few days around this time. What is important is that, in Pritchard's words, "to no eye however weak could the planets have been diffused into one. On the contrary, the planets never appear during that year to have approached each other within double the apparent diameter of the Moon." He continued his calculations to see which conjunctions between Jupiter and Saturn had occurred in that part of the sky before 7 BC. In 66 BC, about two orbital revolutions of Saturn and five of Jupiter before the 7 BC happening, the two planets had a single conjunction, being only 55′ (minutes arc) apart on 20 February. The actual longitudes and latitudes are given in Table 6.1. None of this,

Table 6.1 Pritchard's two conjunctions

	February 20th, 66 B.C. Paris Mean Midnight						December 4th, 7 B.C. 6 p.m., Paris Mean Solar Time					
	Geocentric						Geocentric					
	Longitude			Latitide			Longitude			Latitude		
	°	′	″	°	′	″	°	′	″	°	′	″
Jupiter	338	31	0.7	1	10	32	S 345	30	5.1	1	28	27.9S
Saturn	338	24	16.6	2	4	47.8	S 345	33	44	2	31	8 S

however, convinced Pritchard that any of the conjunctions was the star of Bethlehem.

What do we know about the partners in the conjunction, Jupiter and Saturn? Jupiter, which is surrounded
by at least thirteen satellites including Io, Europa,
Ganymede and Callisto, is the giant of the solar system. If we list the masses of the planets and the Sun,
using the Earth's mass as the unit (putting the mass of
the Earth equal to 1), we can make the following
comparison:

Sun	Mercury	Venus	Earth	Mars	Jupiter	Saturn	Uranus	Neptune	Pluto
333,000	0.06	0.8	1.0	0.11	318	95	15	17	0.003

As can be seen from Figure 14, Jupiter is the largest
planet with two and a half times the mass of all the
other planets combined. In comparison with our small
planet Earth, Jupiter has an equatorial diameter of
142,600 km (88,600 miles), about 11 times that of
Earth. Its composition, however, is entirely different.
This is obvious when we consider its relative density.
Jupiter is 1.34 times the density of water in comparison
to Earth, which is mainly rock and iron and has a
density 5.5 times that of water. Jupiter is composed
largely of hydrogen and helium, with an overall composition similar to that of the Sun, seventy-five per
cent hydrogen, twenty-three per cent helium and two
per cent of other matter. For our investigation the
most important point about Jupiter is its orbital speed.
If we list the planets in order of increasing distance
from the Sun, taking the Earth's orbit as 1—in other
words the mean distance between the Sun and the
Earth as one unit (an "Astronomical Unit," with a
length of 149,597,910 km or 92,955,832 miles)—we
arrive at this comparison:

Mercury	Venus	Earth	Mars	Jupiter	Saturn	Uranus	Neptune	Pluto
0.39	0.72	1.0	1.52	5.2	9.5	19.2	30.1	39.4

From this listing we can see that the distance between
Jupiter and the Earth will vary as both planets move

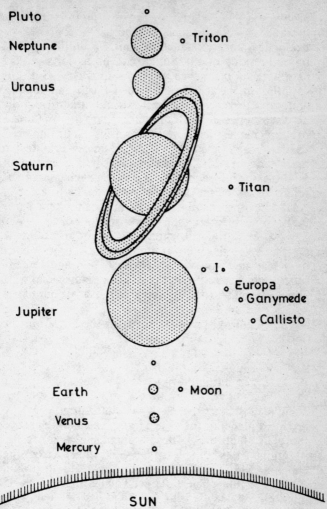

Fig. 14 The sizes of the planets in the solar system in relation to the Sun

around the Sun. When they are both on the same side
of the Sun the distance can be as little as 4.2 astronomical units (590,000,000 km). When they are on
opposite sides of the Sun it can be as large as 6.2
astronomical units (965,000,000 km). Because of this
variation in the distance between Earth and Jupiter,
and to a lesser extent because of variation in the
distance between the Sun and Jupiter, the brightness
of the planet as seen from Earth varies. At its faintest it
has a "magnitude" of -1.2 and at its brightest a
magnitude of -2.5. "Magnitude" is a measure of
brightness. For each unit decrease in magnitude the
brightness of a star or planet increases by a factor of
2.512. In other words a planet of magnitude -2.0 is
2.512 times brighter than one of magnitude -1.0 and
2.512×2.512 times brighter than one of magnitude 0.
On this scale the faintest star we can see on a clear
moonless night has a magnitude of $+6$ and the full
Moon, which is so bright that we can easily see to walk
about at night in full Moonlight, has a magnitude of
-12.6.

The brightest star we can see in the sky from the
northern hemisphere of Earth is Sirius the Dog Star,
Alpha Canis Majoris. This has a magnitude of -1.4, so
that when Jupiter is at its faintest it is just fainter than
the brightest star in the sky. At its brightest it is nearly
three times brighter. With the exception of one of the
planets closer to the Earth—Venus—Jupiter is the
brightest planet in the sky. Through a small telescope
the planet appears to be flattened, the distance between the poles being less than the distance across the
equator. This is due in no small part to the rapid
rotation of the planet. Jupiter rotates in 9 hours 55
minutes, its "day" being less than half the length of
the Earth day. The telescope also reveals that Jupiter
is covered by clouds which act as an excellent reflector
of the incident sunlight and so help to make the planet
appear all the brighter.

The disc of the planet is crossed by rich orange, red,

brown and cream bands which run parallel to the equator. It is a cold, inhospitable place surrounded by a complex system of radiation belts. Because of the large distance between Jupiter and the Sun the mean temperature of its hydrogen, helium, methane and ammonia clouds is $-150°C$. Jupiter's year is much longer than the Earth year, for it takes Jupiter 11.86 Earth years to travel all the way around its orbit. This slow progress means that, as viewed from Earth, Jupiter spends about one year in each of the constellations of the zodiac and only returns to the same constellation after about twelve years.

Saturn, the partner of Jupiter in this triple conjunction, is considered by many to be the most beautiful planet in the solar system when viewed through a small telescope. It is Jupiter's neighbor and is farther away from the Sun, being the most distant planet known to antiquity. Saturn is the second biggest planet in the solar system, 95 times more massive than Earth, and has a density of 0.7 times that of water. Being smaller in diameter than Jupiter—120,200 km as against 142,600 km—and being nearly twice as far away from the Sun, Saturn is less bright. It has a fascinating system of rings, made up of a myriad of small ice-covered dust particles which are individually orbiting the planet in a very thin disc-shaped layer in the plane of the planet's equator. This ring system is about 270,000 km in diameter and 2 to 3 km thick.

Saturn was thought to be the only planet in the Sun's family with a ring system, but on 10 March 1977 the planet Uranus "occulted"—in other words, went in front of—a faint 10th magnitude star and was found to have a series of small satellite-like objects orbiting in its equatorial plane, so that Saturn's ring-system is now known not to be unique. The Voyager spacecraft also discovered rings round Jupiter when it passed by in 1979. The brightness of Saturn depends not only on its distance from the Sun and Earth but also on the inclination of the plane of the ring system to our line of sight. When we see the rings edge-on they contribute nothing to the brightness of Saturn. In fact they disappear—a telling indication of how thin they are. At their maximum inclination (about 27°) they contribute considerably, and they can even be brighter than the rest of Saturn. The brightness of the planet can vary from about magnitude −0.23, when the rings are at their maximum inclination and the planet is nearest to Earth, to +0.96, when the rings are edge-on and contribute nothing to the brightness and when Saturn is farthest away. This is a variation of times three in brightness.

Saturn is farther away from the Sun than Jupiter, its orbit is larger and it also moves more slowly around its orbit. It takes 29.46 years for Saturn to go completely round, during which time the brightness variation has passed through two cycles. Through a small telescope Saturn is a fine sight. It has bands and belts like those on Jupiter but they are more diffuse, fewer in number and only rarely show much detail. Saturn has much less pronounced color variation than Jupiter and in the main is a golden yellow, the equatorial regions being yellowy white and the polar regions appearing greenish. As it is farther from the Sun than Jupiter, Saturn is colder, the cloud tops being −170°C. Even the ammonia in the atmosphere has frozen into cloud crystals.

What do we know about the conjunctions of these two planets? In astronomy a conjunction is the apparent coming together of two planets in the sky. Needless to say, they do not come together in reality. In their orbit around the Sun (Figure 15) Earth, Jupiter and Saturn always keep a large distance between them. From time to time the three planets are in line and are then said to be in conjunction. Looking from Earth, Saturn and Jupiter appear to be close together against the stellar background. The orbits of Saturn and Jupiter are inclined at 2.489 and 1.305 degrees respectively to the Earth's orbit plane. This plane is

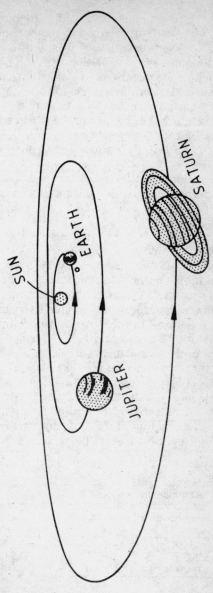

Fig. 15 The orbits of Earth, Jupiter and Saturn

known as the ecliptic plane. According to the position
of these two planets in their orbit, the minimum separation at conjunction can vary from 3.8 to zero degrees. (In a more exact definition than the one given
above, conjunction occurs when planets have the same
ecliptic longitudes. In this system the bowl of the sky
is divided into latitude and longitude rather like the
globe of the Earth, but instead of the equator we have
the ecliptic and the Greenwich meridian is replaced by
a point on the ecliptic known as the first point of
Aries.)

The most important factors in conjunction calculations are the mean planet-Sun distance, the planet year
(in other words the time it takes the planet to go
completely round its orbit) and finally the average
angular movement of the planet across the sky per
year (Table 6.2). When a conjunction of Saturn and
Jupiter occurs the two planets are very close together
and have the same ecliptic longitude. Since Jupiter
moves across the sky faster than Saturn, the next
conjunction will occur when Jupiter has gained 360
degrees on Saturn—in other words when Jupiter has
lapped Saturn. By comparing the average angular
movement of the two planets per year it is possible to
calculate that a conjunction will take place every 19.86
years. This is only an approximation, for two reasons.
In the first place, the angular speeds are average values
and when the planet is at perihelion (the point in its
orbit closest to the Sun) it moves faster than when it is
at aphelion (the most distant point in its orbit). Sec-

Table 6.2

	Mean Planet-Sun distance (astronomical units)	Orbital period (years)	Mean yearly motion (degrees per year)
Saturn	9.53884	29.4577	12.2209
Jupiter	5.202803	11.86223	30.3484
Earth	1.000000	1.0000	360.0000

ondly the 19.86 years is strictly the time between conjunctions as seen from the Sun and not from Earth. As Earth is moving around its orbit, Jupiter and Saturn are seen from an ever-changing viewpoint and so 19.86 years is only the average time.

Now a triple conjunction is a rarer occurrence than a single conjunction. For a single conjunction Earth, Jupiter and Saturn have to line up approximately. For a triple conjunction we need a near alignment of Earth, Jupiter, Saturn and the Sun. If we start with an assumed triple conjunction at year zero, single conjunctions will then occur approximately at years 19.86, 39.72, 59.58, 79.44, 99.30, 119.16, 139.01, 158.87, 178.73 and so on, each number being 19.86 larger than the preceding one. Again, of course, these are conjunctions as seen from the Sun, but for the sake of simplicity and because from Jupiter and Saturn the Earth is always "near" the Sun, we shall assume this analysis holds for conjunctions seen from Earth as well.

We had a triple conjunction at year zero, and the next triple conjunction will occur when the number given in the list above is very nearly a whole number, because only then will Earth, Jupiter, Saturn and Sun be in line again. Looking at the list of numbers we see that 139.01 is nearly a whole number, whereas all the rest have considerable fractions of a year associated with them. Triple conjunctions therefore only occur at year 0, 139.01, 278.03, 417.06, 556.06 and so on. In fact we get a triple conjunction about every 139 years, so that it is a considerably rarer event than a normal conjunction, which occurs every 20 years or so.

Let us now take this rough calculation one step further and assume that the first triple conjunction occurred in Pisces, a zodiac sign on the ecliptic plane, in other words the plane in the sky around which the Sun, Moon and planets appear to move as seen from Earth. The ecliptic plane, the zodiac and the planetary positions at the first triple conjunction are illustrated in

Figure 16, while Table 6.3 lists the triple conjunction years starting from the arbitrary year zero when the conjunction was in Pisces. This first Piscean triple conjunction is important as it is thought to be the probable star of Bethlehem. If we know the mean angular velocity of Saturn and Jupiter around the ecliptic, it is an easy task to calculate the zodiacal constellation in which subsequent triple conjunctions occur and these are listed in Table 6.3 also. The angle θ in this table is the one between the listed triple conjunction and the zero year Piscean triple conjunction measured in the anticlockwise direction. It can be seen from this table that Piscean triple conjunctions are rarer still and in the last three millennia they have only

Table 6.3 Triple Conjunction of Saturn and Jupiter listed with respect to the reference year zero

Occurrence time relative to arbitrary year zero	θ	Constellation	Probable occurrence
−993.0	105	Cancer	1000 BC
−854.0	4	Pisces	861 BC
−695.1	146	Leo	702 BC
−556.1	44	Taurus	563 BC
−417.0	303	Capricorn	424 BC
−278.0	202	Libra	284 BC
−139.0	101	Cancer	146 BC
0.0	0	Pisces	7 BC
139.0	259	Sagittarius	AD 134
278.0	158	Leo	AD 273
417.0	57	Taurus	AD 411
556.1	316	Aquarius	AD 550
695.1	214	Libra	AD 690
854.0	356	Pisces	AD 848
993.0	255	Sagittarius	AD 988
1132.0	154	Leo	AD 1127
1271.0	53	Taurus	AD 1266
1410.0	312	Aquarius	AD 1404
1549.0	211	Libra	AD 1544
1688.0	109	Cancer	AD 1682
1827.1	8	Pisces	AD 1822
1966.1	267	Sagittarius	AD 1961

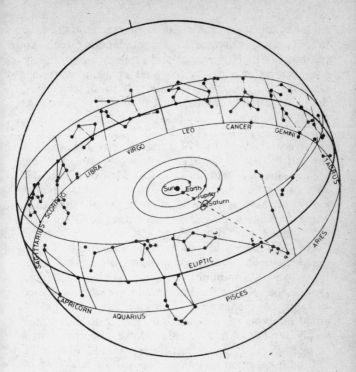

Fig. 16 The triple conjunction of Jupiter and Saturn against the
background of the ecliptic plane

occurred in 861 BC, 7 BC, AD 848 and AD 1822, about
every 900 years or so.

The actual paths of the two planets Jupiter and
Saturn through the constellation of Pisces during the
triple conjunction of 7 BC are shown in Figures 17 and
18, where it can be seen that most of the time the
planet is moving from right to left across the sky in
what is called direct motion. For about a hundred
days, however, the planets move backward, in retrograde motion, from left to right. This direct and
retrograde motion mystified ancient astronomers because they were convinced that the Earth was at the

center of the solar system and universe. To reproduce the observed movement of the planets Greek astronomers like Hipparchus and Ptolemy had to invent complicated eccentric circle and epicyclic systems. Once the Sun is taken as the center of the solar system, the explanation becomes much simpler. The retrogade motion of the planets is a perspective effect caused by the changing positions of both the planet and the Earth relative to the backdrop of stars. The size and shape of the retrograde loops vary. Some loops are below the mean planetary track as shown in Figures 17 and 18, some are above and some are so thin that the planet appears to stop in its track, move backward for a time along the same track and then recommence its forward, direct movement from right to left.

How is a loop produced, as seen from Earth? Let us imagine an observer looking down onto the system from a vantage point above the orbital plane. The dots around the orbit of the Earth and the planet in Figure 19 represent planetary positions and are separated by equal intervals of time. Initially the Earth and planet can be thought of as being at the lowest points on their respective orbits. From Earth the planet appears to be at the lowest point on its path against the backdrop of the more distant stars. By moving along the two orbits and joining the points it is possible to see how the retrograde loop is produced and also that the maximum retrograde speed occurs when Earth and planet are lined up with the Sun at the midpoints. The scheme illustrated in Figure 19 was first propounded by Nicolaus Copernicus in his great book *De revolutionibus orbium coelestium* ("On the Revolutions of the Heavenly Spheres"), published in early 1543. The wise men and astrologers 1500 years before this date would still have regarded the retrograde motion of the planets as a mystery and it was probably one of the main problems of the astronomical science of the day awaiting a satisfactory explanation.

In Figure 18 the brightest stars are Epsilon (ϵ) Pisces,

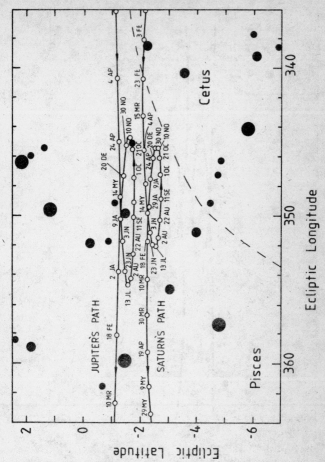

Fig. 17 The path of Jupiter and Saturn in the constellation of Pisces during 7 and 6 BC

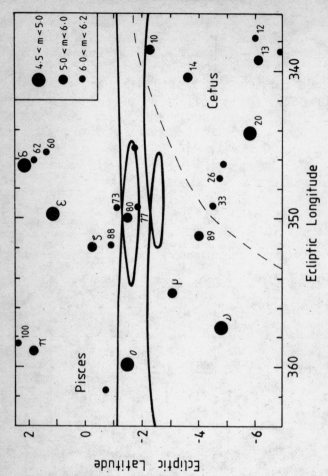

Fig. 18 The stars in Pisces and their relationship with the paths of Jupiter and Saturn in 7 and 6 BC

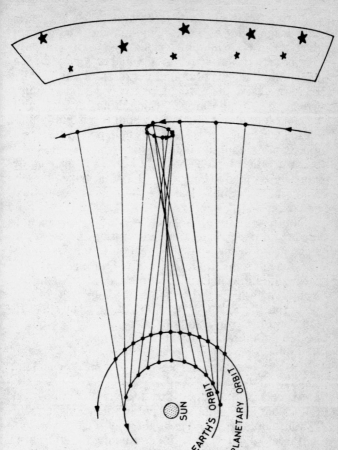

Fig. 19 The method by which the retrogressive loops are formed

Omicron (o) Pisces, Delta (δ) Pisces and Nu (ν) Pisces
with magnitudes of 4.45, 4.50, 4.55 and 4.68 respectively. These are all faint "naked eye" stars which in
our modern profusely lit cities would only just be seen
in the sky. In the profound darkness of the Middle
Eastern desert they would be easily visible. Jupiter
would be at "opposition," which means that it would
be closest to planet Earth, with both Earth and Jupiter
on the same side of the solar system and in line with
the Sun. At opposition Jupiter is at its brightest and
because of its altitude above the horizon its magnitude
can be estimated to be about -2.3. This makes Jupiter
500 times brighter than the four stars mentioned
above.

Saturn is also at opposition, but its opposition
brightness depends to a great extent on the angle the
rings make to the viewing direction (often known as
the "line of sight"). The more of the rings we can see,
the brighter the planet is. This angle varies with time in
a periodic fashion, this period depending on the orbital
period of the Earth (1 year) and of the planet Saturn
(29.5 yrs.). Extrapolating back from the ring viewing
angle of the present day it is found that at the 7 BC
Saturnian opposition the angle was about $-7°$. The
negative sign indicates that we are looking down on the
rings from a northern vantage point. We also see the
north pole of Saturn. At this angle and at opposition
Saturn has a magnitude of about $+0.5$, making it about
38 times brighter than the brightest of the nearby stars
in Pisces. Jupiter is 13 times brighter than Saturn.
They would therefore both be most impressive celestial objects dimming the nearby stars into relative
insignificance.

In the triple conjunction of interest to us Jupiter and
Saturn come together three times in the sky. Bryant
Tuckerman has prepared a series of tables giving the
positions of the Sun and the major planets at 10 day
intervals and the positions of Venus, Mercury and the
Moon at 5 day intervals for the period 601 BC to AD

1649. These positions are given in terms of planetary ecliptic latitude and longitude. With these tables as a starting point it is easy to calculate the angular separation between Saturn and Jupiter as a function of time. This separation is shown in Figure 20 for the period around the triple conjunction. During late 8 BC and early 7 BC the planets are coming together at a rate of nearly 3.5 degrees per month. On 27 May 7 BC they are 1.0 degree apart. The separation then increases for a while until they are about 2.9 degrees apart on 27 July. They then come together again, being once more

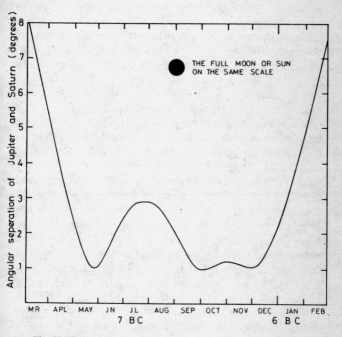

Fig. 20 The angular separation of Jupiter and Saturn during the 7 BC triple conjunction

1.0 degree apart on 6 October. They separate slightly to become 1.2 degrees apart by 1 November, and then return to a 1.05 degree separation for the last time on 1 December 7 BC. They move apart during early 6 BC as quickly as they came together in early 7 BC.

Now a one degree separation at conjunction is not spectacularly close, and we shall see later that other planets came closer to each other than this in the twenty or so years around AD 1. One degree is slightly less than the angle subtended at a person's eye by the little finger held out at arm's length. The Sun and full Moon have discs which are both about half a degree across, so that at conjunction Saturn and Jupiter would be two full Moon diameters apart. Under no circumstances would their two images coalesce to appear as one "star."

How, then, does this triple conjunction fit in with the seven conditions listed at the beginning of this chapter? Generally it fulfills the requirements quite well. In particular, as we shall see, from the astrological point of view Jupiter, Saturn and Pisces do have profound meaning in Jewish and Babylonian astrological lore and can easily be interpreted to signify a Jewish king born in Israel. As for the acronychal rising of the star and its heliacal rising, the Magi told Herod that when they were in the east they had seen the star rise acronychally, and later on in the conversation Herod asked when the star had risen heliacally. In the acronychal rising (Figure 21) the planet and Earth are both on the same side of the solar system and the planet will be at its brightest. Five planetary positions marked 1, 2, A, 3 and 4 are shown in the top diagram. In positions 1 and 2 the planet will rise in the east after the sun has set in the west. In positions 3 and 4 the planet will already be in the sky at sunset and will "come out" like the stars. Position A is the acronychal rising position. Here the planet just rises in the east as the Sun sets in the west. In a coordinate system in which both the Sun and Earth are at rest, such as that

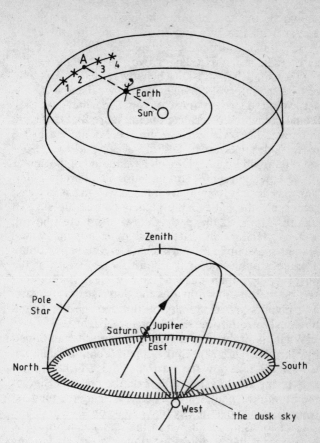

Fig. 21 The acronychal rising

shown in the top diagram in Figure 21, the planet
moves from 1 to 2 to A to 3 to 4 as time progresses.

Babylonian astronomers would be able to time the
acronychal rising to a day or two. They would see the
planet rising after sunset (when it was at 1) and as time
passed the interval between the planet rising and sunset would decrease until on one specific day they
would coincide (lower diagram in Figure 21). Here, we
illustrate the sky as seen from the Middle East at a
place with an assumed latitude of 30° north. The observer should imagine himself as standing in the center
of the hatched region with the horizon all around him.
The dark line moving up over the sky from east to west
represents the path of the planets across the sky. In
Figures 21 and 22 this path is drawn for planets having
a zero declination. After rising acronychally the
planets move up in the dark night sky, attain maximum
altitude around midnight when they are south of the
observer and then descend to the western horizon,
setting there at dawn just as the Sun rises in the east.
The planets are in the sky all through the night, and
obviously make a fine and impressive sight.

What about the heliacal rising apparently mentioned
by Herod (Figure 22)? In the upper "ecliptic" diagram
we can see that now the Earth has moved to the other
side of the solar system and is on the opposite side of
the Sun to the planet. For a heliacal rising the planets,
when seen against the sky, have to be on the right hand
side of the Sun, as shown in the upper diagram. The
observer in the Middle East (lower diagram) looking
over toward his eastern horizon would see Saturn and
Jupiter at a low altitude, but because the Sun is just
below the horizon the eastern sky would be pink with
the first rays of dawn. As the day advanced the Sun
would rise and Saturn and Jupiter would fade as the
surrounding sky became brighter. Finally they would
"go out" altogether (Saturn first, being the fainter of
the two) as the Sun's rays dazzled the observer and the
sky changed from a pinky hue to a light blue.

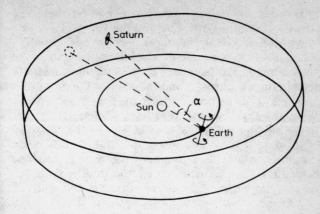

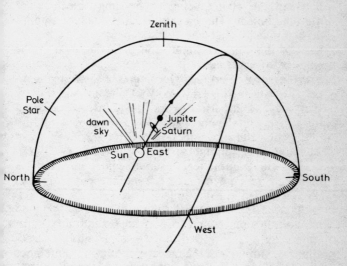

Fig. 22 The heliacal rising

The date of heliacal rising depends on the angle between the Sun-Earth line and the Earth-planet line (the angle marked in the upper diagram of Figure 22). When the angle is negative, which is the case when the angle is on the left hand side of the Sun, the planets are seen in the evening sky and they follow the Sun down as it sets. They do not feature in the morning sky at all. When the angle is close to zero the planets are so near to the Sun in the sky that they cannot be seen because of its glare (Figure 22 shows a positive angle). When the angle is a little above zero the planets just rise before they are blotted out by the Sun, a most unspectacular sight, difficult to observe and only of significance to a student of astrology. The heliacal rising can be thought of as the end of the transition between the planet being an evening object and a morning object. The magnitude of the angle required for a noticeable heliacal rising depends on the brightness of the star or planet, and the brighter it is the smaller the angle needed.

Professor K. Ferrari d'Occhieppo of the Astronomical Institute in the University of Vienna has done a great deal of important work in the interpretation of the star of Bethlehem, especially from the standpoint of the planetary conjunction and its significance for Babylonian astronomers. They were very much concerned with the practical observable phenomena of the planetary movement, and among these phenomena they included the stationary points in the planets' paths across the celestial sphere. These can be seen easily in Figures 17 and 18. Jupiter, for example, stops in the sky in July 7 BC, its celestial longitude hardly changing throughout the month. In August, September and November of that year it moves in a retrograde direction, and its longitude decreases. Retrograde movement stops in November and we have the second stationary point.

Professor Ferrari d'Occhieppo produced a table of results which shows the principal, astrologically

significant, phenomena of the celestial journeys of
Jupiter and Saturn in the year 305 of the Babylonian
Seleucid era, the equivalent of 7 to 6 BC. These data
have been calculated according to late Babylonian
planetary theories and compared with data preserved
in Babylonian calendar tablets (Table 6.4). He states
that fortunately almost complete information is available about the Babylonian special parameters used to
calculate the longitude of the acronychal risings and
second stationary points of Jupiter and Saturn. These
longitudes are given in Table 6.4 to the nearest minute
of arc. The other longitudes in the table are given
roughly to the nearest degree and are rough guesses
from Babylonian procedure texts. The zodiacal signs
zib-me and hun are approximately equivalent to Pisces
and Aries, though there is apparently a five to six
degree difference between the zero-point of the
Babylonian zodiac and the Greek zodiac as defined by
Hipparchus (the one that starts at the first point of
Aries). The Babylonian table (Table 6.4) has been
checked by reference to Tuckerman's tables of plane-

Table 6.4 The principal, astrologically significant, phenomena of Jupiter and Saturn, 7 BC—6 BC, according to late
Babylonian planetary theories
(after Ferrari d'Occhieppo)

Phenomenon	Babylonian Date	Babylonian Ecliptic longitude	Roman Date
Jovian heliacal rising	304 Adaru 13	zib-me 10°	7 BC 15 March
Saturnian heliacal rising	305 Nisanu 3	zib-me 19°	4 April
Jovian 1st stationary point	305 Duzu 22	zib-me 29°	20 July
Saturnian 1st stationary point	305 Duzu 29	zib-me 28°	27 July
Jovian acronychal rising	305 Ululu 21	zib-me 25° 17'	15 Sept
Saturnian acronychal rising	305 Ululu 21	zib-me 24° 16'	15 Sept
Jovian 2nd stationary point	305 Arah' 20	zib-me 20° 13'	12 Nov
Saturnian 2nd stationary point	305 Arah' 21	zib-me 20° 16'	13 Nov
Saturnian heliacal setting	305 Adaru 25	zib-me 29°	6 BC 15 March
Jovian heliacal setting	305 Ad. II 1	hun 9°	21 March
Saturnian heliacal rising	305 Ad. II 28	hun 3°	18 April
Jovian heliacal rising	306 Nisanu 2	hun 16° 43'	21 April

(305 is the year of the Babylonian Seleucid era, Arah' is Arah'samna the 8th
Babylonian month and Ad. II is the intercalary Adaru, the thirteenth month
sometimes added to the year. Zib-me is approximately Pisces and hun is
approximately Aries.)

tary lunar and solar positions. These results are given in Table 6.5 and are also represented diagramatically in Figure 23. The heliacal rising and setting times are indicated in the figure but are not given in the table because they depend to an extent on observational ability and the seeing conditions at the observation site. Instead we list the times of conjunction and opposition which can be obtained exactly from Tuckerman's tables. Heliacal setting occurs just before conjunction and heliacal rising just after. The acronychal rising occurs at opposition. The general agreement between the dates given in Tables 6.4 and 6.5 is encouraging.

Table 6.5 The principal astrologically significant phenomena of Jupiter and Saturn during 7 BC and 6 BC using Tuckerman's data as the basis for the calculation

Phenomenon	Ecliptic longitude	Date
Jovian conjunction with Sun	330.92	7 BC 21 Feb
Saturnian conjunction with Sun	342.12	4 March
Jovian 1st stationary point	354.71	17 July
Saturnian 1st stationary point	352.13	6 July
Jovian opposition to Sun	349.78	15 Sept
Saturnian opposition to Sun	348.66	14 Sept
Jovian 2nd stationary point	344.74	11 Nov
Saturnian 2nd stationary point	345.27	19 Nov
Saturnian conjunction with Sun	355.26	6 BC 18 March
Jovian conjunction with Sun	7.55	31 March

Is it possible to identify the star of Bethlehem among the plethora of "happenings" that Jupiter and Saturn went through during 7 BC? During late 8 BC the two planets were coming closer together very quickly. In February 7 BC they set heliacally. This means that they were just visible to the left of the Sun as it set in the west and they were seen in the sky for only a short time as they quickly followed the Sun down below the horizon. At the end of February the two planets could not be seen as they were too close to the Sun. In mid-

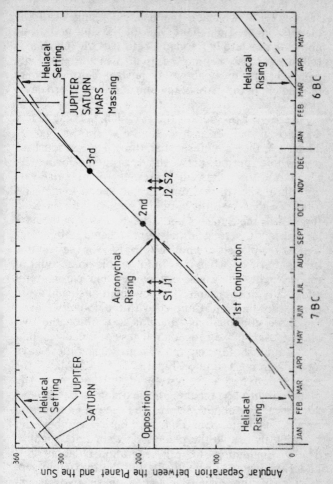

Fig 23 The angular distance between the Sun and the planets Jupiter and Saturn during 7 BC

March 7 BC we have the heliacal rising, with the planets on the right hand side of the sun and rising above the eastern horizon just before dawn. The Sun is following close behind so that planets have only climbed a short way above the horizon before they are blotted out in the glare of the Sun and the eastern dawn sky.

As the year progresses the two planets come closer and closer together and, as can be seen from Figures 20 and 23, they are closer than three degrees apart for the whole period between April and December. Furthermore, as the year passes, the planets rise earlier and earlier in the morning and spend longer and longer in the sky until by mid-September they rise in the east as the Sun sets and then they stay in the dark sky all night, setting in the west at dawn. After September the planets are not seen to rise, for they do this in the afternoon when they are invisible on account of the daylight. They also set earlier and earlier until eventually, by March 6 BC, they set at dusk and again can hardly be seen. Coupled with the above we have the three conjunctions, the times at which the two planets come closest together. These times correspond to the minima of the curve in Figure 20 and these have again been marked in on Figure 23. The 27 May 7 BC conjunction has a separation of 0.98 degrees. The planets then part, reaching a maximum separation of 2.9 degrees by about 28 July. The second conjunction occurs on 6 October and the third on 1 December, and between these two the planets only separate slightly. These conjunctions have a separation of about 0.98 and 1.05 degrees respectively and the maximum separation of the planets between these two occurs around the end of October and is only about 1.2 degrees. There is a distinct possibility that the Magi and any other astronomer of those times would simply not notice this slight parting and would conclude that there was just one conjunction during October and

November, followed by a speedy separation of the planets.

In view of all this, what did the wise men see in their own country? Astrologically the heliacal rising was thought to signify birth. One possibility therefore is that the wise men saw the heliacal rising in the eastern sky when they were in the east, in their own country. This occurred in March 7 BC and an astrologer would have taken the heliacal rising of Saturn and Jupiter to mean that the Messiah, Christ, was born in March 7 BC.

A second possibility is that the "star" seen in the east by the Magi was the acronychal rising which occurred in mid September 7 BC, an event preceded by both the heliacal rising in March and the first conjunction at the end of May. In support of this view there is the possibility that in Matthew 2:2 the Magi were in effect saying "we have seen the acronychal rising." Nevertheless, the real problem with the March and September 7 BC dates and with the triple conjunction hypothesis as a whole is the second appearance of the star. Is it correct to interpret Matthew 2:10, "When they saw the star, they rejoiced with exceeding great joy," as an indication of the happiness of the Magi upon their rediscovery of the star of Bethlehem, which they had first seen in the east, after a period during which it was invisible in the sky? If it is, then Saturn and Jupiter present a difficulty, because from the time of their heliacal rising, March 7 BC, right through to the time of their heliacal setting a year later in March 6 BC, these two planets could be clearly seen in the sky for at least some part of the night. The period of observation occurred in the morning before September, throughout the night during September and in the evening afterward. They only disappeared when they were too close to the Sun to be seen and this only happened (in the time interval under consideration in Figure 23) during late February, early March 7

BC, and March and early April 6 BC. A rather tortuous way out of this dilemma is to refer back to Figure 20 and bring in the second and third conjunction in October and November. Could this have been the second appearance of the star?

The Magi have to travel from the east to Jerusalem and it has already been concluded in Chapter 3 that this would take three to four months or more. The list of time intervals between the phenomena we have mentioned (Table 6.6) seems to rule out the acronychal rising as the first star unless the wise men traveled at almost superhuman speed. We cannot regard the heliacal, acronychal or first conjunction as the first star of Bethlehem and something completely different as the second, unless of course we completely disregard Matthew 2:9 which specifically states that when they left Jerusalem for Bethlehem "the star, which they saw in the east, went before them." Furthermore, how significant is a conjunction or a heliacal or an acrony-

Table 6.6 The time interval between the events illustrated in Figure 23

Possible 1st Star	Possible 2nd Star	Time interval between them
heliacal rising	1st conjunction	3 months
heliacal rising	acronychal rising	6½ months
heliacal rising	2nd conjunction	7 months
heliacal rising	3rd conjunction	9 months
heliacal rising	2nd & 3rd conjunction together	8 months
heliacal rising	planetary massing	12 months
acronychal rising	2nd conjunction	½ month
acronychal rising	3rd conjunction	2½ months
acronychal rising	2nd & 3rd conjunction together	1½ months
acronychal rising	planetary massing	5½ months
1st conjunction	2nd conjunction	4 months
1st conjunction	3rd conjunction	6 months
1st conjunction	2nd & 3rd conjunction together	5 months
1st conjunction	planetary massing	9 months

chal rising of Saturn and Jupiter when the minimum separation is only one degree, twice the angular diameter of the Sun or the full Moon? Is it something that would have made people look up and take notice?

In the Middle East at that time, clear skies were not unusual and there would not have been much surprise when two perfectly ordinary and well-known planets happened to get fairly close to each other in the sky. A one degree separation might have been of passing interest to the amateur stargazer of the day but it would not have been so amazing as to become a topic of public conversation. Herod and his advisers could have easily missed it and been surprised later on by the significance that the Magi attributed to the event. The importance of the event obviously lay in its astrological message, as we shall see in chapter nine.

How well does the triple conjunction fit in with Matthew's reference to the star as "going before" the Magi and "standing over" Bethlehem? As far as these two improbable characteristics are concerned we must conclude that the conjunction theory stands up as well as any other astronomical theory would. Planets and comets do of course move against the fixed background of stars, but this movement is slow and usually takes much longer than one night of observations to detect. In any case, planets still rise in the east and set in the west and in the meantime move with the celestial sphere in a well behaved and well understood fashion just like the stars do, attaining their highest altitude above the horizon when they are due south of the observer. Jupiter and Saturn rise ever earlier in the east as the months progress. If an observer looks at the sky at one specific time of night, the positions of the stars and planets change as the weeks pass. The constellation of Pisces, in which the conjunction, stationary points and acronychal risings all take place, rises at about 2:00 a.m. during May 7 BC, 10:00 p.m. during July, 7:00 p.m. in September, and at 12:00 noon in December.

The time of day when this constellation and the two planets can be seen due south of Jerusalem, in the direction of Bethlehem, varies as the months progress. This occurs about midnight during September and in the early evening (7:00 p.m.) during December. For other times, of course, we can interpolate between these two values. What is important is that the planets can truly be said to be pointing the way to Bethlehem, even if they do not physically "go before." Furthermore, when they are due "south" they are also closest to the zenith, the spot in the sky directly above the observer's head. This is the nearest these planets get to "standing over." We must remember, however, that they appeared to be over all the regions of the Middle East at this particular time and not just over an individual town, even less over a stable in that town.

Matthew does not refer to the brightness of the star and it is only in the Protoevangelium of James that it becomes "an indescribably great star which dimmed the surrounding stars." Jupiter and Saturn are bright, in fact they are 500 and 38 times brighter respectively than the surrounding stars in Pisces shown in Figure 18, so this criterion is partially satisfied. No one, however, then or now would describe either as "an indescribably great star."

There is one point that should worry all adherents to the triple conjunction hypothesis and that is the constant use of the term "star" in Matthew, James, Ephesians, Ephraem Syrus and Origen, whereas Jupiter and Saturn were two planets, not one star. Attempts have been made to meet this objection by claiming that the Greek word for "star" (aster) in the New Testament could mean one star or several stars, rather like the English word "fish" means a fish or a whole collection of fish. As against this, New Testament Greek had a perfectly good plural of the same word, and if Matthew had meant more than one star he could have easily used the plural, asteres. As it happens, he used the singular form "star," in several places in his account of the star of Bethlehem—2:2, 7, 9, 10.

In biblical times people could distinguish both visually and linguistically between the fixed stars and the planets. A planet, which was regarded as a special type of star wandering about among the constellations of the zodiac, was usually referred to in Greek as *planes aster,* a "wandering star," or simply as a *planes,* a "wanderer"—the origin of the English word planet. If Matthew had meant to describe the movement of Saturn and Jupiter, why did he not call them planets instead of using the term star? Whether or not Matthew was a Greek, it is likely that his choice of words was influenced here by the language of the Greek Old Testament, the Septuagint. The word for a planet does not appear anywhere in the Greek Old Testament, whereas the word for star occurs twenty-four times, so that even if Matthew knew the proper Greek word for a planet he might well have avoided using it and substituted the more familiar term *aster,* star.

We now have an explanation of Matthew's mention of "star" rather than "planet," but what more can we say about the singular rather than the plural? According to one view, which draws upon the astrological traditions of the Babylonians, Jupiter was the planet associated with kings, while Saturn was the protector of the Jews and the planet which reigned over their religion. Matthew's single "star," it has been argued, was simply Saturn, the star of the Jews and the symbol of their Messiah. But we can go beyond this. Mention seems to have been made of the triple conjunction and planetary massing in the cuneiform texts of the day. There are two surviving versions. One, the Berlin Table, is copied on Egyptian papyrus and is an ephemeris or table of planetary positions for the years 17 BC to AD 10. The second is the Star Almanac of Sippar, a city on the banks of the river Euphrates about thirty miles north of Babylon in which recent excavations have brought to light many cuneiform tablets. This is a single year ephemeris and gives the computed positions of the Sun, Moon and major planets during the year. The text (Plate 2) is positively dated to the year 305 of the Seleucid era, a year which began on 1 Nisanu, equivalent to 2 April 7 BC in our calendar. The portion of the text that has been found only covers the first seven months of the Babylonian year from Nisanu (our March/April) to Tashrita (September/October). The tablet contains references to the summer solstice, to a solar eclipse and also to the conjunction of Jupiter and Saturn in the constellation of Pisces. This is ample proof that the Babylonians regarded these conjunctions as matters of importance and that they could and did predict such astronomical events.

The Magi would therefore have known that the conjunction, the heliacal and acronychal risings and settings and the massing of Jupiter, Saturn and Mars were going to occur. Nothing here would have taken them by surprise. The situation seems to be similar to that of a modern observatory predicting a solar eclipse and organizing an eclipse expedition. The Magi could have planned the start of their journey and have arranged to arrive in Jerusalem at a specific time. The actual sighting of the "star" when they were in Mesopotamia (assuming, that is, that they started from there) and their second sighting in Jerusalem would merely have confirmed their previous predictions. It is also clear that the Magi understood very well the rarity of such an occurrence.

One further ancient record of the conjunction is known and this is in the oldest preserved manuscript version of the Protoevangelium of James known as the papyrus Bodmer. This is a secondary copy of the work but it contains on pages MA[1]/MB[1] what must have been a popular description of the Magi's visit, albeit one that was written after the account given in Matthew. Here too the Magi wanted to pay homage to the King of the Jews whose star (singular) they had seen at its rising. In the manuscript the writer seems to make a reference to what had really been observed in the sky: "And behold they saw [2] stars [plural] in the [acronychal] rising [singular], and they went before them." This translation presupposes that the cipher 2, which in Greek is given by the letter beta and a vertical stroke, has been forgotten by the copyist. In any case the manuscript refers to more than one star occurring in one and the same *anatole,* acronychal rising, and states that these stars went before the Magi. We therefore have here an accurate description of the acronychal rising of Jupiter and Saturn in conjunction as depicted in Figure 23.

Although Saturn and Jupiter and their triple conjunction fit most of the requisites of the "star of Bethlehem" and are in my opinion at the top of the list of likely candidates, the fact that they could never have been seen as "one star" leaves a feeling of uncertainty, even if the problems of the Greek text are overcome. Their closest approach was 0.98 degrees, which astronomically speaking is not close at all. Roger W. Sinnott decided to look in detail at conjunctions that occurred between 12 BC and AD 7 to see if any came closer than the 0.98 approach of Saturn and Jupiter. Turning to Bryant Tuckerman's table of planetary positions, he searched for two types of event. First he looked for a grouping of three or more planets in a small area of sky. This would result in a most impressive tiny geometric figure in the sky. Tuckerman's tables list planetary positions to a precision of 0.01 degree, so that by interpolating between two values the position of any planet at any time can be found to within an accuracy of only 0.02 degrees. The conditions imposed on this grouping were that all three planets should fit within an imaginary small circle on the celestial sphere three degrees in radius, and the center of this circle had to be more than fifteen degrees away from the Sun. This ensures that the planets can be seen easily and are not lost in the Sun's glare and also that they remain in the sky at night for a reasonable length of time.

The groupings that Sinnott found in the time interval under consideration are given in Table 6.7 and in this table the elongation is the angular distance between the center of the imaginary circle and the Sun. All these are westward and are equivalent to the angle α in Figure 22. The M next to this value indicates that all the groupings can be seen in the early morning. The angular diameter given is that which will encompass all the planets involved. The astronomical term given to this grouping of more than two planets is a "massing" and the best one of the set given in Table 6.7 is the massing that occurred on the morning of 22 January, 12 BC, when Mars, Saturn and Venus came within a circle of diameter 0.8°. Unfortunately this occurred when the planets were very close to the Sun and would have been seen only briefly in the dawn sky. Also, like all the massings in this table, this would occur once only. In January 12 BC Saturn and Mars were close to superior conjunction and were almost diametrically opposite to the Earth in the sky and on the other side of the Sun.

As seen from Earth, planets at superior conjunction have their minimum brightness, and Saturn and Mars would have had magnitudes of about +1.0 and +2.0 respectively. The main problem which rules out all the massings given in Table 6.7 is that they are untimely.

Table 6.7 Compact planetary configuration between 12 BC and AD 7
(after R. W. Sinnott)

Date	Planets	Elongation	Diameter	Constellation
12 BC 22 January	Mars Saturn Venus	18.5° M	0.8°	Capricorn
AD 1 5 November	Jupiter Mars Mercury Venus	17° M	2.7°	Libra
AD 4 19 January	Jupiter Mars Mercury	24.5° M	1.4°	Capricorn
AD 6 29 March	Jupiter Mars Mercury	23.5° M	3.0°	Pisces

The 12 BC one is much too early, occurring way out-side the range we established in Figure 6 for either the first or second appearance of the star. The other three occurred well after the death of Herod the Great and can be ruled out for that reason alone.

Sinnott then went on to list all the conjunctions of two planets occurring between 12 BC and AD 7 and in doing this he introduced certain selection criteria. First the conjunction had to be visible from the Middle and Near East. Secondly the minimum planetary separa-tion had to be closer than 12 minutes of arc (there are 60 minutes of arc in a degree, and 12 minutes of arc are equivalent to about one third of the diameter of the full Moon). The third criterion is that the conjunction had to occur when the planets were more than 15 degrees away from the Sun so that the conjunction was visible for a reasonable time in the morning or evening. In his list of conjunctions (Table 6.8) M and E refer to the morning and evening sky and the time of the day when the conjunction could be seen. The column headed "local time" gives the time period throughout which a Babylonian observer could see the conjunction, these periods stretching from the rising of the planet to dawn or from dusk to the setting of the planet, according to whether it was a morning or evening phenomenon. The word "local" means that the time was such that the Sun would have been due south of the observer at 12:00 noon. The separation is given in minutes of arc and is the minimum observed distance between the

Table 6.8 Close twin planet conjunctions between 12 BC and AD 7
(after R. W. Sinnott)

Date	Planets	Elongation	local time	Separation	RA (1950.0)	Dec
3BC 12 August	Jupiter-Venus	20.7 M	3.44- 5.23	12'	9h41m	+14.7°
2BC 17 June	Jupiter-Venus	45.4 E	19.04-22.02	3'	10h30m	+10.6°
AD 5 3 June	Mars-Saturn	57.3 E	18.57-22.52	11'	10h28m	+11.3°
AD 5 16 June	Mercury-Venus	20.7 E	19.04-20.32	9'	8h53m	+19.3°
AD 5 11 August	Mars-Venus	34.7 E	18.47-20.26	9'	13h05m	- 6.5°
AD 6 29 March	Mars-Jupiter	22.6 M	4.58- 5.58	12'	0h40m	+ 3.1°

planets. Sinnott selects the two conjunctions of Venus
and Jupiter, the brightest planets in the sky, as the
most likely contender for the role of star of Bethlehem.
The first occurred on 12 August 3 BC and was visible
in the eastern dawn sky, close to the heliacal rising, the
Sun coming up at about 5:30 a.m. In 2 BC, about ten
months later, a similar event occurred in the evening
sky on 17 June.

Sinnott paints a fascinating picture of these events:
"We can readily imagine the ancient scene: As the sun
sets over the broad Euphrates River, three Babylonian
priests made their evening climb up the mammoth
ziggurat temple in ancient Sippar, to watch the stars
come out. In the east the Moon was rising and in the
west Venus shone high above the sunset. Just beside it
Jupiter could be seen, dimmer and yellower. The
priests had been watching the pair for some weeks
now, but tonight there was a difference. The two
planets were closer together than anyone had seen
them in many years. As the sky darkened this brilliant
"double star" sank lower, the planets drawing nearer
and nearer. At last they were fused into one, gleaming
like a great beacon over Judea in the west." Venus had
just passed its greatest eastern elongation and would
have had a magnitude of around −4.0, very close to its
greatest brilliance. Jupiter would have been at about
−2.0 magnitude. Just after sunset the observer would
still have been able to resolve them as two individual
points of light even though they would have been
closer than the two stars Mizar and Alcor, the famous
double in the tail of the constellation known as Ursa
Major (the Great Bear). Two hours after sunset it
would have taken the sharpest eyesight to distinguish
the conjunction as two individual planets.

Twinkling caused by the turbulent atmosphere
would have blended Venus and Jupiter together, pro-
ducing one brilliant star in the western sky. This fusion
would have been a rare and awe-inspiring event, and it
would have looked as if Venus had swallowed up

Jupiter. Venus had a magnitude of −4.0 and Jupiter a magnitude of −2.0, so that the brightness of Jupiter, the energy we receive on Earth from that planet, is only 15.8 per cent of the energy we receive from Venus. When the two objects are very close together in the sky they produce a combined object which has a total brightness of only 15.8 per cent more than that of Venus alone. This means that the combination of Venus, which had a magnitude of −4.0, and Jupiter would together have produced a light in the sky of magnitude −4.161. Even now it would take a trained observer to detect the increase in brightness, so the idea that two bright objects coming together in the sky produce between them a new brilliant star much brighter than either of them is entirely incorrect. All that happens is that the brighter planet simply swallows up the smaller one to give a combined object which is only marginally brighter. Table 6.9 lists the sequence of events in detail.

The conjunctions of 17 June 2 BC and 2 August 3 BC both occurred in the constellation of Leo (Plate 3), on each side of the brightest star in that constellation, the star Regulus or Alpha Leonis—the "Royal Star." In ancient times the Sun passed in front of this star on midsummer day. From early times, Leo (the Lion) has

Table 6.9 The Jupiter-Venus conjunction of 17 June 2 BC (after R. W. Sinnott) as seen from Babylon

Local time at Babylon (pm)	Altitude of Planets above western horizon	Planetary Separation	Comments
7.04	37°	8′	Sunset
7.35	31°	7′	civil twilight ends bright stars come out
8.10	24°	6′	nautical twilight ends horizon indistinguishable
8.45	16°	5′	astronomical twilight ends no sky glow in west
9.15	10°	4′	Planets nearly unresolvable
10.02	0°	3′	Planets setting

been one of the traditional symbols of the Jews. Jacob addressed his son Judah as "a lion's whelp" (Genesis 49:9). Balaam's prophecy, "a Scepter shall rise out of Israel" (Numbers 24:17), is echoed in Genesis 49:10, "The scepter shall not depart from Judah, nor a lawgiver from between his feet, until Shiloh come; and unto him shall the gathering of the people be." Alfred Jeremias, the German scholar, wrote in 1911 that the "lawgiver between his feet" was probably the star Regulus, Alpha Leonis, and he thought it possible that Balaam was forecasting the rising of the star Regulus as a special feature of the horoscope of the new Messiah. Certainly a conjunction near Regulus would have been a most impressive sight.

Unfortunately none of the close conjunctions suggested by Sinnott satisfies one of the most important points in the list given at the beginning of this chapter: none of them occurs both before the death of Herod and after the census decree of Augustus. What about the alternative suggestion that the star of Bethlehem was nothing more than the planet Venus? This suggestion can be dismissed fairly quickly, mainly because Venus is a common sight in the sky and it seems most unlikely that something seen so frequently could motivate the Magi to undertake such a long journey. Furthermore, as Venus is visible so often, it is hard to see why one sighting was taken to be the star of Bethlehem while others were not.

Venus is about the same physical size as the Earth, but unlike our planet it is completely surrounded by a dense carbon dioxide atmosphere, ninety times heavier than our nitrogen and oxygen atmosphere. The surface of Venus cannot be seen from "outside" because the upper atmosphere is full of pale yellow clouds which are now thought to consist mainly of sulphuric acid. These clouds are excellent reflectors of sunlight and their reflectivity of about 72 per cent helps to make Venus the brightest of all the planets. This brightness is also enhanced by the fact that Venus is closer to the Sun than is the Earth, its mean distance being 108 million kilometers, so that the sunlight incident on its upper atmosphere is more intense than that incident on the Earth.

Lieutenant Colonel G. Mackinlay, who wrote on the subject in the nineteenth century, is the chief supporter of the hypothesis that Venus was the star of Bethlehem and his book on the Magi contains many interesting points. Mackinlay stresses the fact that Palestinian and Babylonian life at the time of Christ was governed by the hours of daylight. Early rising must have been very prevalent because many events occurred very early on in the day. The Hebrew morning sacrifice took place in the morning twilight, so that many of the people praying outside the temple at that time must have left their homes while it was still dark. The Bible itself is full of examples of early morning activity.

Since there were no clocks, Venus the morning star, the herald of the dawn, was readily recognized as a time keeper. Furthermore, Palestine and Babylon were at a latitude of about 30 to 35 degrees north, so that the celestial paths of the rising Sun and planets were more steeply inclined to the eastern horizon than they were in the more northern latitudes, where London and New York lie. Consequently the Sun appeared to rise much more suddenly and the dawn twilight was a much shorter phenomenon. Twilight therefore gave very little warning of the dawn. In many countries the rising of the "Morning Star" was taken as the herald of the day.

The practicality of Venus transformed it into one of the chief objects of worship among the ancients. In Babylon it was known as Istar and was at one time a rival to the greater divinities of the Sun and the Moon. It is obvious that the Morning Star was a far more familiar object to ordinary people in biblical times than it is to the majority of us at the present moment. Then as today, it was the brightest object in the heavens next to the Sun and Moon. Venus is both the morning and the evening star and the reasons for this are illustrated in Figure 24. If one imagines the Earth, and particularly the plane through the Earth which divides day from night, as rotating in an anticlockwise direction, it is possible to see that for all the positions of Venus to the right of the Earth-Sun line Venus rises in the east before the Sun does and is therefore a morning star. On the left hand side of this line Venus is an evening star. The synodic period of Venus—the time between similar Earth-Sun-Venus configurations—is 584 days (19½ months). During this time interval Venus spends about 292 days, or 9½ months, as an evening star and a similar time interval as a morning star.

The apparent size of Venus also changes (Figure 24). At superior conjunction, when the planet is about 1.72 astronomical units away from the Earth, Venus is a small disc, as shown in 1. Venus revolves around the Sun in an orbit interior to that of the Earth and so it exhibits phases in solar illumination in much the same manner as the Moon. As it moves from superior conjunction its apparent diameter increases, simply because the planet is getting closer to the observer, and this tends to balance out the effect of the diminution of the illuminated portion of its disc. The planet therefore gets brighter. Because of a combination of the phase and distance effects, Venus reaches its maximum brightness not when it is closest to the Earth but about 36 days before or after inferior conjunction (in the latter case at position 4 in Figure 24) when the elongation is 39 degrees from the Sun. At this time Venus is bright enough to cast shadows at night and can even be seen with the naked eye in full daylight. At greatest elongation Venus gives the longest announcement of the coming of dawn, but as superior conjunction is approached the planetary herald gets closer and closer in time to the event it is announcing. Eventually it gets so close to superior conjunction that it disappears in

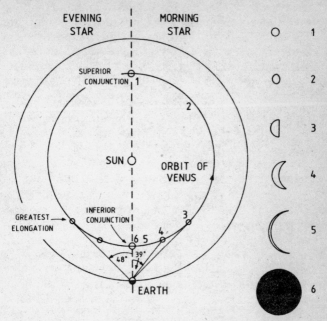

Fig. 24 The apparent variation in the size of Venus as a function
of orbital position

the brightness of the rays of the rising Sun. It then
becomes an evening star and is not seen in the east for
another eleven months.

Using the criteria given in Chapter 4, Mackinlay
concludes that the nativity took place on 20 September
8 BC and that the visit of the Magi took place toward
the very end of the period during which the morning
star shone. This conclusion is reached merely because
it lengthens the period between the birth and the visit
to its maximum of nearly 9½ months. Though this

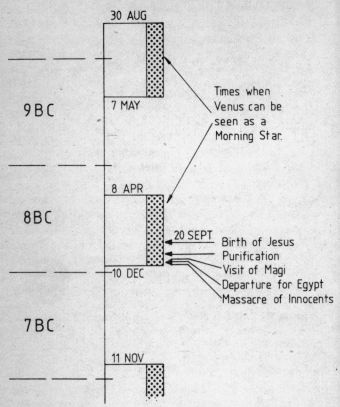

Fig. 25 The times when Venus can be seen as a morning star

length of time is far short of the "two year and under" criterion for Herod's massacre of the innocents, it is the best argument that can be put forward if the birth and visit occur in the same "morning star period." The times when the morning star was visible from Babylon and Palestine around the time of birth of Jesus are shown in Figure 25. In the important period discussed by Mackinlay the star was visible in the east from 8 April to 10 December 8 BC. These dates are only approximate and have been calculated on the basis of Tuckerman's tables and on the assumption that the planet is easily visible only when it is more than 10 degrees in longitude away from the Sun.

Now it is obvious that much more importance was attached to Venus and its role as a morning star and herald of the dawn in biblical times than is today. But when we consult our list of points that the star of Bethlehem must satisfy, Venus fails lamentably in many of them. It has no astrological message, and its appearances were so regular and apparently normal that this planet by itself would not have provided any reason for the Magi to make their long journey. Venus did not appear twice nor did it rise acronychally, and like all astronomical objects it could not "go before" or "stand over." It is invariably seen in the eastern or western skies, depending on whether it is a morning star or an evening one. Either way, it would not have been south of Jerusalem pointing the way to Bethlehem. In its favor we must say that Venus is the brightest "star-like" object in the sky. As such it is a wonderful sight in the dawn sky or in the clarity and darkness of an Arabian night. These features, however, cannot overcome all the problems—Venus was not the star of Bethlehem.

Halley's Comet as depicted in the Bayeux Tapestry

Two typical star-laden
Christmas cards

Zodiacal light above Bethelem (after Occhieppo)

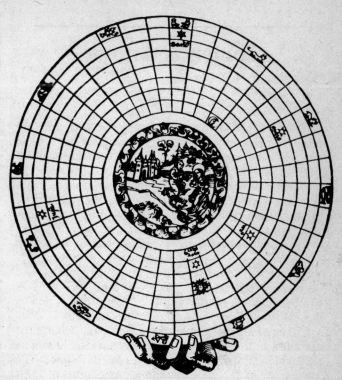

Cardan's horoscope of Jesus

7

Comets and novae

Apart from planets and their groupings and conjunctions, various other astronomical objects have been put forward as the explanation for the star of Bethlehem.

Comets have always been objects of great fascination and wonder to mankind. They can be remarkably bright, easily visible to the naked eye, but spectacular ones appear only a few times each century. As they move slowly across the heavens against the backdrop of stars, comets can be majestic and awe-inspiring. Some are visible for several weeks, even months, and they can often be seen twice, once on their way in toward perihelion (the point in their orbit which is closest to the Sun) and again on their way out.

Comets look like fuzzy, hairy stars, and when they are close to the Sun they often develop long luminous tails which stretch millions of miles out into space. The longest tail on record is that of the great comet of 1843, stretching nearly 400 million kilometers across the sky, equivalent to the distance from the Sun to beyond the orbit of Mars. Sometimes comets are so bright that they are visible even during the day. The comet of 344 BC was likened to a flaming torch, one in 146 BC was said to be as bright as the Sun, and the tail of the comet of AD 530 stretched from horizon to zenith, the point in the sky directly above the observer. It is therefore not surprising that these spectacular comets produced more excitement among members of the public than other celestial objects. They also aroused the interest of astrologers, especially in ancient times. The ancients thought that comets occurred at random, because they did not know where they came from or where they went to when they disappeared from sight. In the fourth century BC Aristotle thought that comets were caused by hot dry exhalations rising up from the Earth's surface. These exhalations were then thought to be carried along by the motion of the sky, this causing them to heat up and burst into flames. This idea persisted for many centuries, and Galileo thought that comets were simply the refraction of sunlight in vapors rising up from the Earth.

Comets came unheralded to the ancient world, were conspicuous for a short time and then faded away into obscurity. Their appearance was regarded as a sign from heaven of impending calamity and divine displeasure. For example Daniel Defoe in his *Journal of the Plague Year* described the comet of December 1664 as being faint, dull, languid in color, and in its motion very heavy, solemn and slow, so that it foretold "a heavy judgment, slow but severe, terrible and frightful, as was the Plague." This same comet so dismayed the commander of the then recently established settlement at the Cape of Good Hope that he introduced strict regulations for keeping the Sabbath so as "to ward off the punishment that hangs over our heads, of which we are warned by the long rayed star . . . a terrible sign of vengeance which threatens us nightly from the heavens." Plutarch told of the brilliant comet which shone for seven nights in the sky over Rome after the assassination of Julius Caesar, and in *Julius Caesar* Shakespeare was to write:

When beggars die there are no comets seen:
The heavens themselves blaze forth the death of princes.

Even in the early 1970s some people predicted that Comet Kohoutek, which appeared unspectacularly in

1973, would herald the destruction of the Earth (Plate 4).

Of all the comets observed since the dawn of history, Halley's Comet is the most famous. Although brilliant comets tend to appear unexpectedly some comets are periodic and predictable. These move in elliptical orbits, the Sun being at one of the foci of the ellipse, and are only visible when close to the Sun. Halley's Comet falls into this category and it takes a regular 76 years or so to traverse its orbit. The last time it passed close to the Sun was in April 1910. On this basis we can calculate that it appeared also in the autumn of 12 BC, twenty-five solar passages previously. Because of the closeness of this date to the birth of Christ, Halley's Comet has often been suggested as a possible star of Bethlehem. The biblical scholar Lagrange and the Hamburg astronomer Stenzel led the field in this belief.

The comet is named after Edmond Halley, an English mathematician and astronomer. In 1705, when he was Savilian Professor of Geometry in the University of Oxford, Halley published a book entitled *A Synopsis of Cometary Astronomy* in which he showed that comets move around the Sun in accordance with the theory of universal gravitation recently propounded by Isaac Newton, Lucasian Professor of Mathematics in the University of Cambridge. Several bright comets had been observed with reasonable accuracy before 1705 and Halley set out to calculate their orbits. He noticed that three of these, for the comets of 1531, 1607 and 1682, were very similar, and he inferred from this that they were the orbits of one and the same comet. From his calculations Halley predicted that this comet would return to the neighborhood of the Sun and Earth in about 1758. In fact the comet takes about 76.1 years to go all round its orbit (this orbit is shown in Figure 26).

Unlike most planets, which have almost circular orbits, Halley's Comet has an extremely elliptical one.

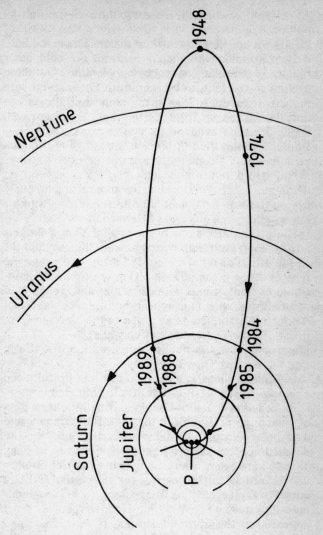

Fig. 26 The orbit of Halley's Comet

At perihelion, when it is closest to the Sun, it is only 89 million kilometers away, well within the orbit of Venus. At aphelion, its furthest distance from the Sun, it is 5250 million kilometers away in the cold outer regions of the solar system beyond Neptune. Out there it is much too faint to be seen from Earth, even with modern telescopes. Like many comets, Halley's can only be picked up from Earth when it has got well inside Jupiter's orbit on its way in toward the Sun. Edmond Halley died in 1742, at the age of 86, sixteen years before the comet returned to confirm his theory. When it did return the comet was first sighted on Christmas Day 1758 and astronomers unanimously agreed to name the comet after him. As far as we now know, Halley's Comet was first seen in 467 BC.

Halley's Comet is one of the brightest known and is a truly impressive sight when it nears the Sun and the Earth. It has also been recorded many times, and the returns of the comet (Table 7.1) have often been associated in men's minds with calamities and incidents of divine displeasure. One appearance of Halley's Comet has been interpreted as an omen of the Norman Conquest in 1066. The comet was considered to be of such importance that a symbolic representation was woven into the Bayeux Tapestry (Plate 5).

In biblical times Halley's Comet was first noticed about 25 August 12 BC near the star Mu Geminorum. It moved slowly across the sky during its sixty nights of visibility, passed near the star Beta Leonis and disappeared in the constellation of Scorpio. A more detailed account of this sighting is given in Ho Peng Yoke's catalogue, where he lists it as object number 61. According to this source, on 26 August 12 BC a comet was seen at the Tung-Ching (the 22nd lunar mansion) treading on Wu-Chie-Hou (Gemini). Later it appeared at the north of Ho-Shu (Canis Minor and Gemini) and moved to Hsien-Yuan (Leo) and the Thai-Wei (one of the three major Chinese star enclosures which contains Virgo, Leo and Coma Be-

Table 7.1 The returns of Halley's Comet (after Ralph S. Bates)

BC	
467	Perhaps first recorded mention of the Comet
240	Chinese record of comet
12	Description by Dio Cassius and in Chinese records; Comet thought to be the herald of the death of Agrippa
AD	
66	Probable Chinese records. Probably also mentioned by Josephus as an omen of the destruction of Jerusalem
141	Probably observed in China
218	Thought to be described by Dio Cassius, observed by Chinese
295	Believed observed by Chinese
373	Believed observed by Chinese
451	Observed in Europe. Attila the Hun defeated at the Battle of Chalons
530	Possibly mentioned in European chronicles
607	Perhaps mentioned by Chinese chroniclers
684	Pictured in the Nuremberg Chronicle
760	Observed in Europe and China
837	Vivid description in the Chinese Maluan-lin catalogue
912	Probably observed in Europe and China
989	Probably observed in Europe and China
1066	Regarded as the omen of the successful invasion of England by William the Conqueror, portrayed on the Bayeux Tapestry
1145	Observed in Europe and China, very bright
1222	Regarded as the omen of the death of King Philip Augustus of France
1301	Observed in Europe and China, very bright
1378	Observed in Europe and China
1456	Omen of the fall of Constantinople in 1453, Turks overrunning south-eastern Europe; Pope Calixtus III orders supplications
1531	Described by Apian
1607	Seen and later described by Kepler in his *De cometis*
1682	Observed by Halley who discovered its periodicity
1759	Return predicted by Halley
1835	Comet is considerably dimmer than on former returns
1910	Most recent visit
1985	Next expected appearance

renices). After that it traveled at the rate of more than 6 degrees per day, and was seen in the morning in the east. On the 13th day it appeared in the evening in the west and approached Regulus, its tail passing through Draco, Ursa Major and Camelopardus. After 56 days it disappeared from sight when it was in Scorpio. In spite of all this, however, August 12 BC is far too early for Halley's Comet to be the nativity star, even if it preceded the birth of Christ by two years.

This fact does not deter the Christmas card manufacturers. Many cards show a cometary representation of the star shining brilliantly over Bethlehem with the comet tail pointing down toward the stable. Plate 6 is a typical example. It may look striking and beautiful, but it is scientifically untenable—comet tails do not point down to the horizon at night. They lie fairly closely along the line joining the Sun to the comet and always point away from the Sun. At night, when the Sun has set and is below the horizon, all comet tails point upward, the cometary head being closest to the land. The tail jets off across the sky, just like the Aristotelian "gaseous exhalation."

Although Halley's Comet in 12 BC was reported from all over China and well recorded, no report of its observation in the west has come to light. Could the comet have been the star of Bethlehem? Like many visible comets, it could have appeared twice, once on its way into the Sun and a second time on its way out. In common with most comets Halley's astrological message would be "doom, disaster, disease and despondency," and it would not be regarded as a joyous herald for the King of the Jews. It would be "heliacal" at some time of its observation period and it would be bright. The maximum brightness of Halley's Comet at each of its recorded apparitions is given in Table 7.2 and it can be seen that this brightness is decreasing with time by about 2.5 magnitudes every millennium. The 12 BC apparition could have been of about zero magnitude, a very impressive sight. The brightness and tail length vary as a function of the distance between the comet and the Sun. Usually comets are brighter and have longer tails after perihelion passage. Halley could have risen acronychally, but by then it would have been well past the Earth's orbit and much less impressive than it was when close to the Sun. We must in any case conclude that Comet Halley was about four years too early to be a serious star of Bethlehem contender.

Table 7.2 Brightness of Halley's Comet at recent returns, given in terms of the Comet's absolute magnitude (after Richter)

AD				
	760	2	1378	3.5
	837	2	1456	4.2
	912	1.7	1531	4
	989	3.5	1607	3.5
	1066	−0.5	1682	4
	1145	2	1759	3.8
	1222	?	1835	4.4
	1301	3	1910	4.6

If the star of Bethlehem cannot be identified with Halley's Comet, could other comets have filled the role? Only two other unusual celestial objects shone in the sky around the time of Christ's birth. These are numbered 52 and 53 in Williams' catalogue of comets and we are not sure whether they are comets or novae. A third comet, numbered 54, was seen by the Chinese in AD 13 and is much too late. The problem with 52 and 53 is that they lack any positive astrological significance. They could not have been the star of Bethlehem either.

Comets also move quickly in their journey through the inner solar system. In the days before the telescope and with the clear bright nights common in the Middle East a new comet would probably have been picked up when it reached a magnitude of between +3 and +4. Its brightness would still be increasing at this time. If, for the sake of argument, it had remained visible for two months, it would have reached a brilliant maximum, probably even brighter than Jupiter. Such bright comets move across the sky with a speed of about 10 degrees per day, moving from one constellation to the next every three or four days. In this way comets would be clearly distinguishable simply by their movement.

Origen was one of the first writers to speculate on the real physical nature of the star of Bethlehem. He described the phenomenon as ''a new star unlike any of the other well-known planetary bodies . . . but partaking of the nature of those celestial bodies, which appear at times, such as comets. . . .'' It must be remembered, though, that Origen wrote in the first half of the third century, over 200 years after the occurrence, and he could quite easily have misidentified the star of Bethlehem and be describing one of the bright comets or novae that did occur in the decades around the nativity.

Could the star of Bethlehem be a nova? The name implies a new star, something which suddenly springs into life, but this is entirely misleading. A nova is not really new at all, but a star that has been there all along for many millions of years. What has happened is that the star which was previously unknown flares up in brightness, typically increasing in energy output by a factor of 10,000 to 100,000 times. In terms of stellar magnitudes this is equivalent to a change of between 10 and 13. This astronomical flash is relatively short-lived and the new star then steadily declines in brightness until it returns to its pre-nova magnitude. Of course the period of visibility depends to a great extent on the instrument being used, but if the nova is being observed just with the naked eye or a small telescope a typical visual lifetime is a month or two. Until recent times astronomers thought that novae were normal stars which were readjusting themselves during the fourth stage of their stellar evolution. In this phase of their lives all the nuclear reactions which entail the conversion of hydrogen and helium into other elements with higher atomic numbers have come to an end. The hydrogen and helium fuel has been almost completely depleted and the star is left with only its gravitational potential energy. To put it simply, the star is large and gains energy by shrinking, and the stellar material falls in toward the center with an increase in velocity and temperature.

This picture has changed recently. Astronomers now believe that a nova is produced by a process in which one star in a close binary system literally feeds on the material of its companion. Our Sun is a single star and we are almost certain that there is no other star within about four light years. Out of the stars we see in the sky, fewer than half are single, lonely objects, whereas double and even triple stars are common. Here two stars of relatively similar mass are close together and move in their mutual gravitational field about their common center of mass. If one of these is a white dwarf star and the other a red giant, we have a binary system containing two of the extremes of stellar characteristics. Roughly speaking, we can assume that both stars have masses within a factor of about five times that of the Sun, but the white dwarf is about one hundred times smaller than the Sun with a surface temperature about ten times higher. The red giant can be a hundred times larger than the Sun with a surface temperature of about a half the solar value. Visually it is equivalent to a white apple pip and a red football being gravitationally locked together.

Each star has its own gravitational field of influence and inside this field all the material belongs exclusively to that star. These fields surround each star and are shaped like teardrops, the pointed ends of the teardrops touching each other. If a star overfills its Roche lobe, the name given to the teardrop-shaped field, the overflowing material may fall onto the other star. If hydrogen from the red giant star falls onto the extremely hot surface of the white dwarf, this material may build up to form a surface shell in which nuclear reactions can take place. The surface would then explode and the resulting release of energy would be recognizable from Earth as a nova. Now the total mass drawn in by the white dwarf may only be a small fraction, as little as a few millionths, of the mass of the binary system. The resulting explosion does not penetrate very deeply into the white dwarf, and does not permanently affect its structure. On the other hand, the explosion does accelerate some material at a high enough speed for it to escape from the system and this mass loss leads to an increase in the orbital period of the two stars about their common center of mass. An example of this effect was observed in 1934. In this year a binary in the constellation of Hercules became a nova for a brief time. The mass loss caused the orbital period to increase from 0.1932084 days to 0.1936206 days.

This process of gas build-up, shell formation and nova explosion can and usually does recur, so that a single binary star pair can become a nova many times. The larger the energy release during the explosion, the longer on average is the intervening time interval. Some recurrent novae flare up in this way at intervals of from twenty-five to fifty years, but there are many novae which are much less frequent. In the Milky Way galaxy about fifty novae occur each year among a total of around 100,000,000,000 stars. Many of these are much too distant to be detected from Earth and on average only just over two a year are noticed. Even this small detection number relies on hours of painstaking observation with binoculars and telescopes, and of course the number of novae visible to the naked eye is very much smaller.

To this number we must add the supernovae. As the

name implies, the energy emission is about a thousand times greater than in the case of a nova and the explosion is so enormous that up to ninety per cent of the star can be ejected into space. A supernova is thought to occur when a star in its fourth stage of evolution becomes dramatically unstable, the outer layers are then hurled into space and the central remnant collapses to form a neutron star. A star suffers this fate in our galaxy about every fifty to a hundred years and in the last millennium supernovae have been seen from Earth in AD 1054, 1573 and 1604.

We should be more interested here in the number of novae recorded around the time of the birth of Christ. The study of the movement of the stars and planets, the subject which today we call astronomy, was considerably advanced in the ancient world. Astronomy was important because the movement of the heavenly bodies marked out the time. Days, months, seasons and years were all measured on the basis of planetary, lunar and solar positions. In those days astrology was a sister subject to astronomy. Astrologers used the positions among the stars of the seven major celestial objects—the Sun, Moon, Mercury, Venus, Mars, Jupiter and Saturn—to predict future events. The Babylonian astrologers built up a knowledge of the attributes of the specific planets and constellations by working back from the recorded events in the lives of people to the planetary positions when those events took place. By about 700 BC the Babylonians had divided the map of the observed stars into three concentric circles which were crossed by twelve radii to give thirty-six constellation sectors. The zodiacal, ecliptic constellations are the same as those used today. From this time on, systematic observational work produced two important results. The Babylonians obtained the correct mean values for the chief astronomical periodic phenomena and so were able to make good short-range predictions. They also devised a clever method of making accurate long-range predictions by using a system akin to the present-day Fourier analysis, in which a signal is broken up into a series of different frequencies and amplitudes.

Babylonian mathematics helped a great deal in all this as it was much more advanced at this time than that of Egypt or Rome. They used a base 60 system dividing circles into 360 degrees of 60 minutes or 3600 seconds. They also invented the "place value" numerical notation, so that 51 did not mean 6 as it did to the Romans but meant 5×60 plus 1, i.e. 301, just as today 51 means 5×10 plus 1.

Mesopotamian astronomers have been credited with the invention of the water clock (known as a clepsydra). This had two bowls, one kept full of water and having a small hole in the bottom through which water dripped at about six drops per second, while the second bowl caught the water and also contained a floating pointer indicating the time on a graduated scale. They have also been credited with the invention of the gnomon sundial.

The other ancient astronomers that feature in the quest for the star of Bethlehem are the Chinese. Like the Babylonians they were keen astrologers too and believed that not only did the planets affect the behavior of mankind, but that the reciprocal was true and that our actions on Earth change the movement of heavenly objects. They developed an astrology which supposedly predicted countrywide phenomena as opposed to the more personal individual birth horoscopes. Their observational work resulted in an accurate calendar in which the year was 365¼ days long (established about 2300 BC) and they determined the obliquity of the ecliptic (the angle between the Earth's orbit and its equatorial plane) to a few minutes of arc as early as 1100 BC. The astronomer Shih Shen made a catalogue of the positions of 800 stars some time between 400 and 300 BC. They also kept records of sunspots, eclipses, showers of shooting stars, meteorite falls, comets and novae, the last two of which are of importance to us here.

Usually comets can be distinguished from novae. Comets have tails pointing away from the Sun, a fact known to the Chinese. Ma Tuan Lin wrote that "in general, in a comet east of the Sun, the tail, reckoning from the nucleus, is directed to the east; but if the comet appears to the west of the Sun, the tail is turned toward the west." As comets pass the Sun in their orbit they appear from Earth to move through the constellations. The speed of this movement depends on the comet-Sun and comet-Earth distance. Furthermore, the apparent tail length of the comet depends on how close it is to the Sun, or whether it is on its way in to perihelion or away from it and again on the comet-Earth distance and comet-Sun-Earth geometry. When, for example, the comet is near opposition on the opposite side of the Sun to the Earth, the tail is pointing away from the observer and can be hidden behind the coma, the nebulous envelope around its nucleus. Distant comets often have short tails, and tail length is a function of the age of the comet, or more precisely on the number of perihelion passages it has already had. In the case of short tails, small bright coma and distant slow-moving comets, the ancient observer could easily have confused them with novae, the new stars we have already mentioned.

The Chinese recorded their observations very carefully. One important source of records of events that occurred during the Chou period c 1100-221 BC, and the following Han dynasty, is the Shih Chi, or "Historical Records" of Ssu-ma Ch'ien, who lived c 140-c 80 BC and who completed this great work some time between 100 and 90 BC. This Chinese history was continued later on in the treatise Ch'ien-Han Shu, the "History of the Former Han Dynasty," written by the father, son and daughter of the Pan family. The father, Pan Piao (AD 3-54), concentrated on a year by year record of the emperors and also on biographies of famous men. His son extended this work and the daughter Pan Chao (c AD 47-117) helped the son Pan Ku (AD 39-92) to write a treatise on astronomy.

Much later on in our Middle Ages, Ma Tuan-Lin, working between AD 1240 and 1280, produced his Wên-hsien t'ung-K'ao. Chapter 286 deals with cometary observations prior to AD 1222, and chapter 294 is a list of extraordinary stars. In 1958 Hsi Tsê-tsung, of the Commission of the History of Chinese Natural Sciences, Academia Sineca, Peking, searched through the "Twenty-four Histories," Wên-hsien t'ung-K'ao, T'ung-chih, and the studies of institutions known as the Hui-yao, together with other histories and various Japanese astronomical material and produced a revised and more accurate catalogue of novae. This catalogue includes the three novae which, according to the compiler, occurred in the time period of Christ's birth (Table 7.3). It can be seen from the timing that only the 5 BC nova has any claim to be a possible star of Bethlehem.

Another interesting point arises from the complete novae table and this concerns their frequency. Between 100 BC and AD 1690, 84 novae and supernovae were bright enough to be detected by astronomers and recorded, an average of one every 21 years. This

Table 7.3 Hsi-Tsê-tsung's catalogue of ancient novae, entries from 50 BC to AD 50

No.	Description	Source	Date	R.A.	dec	Comments
10	4th month, 1st year of Ch'u-yüan of Han Star as large as a melon, blue white 4 Chi'ih eas of No 2 of nan-ton (μ, λ, ρ, σ, τ, ξ, Sag.)	Han-shu	48 BC	18hr	$-25°$	East of Mu Sagittarius
11	2nd month, 2nd year of Chien-p'ing of Ai-Ti of Han, sweeping star appearing at Ch'ien-niu (α, β, υ, Aql.) for more than 70 days	Han-shu	5 BC	19h40m	$+10°$	Near Alpha Aquila
12	5th year of Chien-wu of later Han Dynasty, quest star offending Ti-tso (Rasalgethi)	"Biography of Yen Kuang" in Hou-Han-shu	AD 29	17h20m	$+15°$	Near Alpha Hercules

contrasts with the hundreds of years between Piscean triple conjunctions.

As far as comets are concerned, a list was made in 1871 by John Williams, who derived his information from Chinese sources. This list contained 372 comets occurring between 611 BC and AD 1640, which means that an easily visible comet was recorded every five to six years. Number 51 in Williams' list was Halley's Comet of 26 August 12 BC and was too early to be the star of Bethlehem, while number 54 occurred in December AD 13 and was too late. We are therefore left with the intervening two, both of which fall in the reign of the Emperor Ai-Ti of the Han Dynasty, who ruled from 6 BC to 1 BC. The first is number 52 in Williams' list and was recorded by Ma Tuan Lin: "In the reign of the Emperor Ai-Ti, the second year of the epoch chien-p'ing, the second month a comet appeared in Ch'ien-niu for about seventy days." Pan ku, writing in the Ch'ien Han Shu, said that it appeared "for more than seventy days." The epoch chien-p'ing is the equivalent of 6 to 3 Bc, so that the second month of the second year is March 5 BC. Ch'ien-niu is a star division equivalent to our present constellation of Capricorn. The object seen was termed a hui hsing, which can be translated as a "sweeping star" or a "broom star." According to David Clark and Richard Stephenson the object was first seen between 10 March and 7 April 5 BC. The asterism ch'ien-niu contains Alpha and Beta Capricorn and is centered just north of the ecliptic (1950 coordinates are Right Ascension 20h 15m dec-15°, 5 BC coordinates are R.A. 18h 25m, dec-19°, these differing because of the precession of the Earth's spin axis). The term hui hsing is usually applied to a comet with a discernible tail. To quote from Clark and Stephenson, "Its body is a sort of star, while the tail resembles a broom." Clark and Stephenson also note that the 5 BC object had a high galactic latitude ($-25°$).

There seems to be insufficient evidence available today to enable us to decide whether the 5 BC event was a comet or a nova and there is therefore no reason to doubt the statement in the Han-shu that the object was a comet.

It has been claimed by three astronomers—Clark, Parkinson and Stephenson—that there was a second sighting of the object in Korea. In the History of the Three Kingdoms, in the third chapter of the Chronicle of Silla (Samgube Sagi), we find: "Fifty-fourth year of Hyokkose Wang, second month, (day) chi-yu, a po-hsing appeared at Ho-Ku." Ho-Ku is an asterism in Aquila, centered on the first magnitude star Altair. The way in which the Chinese astronomers divided the sky into constellations is described by Ho Peng Yoke. The asterisms of Ch'ien-niu and Ho-Ku are close together in the sky, some 20 degrees apart.

The term po-hsing (a sparkling star) is the standard term used to describe an apparently tailless comet. The Chin-shu states: "By definition a comet pointing toward one particular direction is a Hui comet and one that sends out its rays evenly in all directions is a Po comet." As the record is so brief, Clark and his co-authors conclude that it is uncertain whether the object is a comet or a nova. They also point out that these reports produced in the very early periods of Korean recorded history are of doubtful reliability, the one given above suffering from one certain error. There was no chi-yu day in the second month of the year given. The authors put forward three possible solutions. First, the day could be wrong. As the Chinese characters for Chi and i are very similar and are often confused in manuscript, the above could refer to the i-yu day, 31 March 4 BC. Secondly the month could be incorrect, in which case the event must have occurred at some other time in 4 BC. Thirdly the year might be wrong. This last error, combined with one of the other errors, would put the observation in, say, spring of 5 BC and make it coincide with the Chinese observation that we have discussed previously.

Clark and his colleagues note that if the Koreans did see a po-hsing in 4 BC, it is surprising that the more competent Chinese astronomers did not record it as well. It is on this point, however, that the Cambridge historian Christopher Cullen reverses the argument, for he reminds us that the Chinese observers did record the 4 BC po-hsing. In the eleventh chapter of the Han-shu we read: "(In the third year of the Chien-p'ing reign period) the third month, (day) *chi-yu* (24 April 4 BC) . . . there was a hsing-po at Ho-Ku." This quotation was also reproduced in the twelfth-century Thung Chien Kang Mu and corresponds to "comet" number 53 in the Williams catalogue and object number 64 in the Ho Peng Yoke catalogue. The Samquk Sagi, the Korean work written in AD 1145 and quoted by Clark and his co-authors, followed a common practice in which a blank year in the sparse records of early Korean history was simply filled by copying from an earlier Chinese book, in this case the Han-shu of AD 90. Unfortunately the Korean text has garbled the date by miscopying the month, a matter of omitting a single stroke from the Chinese character for "three," so that the Korean record is not an independent account of the 5 BC event but a copy of a much earlier Chinese observation of the 4 BC object.

A different candidate for the star of Bethlehem was put forward by Ho Peng Yoke, who found that another comet was recorded between Halley's Comet (Williams number 51) and the 5 BC object (Williams number 52) and that it occurred in 10 BC. This is number 62 in the Ho Peng Yoke catalogue, where he quotes from Thung Chien Kang Mu, the only source that mentions it: "During the third year of the Yuan-Yen reign period of po comet was seen at Shê Thi and Ta Chio." Again we must dismiss this comet as being too early to fit in with our estimate of the time when the star must have made its second appearance, though it does creep into the possible time period for the first appearance (see Figure 6).

Of the various comets and novae that appeared about the time of the birth of Jesus (Table 7.4), comets with tails, the hui-hsing or broom stars, seem to be self-evidently comets. The po-hsing are probably also comets which in this instance are viewed either

Table 7.4 Comets and novae that occurred around the birth time of Christ

Ho Pen Yoke Catalogue Number	Date	Description	Position in sky	Comments
61	26 August– 21 October 12 BC (56 days)	po (comet)	Gemini, Leo Boötes, Scorpio	Halley's Comet
62	10 BC	po (comet)	Boötes, Arcturus	
63	March 5 BC (for 70 days)	hui (comet)	Capricornus	
64	April 4 BC	po (comet)	Altair region	
65	December AD 13	hui (comet)		

head-on or end-on, though a small po comet was not easily distinguishable from a k'o-hsing, a guest or visiting star. Ho Peng Yoke concluded that many of the guest stars in his catalogue were actually comets, while he thought that certain of the po comets were probably novae. The term k'o-hsing was used in the Chinese records to identify the new stars of AD 1006, 1054, 1572 and 1604 and these are obviously novae or supernovae. On the other hand there are frequent references, more than twenty in Ho Peng Yoke's catalogue, to moving k'o-hsing, so that here the guest stars are obviously comets. We have to conclude that the terms k'o and po must be treated cautiously.

Could either of these two objects, the 5 BC hui and the 4 BC po, have been the star of Bethlehem? Each of the star groupings given in Figure 27 is based on the Chinese sky maps given in Ho Peng Yoke and it can be seen that both asterisms are close to the ecliptic, which means that there is no problem of heliacal and acronychal risings. Today the Sun passes below Alpha and Beta Capricorni on about 25 January. Because of the precession of the equinox, an effect caused by the

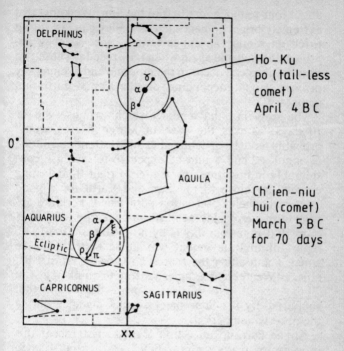

Fig. 27 The positions on the celestial sphere of the 5 and 4 BC objects

Earth's spin axis moving around an imaginary circle on the celestial sphere every 25,725 years, the Sun would pass in front of Alpha and Beta Capricorni earlier in the year in 7 BC than it does today—about 27 days earlier, around 29 December. These two stars, as well as the asterisms Ho-Ku and Ch'ien niu, would set heliacally just before this date, in mid December, and would rise heliacally just after, in mid January. The acronychal rising would occur six months away from the 29 December conjunction, around 30 June.

As both events occurred in March-April the celestial objects would be visible in the late night sky, rising

about four to five hours before the Sun. We know that
extremely bright comets such as Halley can last for up
to 60 days and can appear twice, once as they approach the Sun and again when they recede. These two
observations can occur in the morning and evening sky
or vice versa, depending on the comet-Earth-Sun
geometry.

The problem is that a comet which was observed for
70 days, as was the case in March 5 BC, would
probably have been detected at an apparent magnitude
of about +2 and would be expected to increase considerably in brightness for a time. Bright, long-lasting
comets are close to the Sun and Earth for a good
fraction of their observation period and therefore appear to move quickly against the background of stars
(6 to 10 degrees per day is by no means unusual). No
report of this movement was made in the Chinese
annals about either the March 5 BC or the April 4 BC
object. We therefore have reason to think that the
70-day object in 5 BC was a nova, an idea further
supported by the Sun-object angular distance during
the observation period.

Novae flare up once and then do not repeat this
process for many years. They have a rapid rise to
maximum light followed by a much slower decline in
brightness. In a schematic light curve of an ordinary
nova (Figure 28) the nova reaches maximum brightness very quickly, changing its magnitude by about
eleven in a week or so. The decline is much slower. To
incorporate a time factor into this figure we have
assumed that the nova reaches a maximum brightness
similar to that of the brightest star normally seen in the
sky. We also assume that the nova is lost from view
when it becomes fainter than a magnitude of +6, the
naked eye limit. If this is the case the nova will be
brighter than about +2 magnitude (the average brightness of the constellation stars shown in Figure 27) for
about 30 to 40 days, half the total visual period. If the 5
BC object was a normal nova there seems to be no way

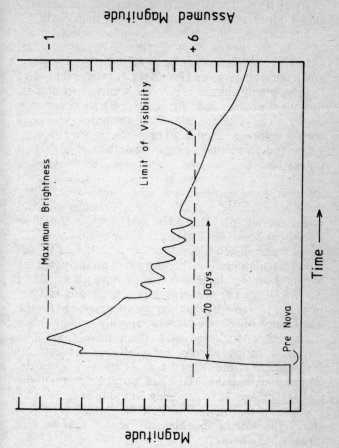

Fig. 28 A typical curve of magnitude as a function of time for a nova

in which it could have occurred twice, and this tends to rule it out as a candidate for the star of Bethlehem.

The astrological significance is also a serious problem. In the words of a nineteenth-century writer, Granville, "We need not be appall'd by blazing stars, and a comet is no more ground for astrological presage than a flaming chimney." To the ancient astrologers, however, comets and novae seemed to occur randomly. The Chinese classified them as "ominous stars," a phrase which sums up perfectly their inauspicious and threatening aspect and their role as evil omens and foreshadowers of disaster. In Babylonian astrology the comets and novae were simply grouped together as unforeseen celestial phenomena. They were not excluded from astrological consideration but could merely play an additional role to the main influences possessed by the planetary positions, which could be predicted a considerable time before by detailed calculations. It is therefore very unlikely that the appearance of a tailless comet or nova in Aquila in April 4 BC or the appearance of a hui comet in Capricorn in March 5 BC had any specific message for the Magi. Such phenomena would certainly not have been significant enough to make them travel over five hundred miles across inhospitable deserts to Jerusalem. On the other hand, Matthew 2 gives the impression that the Magi had no doubts about the stellar message. In questioning Herod they seem to be positive in their assertion that the "star" was "his star," the star of the Messiah, a sign that he had already been born.

If we take the probable date of the death of Herod the Great as 6 December 5 BC and the possible date as being March/April 4 BC, we notice at once that the February 4 BC object occurs after the probable death of Herod and that it must therefore be ruled out. Furthermore, the nine months between the Capricorn hui comet in March 5 BC and Herod's death in December of that year is an extremely short time into which the planning of the journey, the journey itself, the discussions with Herod, the visit to Bethlehem, and the holy family's flight to Egypt must be crammed, and much too short a time if the legendary two years were spent in Egypt. Aquila and Capricorn rose acronychally in May and June, and for the March 5 BC and February 4 BC objects to rise acronychally they would have had to occur in May and June—and they did not.

The astronomical event went unnoticed by Herod and the people of Jerusalem. We are not told how significant or insignificant the two Chinese objects were but we can stress at this point that the Chinese astronomers were much keener and more skilled observers than Herod and his entourage and thus they would be much more likely to pick out faint comets and novae.

All in all, we can conclude that the March 5 BC object is a possible candidate for the star of Bethlehem role, but not a probable one. In my opinion its complete lack of astrological significance, its single appearance, non-acronychal rising and close proximity to Herod's death make it impossible to consider. It does, of course, have its champions, but the great interval of time between the nativity and the present day has enabled people to identify almost any new, unusual bright star that shone around that time as the star of Bethlehem.

According to the historian Christopher Cullen the first reference to the hypothesis that the star of Bethlehem was a nova was made by J. F. Foucquet, an eighteenth-century Jesuit missionary. In his translation of a Chinese chronological table, under the second year of Chien-p'ing, Foucquet inserted a note into the grid of the translation which said "Stella nova in Coelo 70 et amplius dies." This note obviously alludes to the Han-shu reference to the 5 BC object which shone for over seventy days. This was the only astronomical note in the table and its temporal proximity to the date of the birth of Christ gives a strong implication that Foucquet considered it to be the star of Bethlehem. In the eighteenth century Sir Hans Sloane certainly considered this to be the case and in his description of Foucquet's work he commented on "the Appearance of a Star seen in the Heavens upwards of seventy days, the true Year in which our Savior was born." In 1827 F. Münter had a book published on the star of Bethlehem and in it he dated the event in 4 BC, but this was based on a misreading of Foucquet's table.

In this century K. Lundmark (1953) referred to the 5 BC object. He assumed that it was a nova and that as it shone for seventy days the Magi would have had enough time to journey from any eastern country to Jerusalem during the time when the nova was visible. Subsequently Hugh Montefiore (1960) wrote about the problem and dealt with the triple conjunction as well as the 5 BC and 4 BC objects. He conjectured that the Babylonian astrologers saw the conjunctions of 7 BC, and when they remembered the prophecy of a coming world ruler and the tradition that a star would appear two years before the birth of the Messiah, they set out for Jerusalem some time after the conjunction. They were then confirmed in their expectations by the appearance of the March 5 BC object.

There is one almost insurmountable difficulty with this last view. Although there may have been two stars, one appearing to the Magi when they were in their own country and the other just after they left Jerusalem, these were not different stars but two observations of the same star. Matthew 2:9 specifically states that "the star, which they saw in the east, went before them" on the final leg of their journey to Bethlehem. The combination of a 7 BC conjunction and a 5 BC nova is therefore not the right answer.

In his book, published in 1964, on the chronology of the Bible, Finegan reviews all the evidence, including novae, conjunctions, comets, Chinese literature and Babylonian almanacs. He concludes that the 7 BC conjunctions could have attracted attention toward Palestine, and that the comets (or novae) of 5 and 4 BC could be the astronomical phenomenon that lay at the back of the account of the star of Bethlehem. He argued that the comet of March 5 BC could have been the motive for the journey of the Magi. They would have arrived in Judea before the death of Herod, which was between 12 March and 11 April 4 BC. He also thought that the comet of April 4 BC could have been shining at the same time. This interpretation, however, is open to several objections. Herod probably died in December 5 BC. Furthermore, the March 5 BC ''hui'' and the April 4 BC ''po'' were not the same object or the same star. Neither of these objects had an astrological message or rose acronychally and there is no time for the flight to Egypt, or for Herod to worry about the failure of the Magi to return after their visit to Jesus or for him to carry out the massacre of the innocents.

In my review article for the Christmas edition of *Nature,* 9 December 1976, I argued that the star of Bethlehem was to be explained in terms of planetary conjunctions, but I also considered a second possibility in which the conjunctions and objects of 5 and 4 BC all played a role. I now think that this second hypothesis is incorrect.

The next paper dealing specifically with the nova theory was written by Clark, Parkinson and Stephenson and published in late November 1977. They concluded that the March 5 BC object was a bright nova and that this alone was the star of Bethlehem. They retranslated the Babylonian cuneiform almanac for the year 305 of the Seleucid era. It contains predictions for the dates of the equinoxes, solstices and eclipses as well as giving the zodiacal signs for the known planets and the date of entry into these signs where appropriate. The positions of the Sun, Moon and Sirius (the star Alpha Canis Majoris) are also given. There are no predictions for planetary conjunctions in the text, but it does indicate that Saturn and Jupiter remain together in the same constellation for over half a year. The stationary points in the orbital loops of the planets are given. Clark and his co-authors point out that the stationary points are difficult to determine with the naked eye because the planets are moving very slowly on either side of the points. The accuracy of the predictions given on the late Babylonian cuneiform almanacs is most impressive, ranging from one to two hours for the start of a solar eclipse to a few days for the stationary points for Jupiter and Saturn. The authors argue from this that planetary motions were evidently well understood, so that the Babylonians would almost certainly not have been surprised or even especially interested in the planetary conjunction of 7 BC. My own view is that they certainly were not surprised, but they were definitely interested.

Clark, Parkinson and Stephenson take the idea that the 5 BC nova was the star of Bethlehem one step further. They introduce the converse and argue that in the Middle East at that time, only the most spectacular events would have aroused enough interest to be recorded. They think that the star was in this category and therefore one of the earliest instances where a "new star" has been recorded outside the Far East.

The Clark, Parkinson and Stephenson single nova hypothesis is basically the same as the theories put forward by Foucquet in 1729 and Lundmark in 1953, and it shares the defects of these two theories. Another scientist, A. J. Morehouse, seems to have worked independently on a supernova hypothesis at about the same time as Clark, Parkinson and Stephenson. Morehouse concentrates on the April 4 BC event and suggests that it was not a nova but a supernova and that the binary pulsar PSR 1913 + 16b is a remnant of the event. He proposes that the Christmas star consisted of three unrelated celestial happenings. The first was the triple conjunction which in time covered a period of eleven months. It happens that Saturn and

Jupiter were closer together than six degrees for the eleven months between mid March 7 BC and mid February 6 BC. Morehouse goes on to suggest that the second phenomenon was a possible nova which first appeared around 24 March 5 BC, about eleven months after the end of the conjunctions. This nova occurred about the time of the equinox and it may have been close enough to be important to the astrologically minded Magi. The third event, which took place almost exactly eleven months after the second one, was the appearance of another nova. This was first seen on 23 February 4 BC, in the constellation of Aquila, near the point where the winter colure and the equator of that date intersect. Its position may also have been important to the Magi, just as the recurring eleven-month intervals may have been. Morehouse admits that this is speculation, but at least he is the first researcher to bring attention to the time interval similarity.

Before we look into these arguments more fully, it is worth looking at the date of the 4 BC event. It is given as 23 February 4 BC in the third volume of the General Catalogue of Variable Stars by Kukarkin and others. The Korean Sanguk Sagi quotes the time as "second month, (day) chi-yu," which, as Clark and his co-authors point out, cannot be right. The Korean date does not correspond to the Chinese calendar, as the chi-yu day did not fall in the second month that year but only occurred in the first month, on 23 February, or the third month, on 24 April. But the correct Chinese record (Han shu, chapter 11, p. 341) refers to the third month (day) chi-yu, which is the date mentioned above—24 April 4 BC. Furthermore, when Morehouse says that the 5 BC event occurred around 24 March, the original Chinese record simply refers to the second month of the year, 10 March to 7 April. Morehouse has picked the middle of this period but obviously the event could have occurred at any time between these two dates.

We can test the Morehouse equal interval theory simply by dividing the time interval between the 24 April 4 BC po-hsing and the center of the conjunction, 5 September 7 BC, by 2½. The interval obtained is 384 days or about 13 months (Figure 29). In spite of the speculative nature of this argument, it does fit the evidence quite well. The position of the 4 BC object is shown in Figure 27, its coordinates being given as Right Ascension 20h declination +10° for the epoch 1900. The Chinese term "po" has been translated as rayed, bushy, sparkling and scintillating. Morehouse calculates that between 108 BC and AD 390 a po star was recorded on average every 41.4 years. As the brightest novae of this present century occur at intervals of twenty years or so, it seems that there is a possibility that the 4 BC po star was quite bright.

Now if the 4 BC event was not a nova but a supernova, the remnant of this enormous stellar explosion would be a pulsar. Unfortunately within ten degrees of the asterism Ho-Ku there are many pulsars. Kiang identified, albeit with low probability, the pulsar PSR 1929 + 10 with the event, but of the pulsars discovered since 1969 the binary pulsar PSR 1913 + .16b is thought by Morehouse to be a more likely candidate. This pulsar is about 5° 47′ from the star Gamma Aquila in the Chinese constellation Ho-Ku. In 4 BC the position of the star on the celestial sphere is calculated to be Right Ascension 17h 44m 35s declination +14° 38.5′. Like all objects near the ecliptic, this nova would be clearly visible from Babylon and Israel. To take a typical example, Jerusalem has a latitude of 31.8° north, so that if an observer looks from the Old South Gate of Jerusalem, the gate through which the Bethlehem road passed, Bethlehem is 20 degrees west of south. Just before sunrise in April 4 BC this nova would be high in the sky, about 70 degrees above the horizon in the direction of Bethlehem. If it was a bright nova, as Morehouse assumes, this would clearly be a

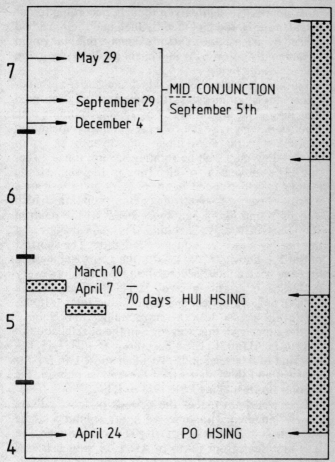

Fig. 29 A schematic illustration of the equal time intervals between the planetary conjunction of the Hui-Hsing and the Po-Hsing

most impressive sight. Even though, according to our calculation, Herod had died by then and the Magi had passed by at least two years previously, this star would be eminently noteworthy and might easily pass into the legends of the time.

Pulsars are radio sources which emit brief pulses of signal at regular intervals. It is now generally accepted that the pulses are produced by rapidly spinning neutron stars, which are the collapsed central remnants of massive stars that have undergone supernovae explosions. They may well be rotating several times a second. The movement of electrons in the very strong magnetic field trapped in these stars gives rise to a narrow beam of electromagnetic radiation which sweeps round like a lighthouse beam as the neutron star spins on its axis. Each time this beam sweeps past the Earth we receive a pulse of radiation. The shortest pulsar we know, NP0531, is in the Crab Nebula and here we have a 0.002 second flash which occurs every 0.033 seconds. This neutron star-pulsar can also be seen to pulse at optical and X-ray wavelengths. It was produced, as also was the surrounding Crab Nebula, by the supernova that was seen in the constellation of Taurus in AD 1054. The Vela pulsar, PSR0833-45, has a period of 0.089 seconds. Together these two are the shortest and third shortest of the known pulsars, the second shortest being PSR 1913 + 16b.

It is well known that the periods of most pulsars slowly lengthen with time, as if the spinning of the neutron star is slowing down. The Crab Supernova was first seen from Earth in AD 1054, which is less than a thousand years ago. The Vela pulsar, however, is between 6000 and 11,000 years old. Michanowsky has recently translated an ancient Sumerian clay tablet that recounts the observation of a short-lived, very bright star in the constellation of Vela. This tablet is about 6000 years old, according to Michanowsky. The

4 BC Aquila pulsar is the second fastest at 0.059 seconds, so that if these pulsars originated with the same period and have evolved in a similar fashion, the Aquila object would have an age between the 1000 and 6000 years of the other two—and 2000 years is reasonable enough.

8

Celestial phenomena

Apart from novae and supernovae, the spectacular explosions of stellar brightness, many other theories have been put forward to explain the star of Bethlehem, including variable stars, meteors, fireballs, ball lightning and zodiacal light. Variable stars are common enough phenomena, whether regular and predictable or irregular and unpredictable. Among the latter, two have been suggested as explanations of what the Magi saw and followed—Mira and a star in the constellation Cassiopeia.

Mira is the star Omicron Ceti in the constellation of Cetus the whale, a long straggling group that runs below and parallel to the ecliptic beneath the zodiacal constellations of Aries and Pisces. It is the type star of a collection of variables with long periods ranging from about 150 to 450 days. All these stars are giants, with diameters of one hundred to five hundred times that of the Sun, and are radiating away into space over a thousand times more energy per second. Mira was first recorded as being variable by Fabricius in 1597. He noticed that it was a third magnitude star in April 1596 but found to his surprise that it had disappeared in 1597. No further records of it appeared until 1638 when the Dutch astronomer Phocylides Holwarda discovered that it was of third magnitude. It was invisible in the summer of 1639 and reappeared in October of the same year. Ismael Boulliau fixed its period at about eleven months in 1667. This is now given as 331.5 days, although the interval between its times of maximum brightness varies from 320 to 370 days. The value of this maximum also varies. Between maximum and minimum luminosity the surface temperature of Mira Ceti changes from 2300 to 1600 degrees Celsius. At maximum luminosity it is about twenty per cent larger than at minimum.

Since Mira is so cool, at least in stellar terms, it radiates most of its energy in the infrared. The extreme variations in its brightness are caused not only by the difference between the temperature and surface area at maximum and minimum, but by the change of energy with wavelength. Much more of the emitted energy is "visible" at the higher temperature. At maximum Mira has a magnitude between +3 and +4, and occasionally it has been known to reach +2, whereas at minimum it is 100 times less bright, with a magnitude in the +9 to +10 range. It therefore changes from being easily visible to the naked eye to requiring a good pair of binoculars to pick it out against the background of stars. In color, Mira is a deep yellowy red.

This change in the brightness of Mira is its most striking characteristic. In view of this, Montague Richardson has recently suggested that the star of Bethlehem is really Mira. He makes five points based on his reading of Matthew's account of the star and on Zaehner's book *The Teachings of the Magi:*

(1) The Magi were Persian Zoroastrians.

(2) The main object of worship of the Zoroastrians was fire, and so the star of Bethlehem must have the color of fire.

(3) The position of the star of Bethlehem on the celestial sphere must be considerably south of the celestial equator in order for it "to be low enough to stand over the one small house that the Magi entered just before dawn." This proviso also fixes the exact time and direction of the Magi's approach to the place where the holy family were.

(4) The star of Bethlehem cannot be explained in terms of planets, because they are "well known," or in terms of novae, because their light is the wrong color. Novae have extremely hot surfaces and shine with a white or blue-white light, not with the "fire" color required. The only stars fulfilling the conditions are red giant stars which are also long period variables. These are the right color and could also have surprised the Magi, since their maximum brightness varies from cycle to cycle. Such a star could, after a long series of faint maxima, have a bright maximum and suddenly look like a new star.

(5) The star went before the Magi until it came and stood over the place where the young child was. The Magi seem to have regarded the star as not belonging to the company of fixed stars, rather as something detached. It must therefore have been a dominant star at its maximum brightness, isolated in an area of the celestial sphere away from other bright stars. At nautical twilight it must have stood out against an apparently starless background.

How do these points stand up to criticism in the light of present biblical and astronomical knowledge? Point (1) is a possibility, but (2) goes against all we know about the astrological side of Babylonian and Zoroastrian religion, and in any case we have no idea whether the color of the star was important to the Magi. Points (3) and (5) are interesting inasmuch as Richardson makes an attempt to explain the statement in Matthew 2:9 that the star went before the Magi and stood over the place of their destination. The idea of a star "standing over" a place when it is behind it near the horizon and not directly above it in the zenith is a new one. The position of the star at the horizon would strictly limit the time as well as the direction of the Magi's approach to the place of the nativity. Point (4) is an obvious problem: novae and planets are dismissed because they are the wrong color, but the justification for the selection of a "flame" colored object is flimsy. Richardson concludes that the star Mira Ceti is the star of Bethlehem, with the right color and declination, and in a region of the sky which contains few bright stars.

When could Mira have been the star of Bethlehem? 4 BC is too late. Richardson assumes the star rose heliacally when the Magi saw it in their own country, but in 5 BC this rising was blotted out by the light of the Moon in its last quarter. In 6 BC the heliacal rising occurred on 19 April and the new Moon on 18 April, so that conditions would have been ideal. Mira's bright maximum is supposed to have been strong enough to interest the Magi but far too faint to attract the attention of Herod and his advisers. Richardson associates its "roundness" and similarity in color to the Sun with the Zoroastrian god of birth, Gayomart, and regards this as the astrological justification for the Magi's use of the expression "his star." Mira would have been lost in the astronomical twilight during May. Apparently the Magi visited Jerusalem about 31 May 6 BC. Leaving Jerusalem early the next morning via the Jaffa gate, they traveled to Bethlehem by way of Mar Elias and Rachel's Tomb. At about 3:50 a.m. local time, from the high plateau of Mar Elias, the Magi would have seen Mira at a magnitude of +1.3 in the otherwise empty sky just above Bethlehem. At 4:16 a.m., as they entered the outer regions of Bethlehem, the star would have been 61° east of south at altitude 18°30′ and therefore directly over the grotto where the Basilica of the Nativity now stands.

Richardson's theory is ingenious but seems to suffer from too many imponderables. The period of Mira is about 331 days, so that maximum brightness would only have lasted for a short time, at most a quarter of the period—about two and a half months. No indication is given as to whether the Magi made the journey during one maximum or between one maximum and another. Furthermore, the astrological significance is rather stretched. Mira's brightening is a well-known phenomenon today, but very few of its maxima differ from the mean magnitude value of +4. Super brightenings are unusual and unexpected, and there seems to be scant relationship between them and any significant astrological predictions. Mira would be rather like a nova in this respect, a portent of general disquiet but not a harbinger of a specific event, particularly one like the awaited coming of a Jewish Messiah. In any case, Richardson's theory needs too tight a timetable for the journey from Jerusalem to Bethlehem, which would have had to take place in the middle of the night, according to his view.

The story of the Magi has been regarded by some as one of the most remarkable instances of astrology in the Bible. The prophecy of Balaam in Numbers 24:17 has been seen as part of an old Chaldean legend associating the coming of the King of the Jews with the appearance of a star. According to Christopher McIntosh, who has made a special study of the history of astrology, in Chaldean astrology the constellation of Cassiopeia was thought to preside over Syria and Palestine. This constellation was known as "the Woman with Child" because every three hundred years or so it brought forth an unusually bright star. To an astrologer the appearance of the star would mean that the Queen of Palestine had brought forth an heir to the throne. If this was the case it would have been of the utmost importance to go and pay homage to the future King.

According to McIntosh it was this other star which appeared just after the birth of Christ and which must therefore have been the one observed and followed by the Magi. Unfortunately McIntosh gives no references to support his claim. The lists of variable stars show that the only bright variable in the constellation was Gamma Cassiopeia, which is a quasi-nova varying

between +1.6 and +3.0 magnitude with an unknown
period. There are, it is true, two fainter variables
which are possible candidates for the star of
Bethlehem. R Cassiopeiae, which varies between +4.8
and a very low minimum of +13.6 every 430.5 days, is
a Mira type, while Rho Cassiopeiae, which varies
between +4.1 and +6.2 with an unspecified period, is
similar to the type star R Coronae Borealis. None of
these stars seem suitable. Perhaps McIntosh is referring to the novae and supernovae that occur in Cassiopeia. By looking at the catalogue of pretelescopic
galactic novae and supernovae given by Clark and
Stephenson in their book *The Historical Supernovae* it
is possible to see that these stars sprang into brightness
in this constellation in December AD 1592, November
1592, November 1572, August 1181 and August 722.
None is recorded as having occurred in Cassiopeia
around the time of the birth of Christ.

In an article in the journal *Planitarium* in 1967 C. St.
J. H. Daniel made the suggestion, among a list of other
more probable candidates, that the star Canopus,
Alpha Carinae, is a possibility: "The wise men might
have observed Canopus for the first time during the
winter months when they climbed to high ground
during a chance journey to the south. The sight of this
great new star together with Sirius, the brightest star in
the heavens almost vertically above Canopus, would
be a sufficient sign to set them on their journey in
search of the Messiah. When heading southward on
the last lap of their journey, from Jerusalem to
Bethlehem, the Wise Men would see these two brilliant stars directly in front of them, pointing to the
place where Jesus would be found." Sirius has a
magnitude of −1.4, while Canopus, the second
brightest star in the heavens, has a magnitude of −0.7.

Now as Daniel pointed out, the whole case rests on
the place of origin of the Magi. If they came from
Nineveh or Asshur in Assyria (present-day northern
Iraq) they may not have seen Canopus before. Further

south we have the lands of Babylonia and Chaldea, regions famous for their astronomical knowledge. Canopus would be well-known to these people. It is still most unlikely, however, that people such as the Assyrians who had studied astronomy for thousands of years, and had close ties with surrounding countries, were ignorant of the fact that different stars could be seen in the southern sky as an observer journeyed south. The suggestion also rests on the unlikely possibility that the discovery of Canopus occurred just before the birth of Christ. Furthermore, the star has no known astrological message, and no newly discovered object could have. Finally, as Canopus is far south of the celestial equator, there is no possibility of any acronychal or heliacal rising.

Daniel also recounted the belief that every time a shooting star—the colloquial term for a meteor—is seen in the sky, then somewhere on Earth a baby is born. But a meteor would hardly have excited the Magi. Meteors, after all, are common enough and on a clear dark night, away from towns and the full Moon, an average of ten meteors can be seen each hour. There is therefore nothing unusual about them, and they seldom last for more than a few seconds.

It is possible that instead of seeing an isolated meteor they witnessed a meteor swarm, a spectacular display of meteors visible on the rare occasions when the Earth intersects a meteor stream close to the parent comet. The Leonids in 1866 and 1966 are a modern example. Again there are many problems. Other people would have seen it too, and it would have probably been brought to the attention of Herod. Furthermore, meteor swarms are short-lived phenomena lasting usually no more than one night, so this does not tie in with the reappearance of the "star" as the Magi journeyed southward from Jerusalem to Bethlehem. In a meteor swarm all the individual meteors shoot across the sky in paths which seem to be radiating from a specific spot on the celestial sphere. This radiant spot rises and sets in a similar fashion to the Sun, Moon and stars. Like these, it does not go before or stand over anywhere. In any case, the ancient records of meteor showers contain no entries for anything remotely near the estimated time of the birth of Christ (Table 8.1).

Meteors are caused by the frictional break-up and deceleration of small dust particles. Such particles, usually with masses in the 0.1 to 10 gram range, impinge on the top of the Earth's atmosphere with speeds in the region between 11 and 74 kilometers per second (25,000 to 160,000 mph). Collisions with the molecules in the atmosphere soon heat the incoming particles to vaporization point and their out-of-the-atmosphere kinetic energy is quickly converted into light, heat and ionization. If the incoming body has a mass of about one ton or more, a brilliant fireball is produced having a luminosity of the same order of magnitude as the full Moon and capable of lighting up the night sky and illuminating all the land around. Sometimes the interplanetary body is large enough to survive its swift passage through the atmosphere and it hits the Earth's surface and can be recovered as a meteorite.

Is it possible that the wise men happened to see a fireball, perhaps with a brilliant train of light, and interpreted it as a sign? They would not have known the cause, and it might have appeared as a miracle. It is possible that they would be seeing a fireball for the first

Table 8.1 Ancient meteor showers near the time of Christ's birth (after Imoto and Hasegawa)

Date	Solar longitude (1950.0)	Probable shower	Record
26 March 15 BC	30°	Lyrids	Stars fell like a shower
Sept-Oct 15 BC			Stars fell like a shower
23 May 12 BC	86°		Stars fell glittering like a shower
15 March AD 36	20°		More than 100 small stars flew
17 July AD 36	138°	Perseid	More than 100 meteors flew thither in the morning

time. Furthermore, if a second fireball had appeared later on, more or less in the same place in the sky as the first one, on their way to Bethlehem, they would have been convinced that the phenomenon was a miracle. A very bright fireball might easily have led them in some particular direction.

This theory has one advantage. Fireballs and meteorite falls are localized. It could have occurred in the east where the Magi lived and have been completely invisible to Herod and the citizens of Jerusalem. The very strong argument against this idea, however, is that fireballs are visible only for a very short time, and there is no way in which they could have led the Magi for more than a few seconds. It is in any case highly unlikely that the Magi would have regarded a meteorite fall as a miracle. 500,000 fireballs occur in the Earth's atmosphere each year, while 500 meteorites hit its surface annually. They might not be common, but in view of the long history of the Persian and Babylonian people that preceded the advent of the Magi it is most unlikely that they would have been surprised by such phenomena. Furthermore, fireballs and meteorites have no astrological message.

For a suggestion that the star of Bethlehem is not astronomical at all but terrestrial—ball lightning—we are indebted to an unpublished manuscript by Professor Michael Kamienski, the late Professor of Astronomy in the University of Kracov in Poland. Kamienski was concerned because he thought that in general the theologians who write on the subject of the star do not have a sufficient knowledge of the fundamentals of astronomy, whereas the astronomers who advance theories do not take into account the whole text of St. Matthew's Gospel but only a minor part of it, neglecting the rest. The neglected aspect that worried Kamienski was the idea in Matthew 2:9 that the star "stood over" and "went before." He calculated that the triple conjunction of Jupiter and Saturn in the constellation of Pisces took place exactly every 854 years and his calculations showed that they occurred around June 7 BC, AD 848 and AD 1702. There is a minor cycle of 238 years and 1 month, and a secondary cycle every 60 years. The fact that Piscean triple conjunctions of Saturn and Jupiter occurred regularly every 854 years led Kamienski to conclude that they are not exceptional and by implication not rare enough or unusual enough to qualify as the star of Bethlehem. In my opinion this is an invalid conclusion. Once every 854 years seems rare enough, being much rarer than the occurrence of bright novae and supernovae, and gives a considerably longer interval than the time period between exceptional comets. To put it another way, such a conjunction would only occur about every twenty-five generations.

Kamienski's second point applies directly to Matthew 2:9. The planets obviously participate in the diurnal motion of the celestial sphere. They rise in the east and move with a constant and uninterrupted angular velocity of 15 degrees per hour around the polar axis. They could in no way have stopped over the place where the infant Jesus was born. Even if they had miraculously stopped in their paths, they would not have been "over" the place. Bethlehem has a geographical latitude of 31.8 degrees north. At the time of conjunction the celestial declinations of Jupiter and Saturn are respectively −4.7 degrees and −6.0 degrees. At the moment of their culmination (the time when they are due south of Bethlehem and at the highest point of their diurnal path) the mean zenith distance of the planets is 37.2 degrees. The only spot in the sky which can be said to be "over" Bethlehem is the point known as the zenith. Saturn and Jupiter would have been 37.2 degrees away from that point and certainly not "over" the place where the babe was lying.

This last stipulation also rules out other planets, comets and novae unless they had a declination on the celestial sphere of exactly +31.8 degrees. Even then they would not have stopped over Bethlehem but would have continued to move across the sky like all celestial objects. Furthermore, as the distance between celestial bodies and the Earth is so enormous compared to the dimensions of the Earth, any celestial object in the zenith appears to be over an area of some hundreds of miles in diameter and cannot be considered as "over" an individual town, let alone an individual house or manger. To the Magi on the last stage of their journey, if the star was over Bethlehem it was over Jerusalem as well.

This is the problem Kamienski was trying to solve. He therefore rejected the idea of the star of Bethlehem as a celestial body and concluded that the phenomenon must have been in the immediate neighborhood of the Earth. Only in this way could it have guided the Magi directly to the newborn baby by stopping over the inn-stable in Bethlehem. The star of Bethlehem had to move about the surface of the Earth at a maximum height of a few hundred meters. Kamienski also argued that Matthew's word for star (aster) referred to a peculiar or individual object rather than to an ordinary star (astron) in the sky.

Kamienski then took the intriguing step of moving into the strange world of the psychic and had recourse to the mystical writings of St. Maria de Agreda, an Abbess of the Order of St. Francis in Spain. There was a belief that Maria often went, in her astral body, to Mexico to convert the Indians, using their own language even though she did not know it. When the missionaries arrived in Mexico some time later they found that the Indians were already prepared for baptism because a certain White Lady had been there and preached to them. These details were supposed to have been confirmed by subsequent missionaries.

In the book written by St. Maria she recounts the following vision concerning the origin and motion of the star of Bethlehem:

At that time the angel who was sent to them [the Magi] from the stable at Bethlehem created in [or "out of"] the air, by the power of God, a star of peculiar splendor, not so great however as those of the firmament, for this star was fixed, not in the sky, but in the lower air, in order to guide the Kings to the stable at Bethlehem. This star was of a great splendor, different from that of the Sun and stars.

With its charming light it illuminated the night like a torch. When they started out from their homes, they all saw the star, although they started from different places. For it was so elevated and at such a distance that all three could see it. After they had left their homes they soon met together and the star was lowered in the air and shone close to them . . . They went where the star guided them and when they arrived in Jerusalem (reasoning that there in the capital city the King of Judea would be born), the star disappeared from their sight. . . . When the Kings set out from Jerusalem, the star appeared in front of them again and led them to Bethlehem where it stopped. Then having come down a little and diminishing [in size and brightness] it went into the cave or stable and diminished more and more slowly, it came to rest over the head of the Divine Child, surrounded it with a marvelous light and finally disappeared.

What is a scientific inquirer to make of the report of the mystical wanderings, in body as well as mind, of a seventeenth-century abbess? And what can one make of the "star" that she describes? Kamienski concludes that the phenomenon is ball lightning. Unfortunately this conclusion simply exchanges one unusual phenomenon for another. Although ball lightning has been seen by thousands of people and many scientists have written about it, it still remains a subject of considerable mystery and debate. One reason for this is that it is extremely varied in appearance. There are two general types, one falling from the upper atmosphere to Earth, a so-called electrical meteor, and the other moving with a path which is generally parallel to the Earth's surface, having been formed relatively close to it. Falling spheres have been reported at the Eiffel Tower in Paris, and at other similar locations at times when ordinary lightning strikes metal.

Ball lightning can vary from the size of a pea to the size of a house. On average it is around 30 centimeters across and is usually spherical in shape, one report stating that the object was so symmetrical that it was not possible to tell whether it was spinning or not. In rarer cases it is non-spherical, and can sometimes even resemble a rod, dumb-bell or spiked ball. Its colors are many and various, and examples have been described as violet, blue, yellow, red, blue-white, and even purplish with a reddish cast. The ball may glide silently around a room and then quietly dematerialize or it can explode violently like a shotgun blast. It can move very slowly, literally hovering in one place. On the other hand more typical speeds have been referred to by such terms as ambling and whizzing. The duration of the phenomenon seems to vary from a few seconds up to a hundred seconds. The ball lightning has been seen to materialize as often in closed rooms and aircraft bodies as in the open. Observers seem to have no doubts that something palpable has visited them and often after the disappearance the room is filled with the typical odors associated with electrical discharges. Usually electrical storms and thunder occur at the same time.

Although instances of ball lightning are well documented, the fact that it is a rare and transient phenomenon that cannot as yet be reproduced in the laboratory means that no accepted explanation of it exists. Theories have been propounded which are based on such things as standing waves in electro-magnetic fields leading to coronal discharges in space charge distributions, molecular recombination in plasma spheres generated by radio frequency fields, and H-type discharges in a closed current configuration. None of these explanations is entirely satisfactory and the problem of how the mechanical or thermal energy is transferred to electrical and radiant energy still remains.

In view of all this, it is highly unlikely that the star of Bethlehem was ball lightning. This phenomenon has scant resemblance to a star, even if Matthew's text does refer to an extraordinary object rather than a normal star—and in any case we cannot assume this. Furthermore, ball lightning would need an accompanying thunderstorm, and it would have been too short-lived to lead and stand over any place for long enough to guide the Magi unequivocally to one specific house, let alone draw them from Jerusalem to Bethlehem. Again, it lacks any astrological message or specific association with the new Messiah. As it turns out, to believe that ball lightning is the explanation behind the star of Bethlehem seems to be tantamount to invoking a miraculous event when more straightforward scientific interpretations have failed. One is forced to conclude that the leading, diminishing, resting, surrounding and disappearing of this "star" in the report of Maria de Agreda rely more on a fertile imagination than on an acquaintance with the physical actuality.

A very different theory, which is an elaboration of the Jupiter-Saturn conjunction idea, relies on the notion of zodiacal light. According to one version of this view, astrological and astronomical reasoning had revealed to the Magi certain information about the forthcoming birth of the new Messiah. They first went to Jerusalem, though this turned out to be the wrong place, and were then directed to Bethlehem because Herod's scribes and Pharisees recalled the prophecy of

Micah. After some uncertainty, they would have considered it as a good omen when at nightfall the brilliant planets Jupiter and Saturn appeared in the dusk just above the direction of their way to Bethlehem. By the intervention of the zodiacal light, the planets would have appeared to point persistently to a certain place on Earth, where finally they found the child Jesus.

What is this zodiacal light? It is a faint lens-shaped illumination of the night sky, with the Sun at the center of the lens. This shape is elongated in the direction of the ecliptic plane—the zodiac of the sky. It can only be seen when the Sun is below the horizon and can be best viewed from a high mountain in the tropics, though it can also be seen elsewhere. In the tropics the Sun sets very quickly and twilight is short, both these effects being due to the fact that the path of the Sun in the sky is inclined at a considerable angle to the horizon. In more northern and southern latitudes this angle is smaller and the zodiacal light tends to be washed out in the horizon glow. In low latitude regions it appears for an hour or so in the western sky after the end of evening twilight, or in the east for a similar period before the beginning of dawn. The narrow cone of light stands up above the horizon and reaches about halfway to the zenith. It shares the apparent diurnal motion of the sky and during the night sinks below the western horizon until, two hours or so after its first appearance, at the end of twilight, only the faint upper portion remains visible. The cone is widest at its base—near the Sun—and here it has a brightness comparable in intensity to that of the Milky Way. Zodiacal light is caused by the scattering of sunlight by a myriad of small, solid interplanetary dust particles which are moving mainly in direct orbits around the Sun.

In the evening sky of 12 November 7 BC the second and third conjunctions of Saturn and Jupiter were taking place (Figure 17). If zodiacal light was visible, it would have led the eye of the observer from the two planets down to a spot on the southern horizon (Plate 7). As the planets sank lower in the sky, the cone would have continued to point out the small house, as long as the observer was moving toward the house along a straight path—a fairly reasonable assumption for the journey of the Magi from Jerusalem to Bethlehem.

To introduce the zodiacal light as a final guide for the Magi is extremely ingenious, but it is not really necessary. The Magi had been told that the Messiah was to be born in Bethlehem, and so they did not need a celestial guide for their two-hour walk. Arriving in Bethlehem they were obviously confronted with an enormous mellay of people, all the inns were full, the town was overflowing. If we assume that Jesus had just been born and that the birth of this child, in a stable, to a stranger, was still fresh in the mind of the local midwife, one or two inquiries would quickly lead the Magi to the place where the holy family was. In Bethlehem the Magi would see the two planets and the zodiacal light over in the direction of Hebron and they would be useless as a further guide.

If, on the other hand, Mary and Joseph actually lived in Bethlehem and the visit of the Magi occurred forty days or so after the birth, we have to recall the fact that Bethlehem had a population of about one thousand at that time and an annual birthrate of around thirty. Possibly the Magi visited a few families before they found the right family. We must rely on the testimony of Mary and Joseph here. They obviously knew that Jesus was the Messiah, especially because of the visitations by the angel Gabriel and the shepherds. Unless the star is to be reduced to the size and the proximity of a phenomenon like ball lightning, we must reject it as the infallible guide to the Magi on the last mile or so of their journey in Bethlehem and must relegate it to a general guide for their travels along the road from Jerusalem to Bethlehem. Zodiacal light would in any case have been a common enough sight to the Magi.

All the objects and phenomena mentioned in this chapter, including zodiacal light, must be ruled out because of their lack of astrological significance. They have no attributes that would relate them directly to the King of the Jews or, to be more specific, to his birth. We must remember that the star of Bethlehem must have been unusual and probably appeared twice, and this means that most of the objects mentioned above remain ineligible. The triple conjunction of Saturn and Jupiter still remains the best candidate for the star.

9

The sign in the sky

Most astronomers and scientists would today dismiss astrology out of hand as a subject unworthy of serious consideration. Belief in astrology, however, is still a fact of life, and only a few centuries ago astrology and astronomy went hand in hand. The Magi themselves were astrologers and they regarded the star of Bethlehem as an astrological sign.

The well-known British astrologer John Addey concluded in the 1950s that the triple conjunction of Saturn and Jupiter in the constellation of Pisces in 7 BC was the strongest claimant for the title of star of Bethlehem. He went on from this to argue that the last of the three conjunctions, the one occurring about the end of November or beginning of December, was the one taking place when the Magi were in Jerusalem and as they traveled from Jerusalem to Bethlehem. He gave the following reasons for this:

(1) Although the Saturn-Jupiter conjunction is the star of Bethlehem, the Magi might have been uncertain as to which of the conjunctions actually coincided with the birth of Jesus. It would then be reasonable to assume that they arrived in Bethlehem for the last of these conjunctions rather than sooner, for in this case they would have had to wait around in Judea or wander about in search of an event which might not as yet have happened.

(2) Given a free choice, the Magi probably would not

have traveled across the Arabian Desert or around the Fertile Crescent at the height of the summer.

(3) Herod questioned the Magi carefully about the appearance of the star. The purpose of this questioning was to find out when they expected the child to be born. The Magi would then have told Herod that Saturn and Jupiter had been in conjunction in Pisces since February, and they must have assured Herod that the child had already been born and was not just expected. Herod must have gleaned from their answer a reasonable idea as to when Jesus was born, because a short time afterward he sent his murderers to Bethlehem to kill all the male children under the age of two.

(4) The final journey from Jerusalem to Bethlehem took place in the evening round about twilight. The last of the three conjunctions "went before them till it came and stood over where the young child was." As for the time interval between the adoration of the Magi and the birth of the child, Addey assumed that the circumcision and purification had taken place before the visit, so that the baby Jesus and the holy family must have been in Bethlehem for at least six weeks.

(5) In working backward six weeks in time from the November-December visit of the Magi to the actual birthday, Addey relied on common sense. He argued that since Joseph was a carpenter and presumably had to earn a living, it is unlikely that the newly married Joseph was willing to leave his work behind for a very long stay near Jerusalem. Joseph and Mary would therefore have reached Bethlehem around August at the earliest. The period to be examined for the birthday therefore stretches from early August to mid October, a period of ten or eleven weeks.

(6) The last clue reduces the choice from ten weeks to ten days and this relies on one of the early Christian traditions about the birthday. This is that Jesus was

born on the day after the Jewish sabbath. If we transfer this statement into our calendar system it is equivalent to saying that Jesus was born some time between sunset on a Saturday and sunset on a Sunday. In the year 7 BC and in the time period under consideration Sunday occurred on 2, 9, 16, 23, 30 August, 6, 13, 20, 27 September and 4, 11, 18 October.

John Addey then used traditional astrology to decide which of these dates corresponded to the birthday of Jesus. The process was relatively simple. An enormous amount is known about the character of Jesus and his life. For those who believe in astrology, this should be predictable from the Sun, Moon and planetary configuration at his birth. On the basis of astrology it would be possible to work backwards from the later life of Jesus and arrive at the date of his birth. According to Addey the symbolism of the Pisces-Virgo polarity is intimately involved in the life and religion of Jesus. (The signs of the zodiac can be arranged around the circumference of a circle, as shown in Figure 30, and a polarity exists between signs that are diametrically opposite each other.) The significant astrological elements are the virgin birth, the word Bethlehem, meaning "a house of bread," which is also the sixth house, and Virgo, the virgin, who is usually represented holding an ear of corn. As an alternative to the sixth and twelfth signs of the zodiac we can have the sixth and twelfth houses as, in matters of this kind, these are interchangeable.

John Addey argued that the horoscope of Jesus should also contain a distinct solar or Leo element. This would give prominence to the dignity, authority and kinginess in Jesus' character and personality. In Addey's view, the emphasis that Jesus continually put on the Father-Son relationship and the absolute trust and devotion that he inspired in his followers suggest that the Sun in the fifth sign or the fifth house would at least be appropriate. John Addey then searched through the set of days after the Jewish sabbath, remembering the sunset to sunset proviso, and found that the time which satisfied his astrological preconceptions was the evening of 22 August—a Saturday to us, but the day after the sabbath to the Jews, because the Sun had set—in the year 7 BC. The horoscope for this time is given in Figure 30.

The signs of the zodiac are drawn in around the circumference of the circle and each sign occupies 30 degrees. The positions of the planets at 4:00 p.m. on 22 August 7 BC are marked as large dots in Figure 30 and each planet is signified by its glyph. The number next to the glyph or symbol represents the position of the planet in the zodiac sign in degrees, the position being measured in the anticlockwise direction. Choosing the time of birth as 4:00 p.m. puts the ascendant in Aries. The ascendant is defined as the point in the sign of the zodiac which is rising on the eastern horizon at the moment of birth. The choice of an ascendant in the case of the horoscope of Jesus immediately fixes the positions of the "houses," which are marked off by numbers in the center of the circle in Figure 30. They start with number 1, which comes immediately after the ascendant, and then each house occupies 30 degrees of the circle, again going round in an anticlockwise direction.

This horoscope is retrospective. The positions of the planets, especially the fast-moving planets like Mercury, Venus and Mars, as well as the positions of the Sun and Moon and the houses, have been fixed by our knowledge of the character and life-style of Jesus and by our rough knowledge of his time of birth. Some astrologers might question the details. John Addey justifies the choice of an Aries ascendant by the fact that "this deposes the planets in very suitable houses. One must always remember that Jesus was a man of action, courage and resolution, as well as a great mystic. The religion he founded has also been a religion of action and many of its greatest votaries have

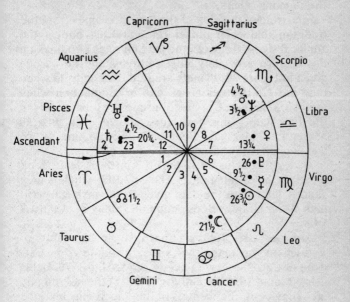

Fig. 30 The birth horoscope of Jesus as drawn up by John Addey

been pleased to regard themselves as "Soldiers of Christ." Of all the great religions of the world, it must, I think, be admitted that Christianity is easily the most Martian. Furthermore the Aries ascendant agrees with such titles as "Lamb of God" and "The Good Shepherd". . . . The conjunction of Mars and Neptune in Scorpio, on cusp 8 and in exact trine to Uranus, is a marvelously apt configuration for many things in the life of Jesus showing a profound, penetrating and yet intensely spiritual will power."

This conjunction of Mars and Neptune in trine to Uranus is just the sort of configuration which could provide the clue by which to choose the correct date from among others.

In astrology the idea of the "ruler" comes from the tradition that each planet rules at least one of the zodiacal signs—for example the Sun rules Leo, making this feature especially noteworthy in the horoscope given in Figure 30. Planets are said to be in trine when they are 120 degrees apart, and in conjunction when they are together. Conjunctions are the focal points in the horoscope, the horoscope shown in Figure 30 having two, Mars and Neptune in Scorpio, and Saturn and Jupiter in Pisces.

Addey's conclusion is that the birth of Jesus took place on the evening of 22 August 7 BC, which is only slightly later than the date given in the mystical writings of the Urantia Book, noon on Friday 21 August 7 BC.

Another astrological approach to the star of Bethlehem was made by Cardan (also known as Cardano or Cardanus), who lived from 1501 to 1576. In his astrogram of Christ's nativity (Plate 8) the holy family are shown at the center of the figure against the background of a spherical Earth surrounded by wispy clouds. The diagram follows the Ptolemaic representation of the heavens in which the Earth is at the center, with the major celestial bodies on circles of ever increasing radius. The Moon, Mercury, Venus, Sun, Mars, Jupiter and Saturn are shown in this order, which is based on decreasing velocity in relation to the celestial sphere rather than on distance from the Earth, which in those days was unknown. A comparison with the planetary positions given in Tuckerman's tables reveals that the Cardan horoscope is for a birth occurring on 25 December 1 BC. A more detailed version of this horoscope for the evening (18.00) of that day at Bethlehem is shown in Figure 31. It is rather an indictment of the strength of astrology and its scientific potential that these two horoscopes, Figures 30 and 31, have been confidently regarded as keys to the life of

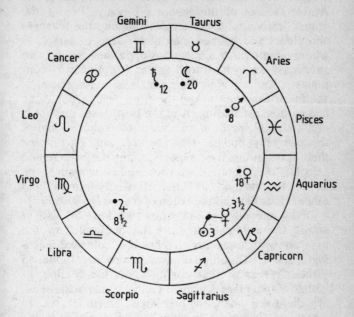

Fig. 31 A diagram of Cardan's horoscope of Jesus

Jesus. It seems to be a fair assumption that the positions of the planets on 22 August 7 BC and 25 December 1 BC have little or no relevance to the birth, life or death of Christ.

In ancient Babylon and Israel, however, there was a strong belief in the power and usefulness of astrology, and even Jesus was regarded as having considerable knowledge of the subject. The report of the twelve-year-old Jesus "sitting in the midst of the doctors, both hearing them and asking them questions" when the holy family had made their annual trip to Jerusalem for the feast of the Passover is told succinctly in Luke's

Gospel (2:41-50), but it is greatly elaborated in the Arabic Gospel of the Savior's Infancy. In this the young Jesus sits in the temple "among the teachers and elders and learned men of the sons of Israel, to whom he put various questions upon the sciences and gave answers in his turn" (verse 50). Verse 51 continues: "And a philosopher who was there present, a skillful astronomer, asked the Lord Jesus whether he had studied astronomy. And the Lord Jesus answered him and explained the number of the spheres, and of the heavenly bodies, their natures and operations; their oppositions; their aspects, triangular, square and sextile; their course, direct and retrogade; the twenty-fourths and sixtieths of twenty-fourths; and other things beyond the reach of reason."

Of all the phenomena which we have looked at among the candidates for the star of Bethlehem, the only one which has any significant astrological meaning is the 7 BC conjunction of Saturn and Jupiter in Pisces. We know that conjunctions, the coming together of two planets against the celestial background, are the focal points in astrological birth charts. In astrology a conjunction gives strong emphasis to the characteristics of the planets and signs involved, and the main mental reactions and the feelings induced by the planets are said to interact strongly, with positive or negative stress according to the sign and house position of the planets concerned.

What would Saturn, Jupiter, and Pisces signify to the Magi astrologers? The problem is that we know little about the details of astrology nearly two thousand years ago. As the New Testament scholar Raymond Brown points out, we cannot be sure how the Jews in the time of Jesus made their zodiacal calculations. The same scholar, however, goes on to say that "Pisces is a constellation sometimes associated with the last days and with the Hebrews, while Jupiter, an object of particular interest among Parthian astrologers, was associated with the world ruler and Saturn was identified as the star of the Amorites of the Syria-Palestine region.'' The claim has been made that this conjunction might have led Parthian astrologers to predict that there would appear in Palestine among the Hebrews a world ruler of the last days, an apocalyptic king. This claim is supported by a recent research paper by Roy A. Rosenberg and much of what follows has been taken from this most useful work. St. Matthew speaks of the ''star'' as having been observed by ''Magi'' from the east, but Rosenberg claims that Matthew is probably reflecting what was essentially at that time a Jewish astrological tradition. From what we know of traditional Jewish astrology, Kepler was correct in his speculation as to the significance of the Piscean conjunction—the Jews did link the appearance of the Messiah, and other great events, with the conjunctions of Jupiter and Saturn.

The Jewish religion has an ambivalent attitude towards astrology. Deuteronomy 4:14 reads: ''And the Lord commanded me at that time to teach you statutes and judgments, that ye might do them in the land whither ye go over to possess it. Take ye therefore good heed unto yourselves . . . lest thou lift up thine eyes unto heaven, and when thou seest the Sun and the Moon and the stars, even all the host of the heavens, shouldest be driven to worship them, and serve them, which the Lord thy God hath divided unto all nations under the whole heaven. But the Lord hath taken you and brought you forth out of the iron furnace, even out of Egypt, to be unto him a people of inheritance, as ye are this day.'' This has been taken to mean that God had allotted the host of heaven for the nations to worship, but had excluded Israel from this, so that in normal Jewish teaching little attention is paid to astrology, especially as a means of divining the time and place of the Messiah's coming. Privately and in folklore, however, astrological speculation persisted from the earliest days of Israel's history.

For an example of Jewish astrology we can turn to

the work of Don Isaac Abrabanel, especially his commentary on the book of Daniel entitled *The Wells of Salvation*. In this book, which was consulted by Kepler, the author discusses in detail the significance attributed by the Jews to the periodic conjunctions of Jupiter and Saturn. This work was completed in 1497 and in it Abrabanel states that these conjunctions occur about every twenty years and that the sign of the zodiac in which they occur changes from one conjunction to another. In astronomical terms this is perfectly correct, and Saturn and Jupiter have the same heliocentric longitudes every 19.859317 years. In calculating this figure we assume that they are moving in circular orbits, the orbital periods being 11.86223 years and 29.4577 years for Saturn and Jupiter respectively.

In true astrological fashion each conjunction was to be taken as a portent of some Earthly event. There were five classes. Small conjunctions (mahberet qetanah) took place every twenty years and foretold such things as wars and the births of kings. Progressively, in order of the increasing importance of the events in human history, Abrabanel had middle conjunctions (mahberet 'emsa'it) occurring every sixty years, great conjunctions (mahberet gedolah) about every 239 years, large conjunctions (mahberet rabbah) approximately every 953 years, and mighty conjunctions (mahberet 'asumah) every 2860 years or so. The mighty conjunctions were portents of such events as the birth of great prophets, miracle workers, revealers of secrets and of course the Messiah.

Abrabanel states that the experience of history must be used to decide which of all the possible conjunctions are in fact the "mighty" ones. This choice would also single out the zodiacal sign which contained the conjunction, and Abrabanel found this to be Pisces. Saturn and Jupiter had a mighty conjunction there in the year 1396 BC, three years before the birth of Moses. This was of considerable importance to Abrabanel because by adding 2860 years one arrived at

AD 1465, a year which occurred during his own life and in which he thought the redeemer of Israel, the Messiah, would come. Just over a hundred years later Kepler calculated that large conjunctions and mighty conjunctions occurred about every 794 and 2383 years respectively.

Abrabanel goes to considerable lengths to explain why Pisces is the zodiacal constellation that hosts the "mighty" conjunctions and also why the sign is associated with Israel. We know that each sign of the zodiac is associated with one of the four astrological elements, earth, fire, water and air. Pisces is watery and this apparently fits in with the many connections between water and the patriarchs and Moses. According to Rosenberg, water falls on the Earth to make it fruitful, and this signifies the role of Israel among the nations. Furthermore, Pisces is the "house" of the planet Jupiter. Abraham, according to an interpretation of Isaiah 41:2, is under Jupiter. We know from the Kabbalistic book Raziel, which dates from the eleventh century, that Jupiter (named Tsedeq or Sedeq in Hebrew) was associated with righteousness. In similar vein Abrabanel states that during the month Nisan, in which the messianic redemption is to occur, the cup of Elijah at the Passover meal preserves in symbolism the idea that the new redemption will come during the same season as the exodus from Egypt. Nisan is associated with Aries, whereas the month preceding Nisan is Adar, which is associated with Pisces. This means that the conjunction which announces the impending redemption should occur in Pisces, the sign of the month before the redemption.

Why is it that a Jupiter-Saturn conjunction has such an overriding significance in the astrological tradition? The answer is apparently related to the fact that these two planets were the slowest moving known in ancient times. Saturn, the outermost, slowest planet was the one closest to the Ptolemaic sphere of the fixed stars and was the planet which communicated motion to the universe of stars. In Babylonian astrology Saturn was closely associated with the Sun, and the Shamash cult of Sippar and Lasa named it the "sun of the night." One of the attributes of Saturn was "star of justice and right" (Kittu u mesar). Kittu and Mesharu are the children of Shamash, the Sun, and are often portrayed as seated before Shamash or as "the ministers of his right hand."

During the time of the Neo-Babylonian empire the god Marduk, who was manifest in the planet Jupiter, also came to be invoked under the names of all the other major deities. Jupiter-Marduk also developed a close association with the Sun and occasionally Shamash was called "the Marduk of justice." In this way Justice and Right, Kittu and Mesharu, the divine qualities of the cult of Saturn and the Sun, became linked with the planet Jupiter as well, and as Jewish astrology was deeply influenced and shaped by Babylonian traditions, this linking carried over. Both the Babylonians and the Jews identified the planets Jupiter and Saturn with "Sedeq," the justice that vindicates the righteous and punishes the guilty. The Messiah is to be the instrument by which this is to come to pass. A Saturn-Jupiter conjunction in Pisces was therefore obviously the sign associated with the coming of a Jewish Messiah.

Rosenberg gives another reason why the Jupiter-Saturn conjunction was so important. From a very early time Yahweh, the God of Israel, was also identified with El, the High Father God of Canaan and Phoenicia. Sanchuniathon, a priest of Beirut, stated in his account of the Canaanite religion that El was the god of the planet Saturn. In Greek mythology, Kronos, who was associated with Saturn, had been dethroned by Zeus, who was manifest in the planet Jupiter. In the Canaanite religion this incident is paralleled by the rivalry between El and Baal. Kronos gives Zeus "all the measures of the whole creation," because Kronos is "the originator of times." If we take the Greek material to be a reflection of a Canaanite idea then there is a possibility that Jewish and Babylonian astrology would also regard a conjunction of Saturn and Jupiter as signifying the transference of power from one planetary supernatural deity to another. To the Greeks and Phoenicians, El (Kronos) had given over all his powers to his son Baal (Zeus). In Jewish theology El, or Yahweh, was still the universal ruler, and the transfer of powers symbolized by the periodic planetary conjunctions meant something slightly different. Yahweh was giving to his Messiah a proportion of his power and authority so that the Messiah might shatter the wicked principalities that hold sway over the Earth, condemn them to punishment and exalt the righteous in their stead. The planet Saturn in this cosmic drama represents Yahweh, while the planet Jupiter represents his son the Messiah.

The association of Sedeq-Jupiter-righteousness with the coming Messiah was commonplace in Jewish tradition. Jeremiah 23:5 says: "Behold, the days come, saith the Lord, that I will raise unto David a righteous Branch, and a King shall reign and prosper, and shall execute judgment and justice in the earth. In his days Judah shall be saved and Israel shall dwell safely. And this is his name whereby he shall be called, The Lord our Righteousness." Jesus is called "the righteous one" (Saddiq) in Acts, and Enoch 46:3 speaks of the "Son of Man who has righteousness (Sedeq), with whom righteousness dwells."

Rosenberg concludes that it is altogether fitting that the Messiah who is the embodiment of Sedeq should be associated in the heavens with Sedeq the planet Jupiter and should receive from his Father (Yahweh and his representative Saturn) a periodic reconfirmation and renewal of his powers in full view of all those who await his coming simply through the workings of the inexorable laws of planetary motion.

We have here ample justification for concluding that the Jupiter-Saturn conjunction in Pisces had a strong, clear astrological message. To Babylonians and Jews alike it heralded the coming of the Messiah, a man of righteousness who would save the world.

The message was unambiguous and obviously impressed the Magi with the importance of the event and the necessity to journey to Jerusalem and Bethlehem. It is also clear that it was only the Jupiter-Saturn-Pisces conjunction that had this message. All other astronomical occurrences around the time of the birth of Jesus were irrelevant in the quest for the Messiah, and this alone is ample justification for ruling them out as candidates for the role of star of Bethlehem.

10

Planets in conjunction

The idea that the star of Bethlehem is inexorably linked with the Jupiter-Saturn conjunction has been firmly established. Regarding Saturn as Yahweh and Jupiter as the Messiah enables a further step to be taken. When the Magi said "we have seen his star in the east" they were referring specifically to Jupiter. It only remains now to establish the precise sequence of events. In particular, how do the two appearances of the star fit the list of relevant astronomical events in 7 BC (Table 10.1)? The first time the Magi saw the star was when they were in their own country, and the second time was when they left Jerusalem after their audience with Herod and were on the last leg of their journey to Bethlehem.

As to the first appearance, present-day opinion divides into two camps. One supports the heliacal rising in mid March 7 BC, the main justification for this being that there is apparently a strong astrological link between heliacal risings and birth. It happens that nearly all the events listed in Table 10.1 occur in the constellation of Pisces, the only exception being the last event, the heliacal setting, by which time Jupiter has moved on into Aries and left Saturn behind. Furthermore, the two planets are close together for nearly all the time, less than four degrees apart between mid April 7 BC and the end of January 6 BC. The second theory is that the first star was in fact the acronychal rising in mid September 7 BC. This theory has strong support from Professor Ferrari d'Occhieppo, who stresses three points. The first is that Matthew 2:2 "for

Table 10.1 The principal dates in the Saturn-Jupiter-Pisces conjunction that occurred at the birth of Christ

Event	Date		Planetary separation (degrees)
Heliacal setting	about 18 February		9.9
Heliacal rising	about 11 March		7.7
1st conjunction	27 May		0.98
1st stationary point of Saturn	6 July		2.5
1st stationary point of Jupiter	17 July		2.8
Mid conjunction	3 September		2.0
Acronychal rising	14-15 September	7 BC	1.34
2nd conjunction	6 October		0.98
Mid-point of 2nd and 3rd conjunction	31 October		1.42
2nd stationary point of Jupiter	11 November		1.44
2nd stationary point of Saturn	19 November		1.46
3rd conjunction	1 December		1.05
Jupiter-Saturn-Mars massing	mid February	6 BC	6.4
Heliacal setting	about 13 March		8.5

we have seen his star in the east,'' and 2:9, "the star which they saw in the east,'' refers to the acronychal rising of Saturn and Jupiter, an event which took place on 14-15 September 7 BC. As the planets were very close together in the sky they both rose acronychally on the same evening. Secondly d'Occhieppo thinks that it is the evening of the acronychal rising that would be regarded as the birth time by the Magi. Obviously it is difficult for us to find the true birth date, but according to d'Occhieppo the Magi were convinced that Jesus was born on 15 September. Thirdly d'Occhieppo turns to the astrological significance. Jupiter was the planet associated with the highest Babylonian deity, and was the more active participant in the conjunction and therefore the only planet to be considered the "star" of the Messiah. Saturn was the celestial representative of the Jews. The central part of the constellation of Pisces, the region in which both planets' reached their second stationary points, was astrologically associated with Palestine. The second stationary points occurred just below the star Delta Pisces (Figure 32).

Unfortunately the Babylonian calendar tablets, of which at least four different copies for the year 305 of the Babylonian Seleucid era (7/6 BC) have come to light (see Table 6.4), do not give the exact date of the conjunctions. Indeed, it would have been extremely difficult, if not impossible, for even a well-trained Babylonian astronomer to predict them. What is important about the conjunction is that the closeness of the planets makes the heliacal and acronychal risings nearly all occur on the same day. Furthermore, we know from the calendar tablets and the state of Babylonian astronomy at the time that the Magi had predicted the close approach of the planets and the dates of the stationary points and risings well in advance of their actual occurrence. We are safe in thinking that nothing took them by surprise. It was all well known beforehand.

The first appearance of the star therefore does not have to be the starting point of the episode. The Magi did not have to wait for it to happen before deciding to make the journey. They could have made up their minds long beforehand, and they could have completed the planning of the journey beforehand. They could even have been well on their way toward Jerusalem by the time the first star appeared. Matthew 2:9 need not be interpreted as "the star which they saw in their own country," for it could simply mean that the acronychal rising occurred sometime—in fact any time—before the Magi arrived in Jerusalem. We shall see, however, that in reality there was probably a gap of over six weeks between the first "star" and the arrival in Jerusalem.

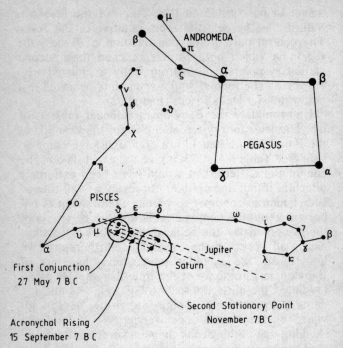

Fig. 32 Jupiter and Saturn in Pisces, 7 BC

What about the statement in Matthew 2:10 that "When they saw the star, they rejoiced with exceeding great joy?" Up to now we have interpreted this phrase as indicating that the star, which they had seen before, reappeared as they made the final stage of their journey—the walk down the road from Jerusalem to Bethlehem. It must be stressed that this interpretation does not fit the Jupiter-Saturn events. These two planets do not leave the night sky from the time of the heliacal rising in March 7 BC to the time of the heliacal setting a year later. The phrase "when they saw the star" is therefore awkward, for they could see Saturn and Jupiter all the time. The sight of a planet that the

Magi had been looking at night after night for months would hardly have been capable of making them rejoice—unless it was the third conjunction that made them joyful, but we cannot be sure.

In working out the sequence of events we can be relatively certain that Saturn and Jupiter and their triple conjunction in 7 BC made the star of Bethlehem. How would this fit in with the nativity story as given in Matthew and Luke? If we follow d'Occhieppo in his supposition that the acronychal rising occurred on the evening of the birthday of Jesus, we would arrive at Tuesday 15 September 7 BC as the birthday, according to the Roman calendar. If, as the Protoevangelium of James says, Jesus was born in the evening, the change of the Jewish day at sunset would bring the time of birth into the next day of the Jewish week, a Wednesday. This would fit about half of Christian tradition as to the day of the week on which the birth took place. The other half still traditionally choose the day after the Jewish sabbath as the birthday.

The sequence of events would be as follows. The Magi, probably being Zoroastrian priests living in Babylon, have predicted most of the events given in Table 10.1 and have decided among themselves that the new Messiah of the Jews is to be born on Tuesday 15 September 7 BC. They have made up their minds to visit the newborn babe and set out on their journey at the end of the hot summer of 7 BC. On their way they see the acronychal rising, which coincides with the birth of Jesus. The events recorded in Luke—the circumcision and Mary's purification—would follow on Sunday 24 September and on about Wednesday 25 October respectively. The interlacing of the nativity accounts in Matthew and Luke (Figure 5) indicates that the Magi visited the holy family some time after the purification. The only predicted astronomical events that happened after the proposed date of the purification were the second stationary points of Jupiter and Saturn (Table 10.1). These occurred in mid

November. Perhaps it was the observation of these stationary points that made the Magi rejoice. If so, the Jerusalem to Bethlehem journey took place some time in the period 11 to 19 November. After the third conjunction, an event which the Magi could not have predicted accurately, the two planets separated quickly, obviously indicating that the momentous event was at an end.

How does Herod come into this picture? Herod called the Magi to him and "inquired of them diligently what time the star appeared." According to the sequence given above, this audience would probably have taken place just before mid December. What would the answer have been to this question? Probably, "We think that the acronychal rising of Saturn and Jupiter on 15 September announced the birth of the King of the Jews, but the two planets have been close companions in Pisces since April of this year." Herod remembered these two dates and a few weeks later, when he realized that the Magi had tricked him and had gone back to Babylon by a different route, he regarded both as possible dates for either the conception or the birth and to be on the safe side he killed all the children under the age of two. Subsequently Herod died in December 5 BC or March 4 BC, about one and a half years after the birth of Jesus, so there are no problems of chronology on this point.

The star was therefore most probably the sequence of Jupiter-Saturn events in 7 BC. Jesus was probably born in mid September 7 BC. This date is consistent with the New Testament passages and fits the date of astronomy and history. We shall see later on that it is possible to arrive at an even more precise date. But mysteries still remain—who were the Magi and where exactly did they come from? And even assuming that Jupiter was the star, which part of the Saturn-Jupiter event resulted in the journey of the Magi, when did they arrive in Bethlehem and how old was Jesus at that time?

11

Miracle, myth or fact?

At some stage we have to ask whether the star of Bethlehem could have been miraculous, an object beyond the bounds of scientific explanation. Alternatively, could it simply be an invention, a story made up to convince Matthew's audience that the Old Testament prophecy of Numbers 24:17, "a star shall come forth out of Jacob and a scepter shall rise out of Israel," found fulfilment in a physical object in the sky?

Many theologians leave the question of a miraculous star an open one. They argue that it is perfectly acceptable and consistent with Christian belief to exclude the idea of a miracle. They argue that the God of Christians does not need to perform a miracle when a natural event serves the same purpose. The star of Bethlehem could therefore have been one of a range of possible natural phenomena. In any case, scientists too are reluctant to turn to a miraculous explanation, even as a last resort.

The opposite view is to suppose that the star of Bethlehem was a special sign in the heavens to announce the birth of Christ, perhaps an exceptional star divinely created for the purpose, or even the appearance of the Holy Spirit in the form of a star. In the third century AD Origen wrote that it was "specially created as a minister to the knowledge of Jesus," while St. Augustine said, "It was not one of the stars that from the outset of creation keep up their journeying in accordance with the Creator's laws, but for the manifesting of Christ a star which had not hitherto existed arose.''

According to a very different and more modern argument, the reference to the star in Matthew is ''midrash,'' which is an exposition or elaboration of a text—in this case a text from the Old Testament book of Numbers—in order to teach or edify the reader. The elaboration generally contains legendary or fanciful elements which often are not straight historical incidents but stories more in line with legend or folklore. If the star were to be explained in terms of midrash, this would mean that the whole idea of the star is an invention, a fiction to give fulfillment to the Old Testament prophecy in Numbers 24:17.

The midrash argument is in some ways the hardest one to answer, for it disposes of the whole problem of the star as a phenomenon and rules out a natural as well as a supernatural explanation. The star becomes merely a literary device. It is true, of course, that stars played a leading role in ancient legends, and for many centuries no significant king was born without mention of some celestial manifestation. Furthermore, people would have found the claim that a star rose to herald the birth of Jesus to be perfectly normal. Nor would they have thought it bizarre that the star led the Magi to the newborn King of the Jews.

Ancient literature contains many fascinating tales of the way in which stars and comets were thought to foretell the birth and death of heroes and kings and a host of other calamities and triumphs besides. Virgil tells of how a star guided Aeneas to the place where the Eternal City of Rome should be founded, and Josephus in his book on the Jewish Wars tells of the siege of Jerusalem and the plight of the inhabitants: ''the wretched people . . . neither needed nor believed in the manifest portent that foretold the coming desolation, but as if thunderstruck and bereft of eyes and mind, disregarded the plain warnings of God. So it was when a star, resembling a sword, stood over the city, and a comet which continued for a year." Tacitus writes in similar vein: "Prodigies had indeed occurred, but to avert them either by victims or by vows is held unlawful by a people which, though prone to superstition, is opposed to all propitiatory rites. Contending hosts were seen meeting in the skies, arms flashed and suddenly the temple was illumined with fire from the clouds."

An incident in which Nero regarded a comet as a portent of doom is related by Suetonius: "It chanced that a comet had begun to appear on several successive nights, a thing which is commonly believed to portend the death of great rulers. Worried by this, and learning from the astrologer Balbillus that kings usually averted such omens by the death of some distinguished man, thus turning from themselves upon the heads of the nobles, he resolved on the death of all the eminent men of the state." Writing about events in AD 60, Tacitus echoes this: "Meanwhile, a comet blazed into view—in the opinion of the crowd, an apparition boding change to monarchies. Hence, as though Nero were already dethroned, men began to inquire on whom the next choice should fall."

There is a particularly interesting late Jewish midrash about a star at the time of the birth of Abraham: "On the night when he [Abraham] was born, Terah's friends, among whom were councillors and astrologers of Nimrod, were feasting in his house, and on leaving at night they observed a star, which swallowed up four other stars from the four sides of the heavens. They forthwith hastened to Nimrod and said, 'Of a certainty a lad has been born who is destined to conquer this world and the next.' " The story continues with a plot between the Magi and the ruling tyrant to kill the child. Terah frustrates this conspiracy by hiding the baby Abraham in a cave for three years.

In the light of these examples and of other legends, some authors conclude that Matthew has simply drawn an elaborate comparison between the early history of the people of Israel and the account of the Jewish-Christian Messiah. They argue that the story has all the characteristic features of a form of midrash known as midrash haggada, in which Old Testament passages were put to ethical or devotional, rather than legal, use. In some religious circles, such as the Essenes, the prophets were studied to find interpretations of happenings in the contemporary scene. These people, knowing of the prophetic oracle of Balaam (Numbers 24:17), would have believed that such a prophecy *had* to be fulfilled. They would even have gone so far as to say that if there was no star, then there was no Messiah. To convince them that Jesus was the Messiah, the argument runs, Matthew would have had to invent a star if one did not already exist.

Such a view cannot be right. If Matthew had invented the story of the birth of Jesus, he would surely have made it much more coherent and plausible. In particular, there is no reason why he should have made do with a very ordinary star or, in view of all the Old Testament prophecies, why he should have omitted any mention of the phrase "that it should be fulfilled" when discussing the star. It is also true that the Jewish religion, as exemplified in this case by Old Testament teaching, was not in favor of astrology. As an example of this attitude, we find the following statement in Jeremiah 10:2: "Thus saith the Lord, Learn not the way of the heathen, and be not dismayed at the signs of heaven; for the heathen are dismayed at them."

What about non-Jewish attitudes to astrology? The Roman historian Pliny speaks against a simplified form of astrology, but later on in the same passage he seems to credit planets with a powerful influence:

Let us return from these questions to the remaining facts of nature. We have stated that the stars are attached to the world, not assigned to each of us in the way in which the vulgar believe, and dealt out to mortals with a degree of radiance proportional to the lot of each, the brightest star to the rich, the smaller ones to the poor, the dim to those who are worn out; they do not each rise with their own human being, nor indicate by their fall that someone's life is being extinguished. There is no such close alliance between us and the sky that the radiance of the stars there also shares our fate of mortality. When the stars are believed to fall, what happens is that owing to their being overfed with a draught of liquid they give back the surplus with a fiery flash, just as with us also we see this occur with a stream of oil when lamps are lit. But the heavenly bodies have a nature that is eternal—they interweave the world and are blended with its weft; yet their potency has a powerful influence on the earth, indeed it is owing to the effect that they produce and to their brilliance and magnitude that it has been possible for them to become known with such a degree of precision.

We can now see that even though certain people in biblical times dismissed astrology, the common man—Jeremiah's heathen, Pliny's vulgar—did regard the subject as one of interest and importance. The appearance of a star to herald the birth of the Messiah would have been thought of as perfectly normal by the people of the time.

In conclusion, the rival explanations of the star of Bethlehem are these:

(1) It was an actual physical object, explicable by scientific law.

(2) It was a miracle, an invention of God for his own specific purposes.

(3) It was a literary invention, a midrash, the author of Matthew making up the appearance of the star to

convince his Jewish-Christian audience that Jesus was the true Messiah.

I am convinced that the first of these three explanations is the correct one. The second is theologically weak because it requires a miracle when none was needed. Of course we cannot say that a miracle did not happen, only that it was not needed, as a perfectly natural phenomenon occurred that fits in with all the information given in the source books. The third explanation, in terms of midrash, is also unacceptable. Far from being just a figment of Matthew's imagination or an invention to tie in with old legends and an embellishment to make the birth of Jesus seemingly more important, Matthew's nativity reads like a simple tale well told. It has the ring of truth. In particular, the simplicity of the star, its obvious ordinariness, shows that it cannot be merely a figment of a fertile imagination.

Epilogue

Our conclusion is that the explanation of the star of Bethlehem lies in a tangible physical phenomenon. It is true that Matthew's gospel, the only book in the Bible that records the star, was aimed at a Jewish audience and that the author frequently cited passages from the Old Testament to prove points to his readers. Matthew therefore probably felt that the star fulfilled the Balaam prophecy of Numbers 24:17. This fact, however, is neutral. Any star or celestial happening around the time of the birth of Jesus would fulfill the prophecy, but this does not of itself mean that the star was an invention.

Could the star be regarded as a miracle, especially since it had the untypical attributes of "going before" the Magi and "standing over" the place? The miracle stories in the gospels probably all reflect the idea that the last days had arrived and that this time was characterized by miracles. Perhaps the star was a miraculous herald, a sign marking the passage of one age and the dawn of another. It is true, of course, that an astronomical event which we can now explain could easily have been a mystery to the people of those times and could have appeared to them as miraculous. But this consideration is also neutral. Even if Matthew thought a star was miraculous, and there is no indication that he did, there is nothing stopping us today, with our present knowledge, from realizing that it was a perfectly normal astronomical happening.

The physical occurrence that made up the star of

Bethlehem was the series of conjunctions, the apparent coming together in the sky and accompanying risings and settings, of the major planets Jupiter and Saturn. This is not a new conclusion, in fact it can be dated back over seven hundred years, but the movements of Saturn and Jupiter in Pisces fit the large majority of the facts. The Piscean conjunction is rare enough to have been considered unusual. This explanation also has the advantage that the Magi did not have to go continually across the desert for every nova, comet or fireball that happened to appear. It was possible to predict the conjunction, and Babylonian magi had done just that, as the cuneiform tablets testify. The phenomenon had an inherent astrological message which equated it directly with "his star" (Matthew 2:2). No comet, nova, fixed star, fireball or whatever could justify this appellation. It was long-lasting, long enough to be seen when the Magi were in their own country, while they were on the journey and on the final leg from Jerusalem to Bethlehem. Historically it occurred at the right time, in 7 BC. And finally, even though it was an extremely significant event to a trained astrologer, in reality it consisted of two perfectly normal planets moving as usual along their ordained celestial paths. This is why Herod and the people of Jerusalem could easily miss its significance.

Does knowing what the star was and when it occurred lead us to a more exact knowledge of the birthday of Christ? It is highly probable that Jesus was born in 7 BC. The month in the year is less certain but the majority of the indications guide us to August or September. The choice of a specific day is really stretching the evidence too much, but if one day has to be selected I think we would be safest with the day that the Magi probably chose, the day of the acronychal rising. This means that Jesus was born on the evening of Tuesday 15 September 7 BC.

Appendix 1

The months of the Hebrew year

1	Nisan	March/April
2	Iyyar	April/May
3	Sivan	May/June
4	Tammuz	June/July
5	Ab	July/Aug.
6	Elul	Aug./Sept.
7	Tishri	Sept./Oct.
8	Hesvan	Oct./Nov.
9	Kislev	Nov./Dec.
10	Tebeth	Dec./Jan.
11	Shebat	Jan./Feb.
12	Adar	Feb./March

The Jewish month is strictly lunar and starts when the first sickle of the new Moon has been observed. The mean time between one new Moon and the next is 29.530588 days and the first sickle becomes visible in the evening twilight glow about twenty-four to thirty hours after the astronomical new Moon. The Jewish month was thus either twenty-nine or thirty days long. The Jewish year was usually twelve months long, i.e. 355 days long. As this is eleven days shorter than the solar year of 365.25 days that we use nowadays, things would soon get out of step if the 355-day year were stuck to rigidly. To get over this problem an extra month of thirty days was added every three years or so. This thirteenth month was known as Ve Adar or Adar II. This prevented Nisan 1 falling too early. The intercalation of the extra month depended on the observation of the equinox, the date on which day and night both equal twelve hours. (In the first half of our year this usually occurs around March 21 and is the first day of spring.) Also the crops and the sacrificial animals were inspected. For example Rabbi Simeon ben Gamaliel wrote to a colleague about AD 50: "We beg to inform you that the doves are still tender and the lambs still young and the grain has not yet ripened. I have considered the matter and thought it advisable to add thirty days to the year."

Appendix 2

Factors affecting the choice of the star of Bethlehem

(1) Noticed by wise men in their own country, which was probably east of Jerusalem.	Matthew 2:1	Behold there came wise men from the east.
(2) Significant in terms of Babylonian astrology.	Matthew 2:2	Where is he that is born King of the Jews, for we have seen his star?
(3) Rose heliacally or acronychally.	Matthew 2:2	in the east, *en te anatolé* "in the first rays of dawn"
(4) Brightness was insignificant, and the star was overlooked by the Jews.	Matthew 2:3	Herod and all Jerusalem were troubled when told by the wise men of the star and the new King.
(5) Possibly appeared twice, once when the wise men were in their own country and again when they were in Jerusalem.	Matthew 2:10	"they rejoiced with exceeding great joy," on seeing the star again.

(6) Went before them as they journeyed south between Jerusalem and Bethlehem.	Matthew 2:9	"the star, which they saw in the east, went before them." As this journey is only about six miles the star must move relatively quickly across the celestial sphere.
(7) Was in the zenith at Bethlehem	Matthew 2:9	"It came and stood over." It must have had a declination greater than 31.8°, the geographic latitude of Bethlehem.
(8) Appeared during the reign of Herod the Great	Matthew 2:1, 3, 7, 12, 13, 15 etc.	Herod probably died in December 5 BC or between March and 11 April 4 BC.
(9) The first appearance possibly occurred 13 months before the birth of Christ.	Matthew 2:7, 16	Herod inquired of them diligently what time the star appeared . . . and he slew all the children from two years old and under.
	Midrashim	"In the fifth year the star shall shine forth from the east and this is the star of the Messiah . . . and at the close of the seventh the Messiah is to be expected."

(10) Christ was born after the taxation decree issued by Caesar Augustus	Luke 2:1	Thought to have occurred in 8 BC.
(11) First appearance occurred between 10 and early 4 BC.		
(12) Bright (contradicting fact 4)	Protovangelium of James 21:2 Epistle to the Ephesians, 19	''an undescribably great star shone among these stars and dimmed them, so that they no longer shone.'' ''its light was beyond description and its newness caused astonishment.''

Bibliography

Chapter 1: The sacred star

A. H. McNEILE, *The Gospel according to St. Matthew*, Macmillan, London, 1915, p. 15.

W. F. ALBRIGHT and C. S. MANN, The Anchor Bible, *Matthew*, Doubleday, New York, 1971.

E. W. MAUNDER, *The Astronomy of the Bible*, T. Sealey Clark, London, 1908.

ARISTOTLE, *Generation of Animals*, V, 1, translated by A. L. Peck, Heinemann, London.

The Observer, letter page, 18 and 25 November 1973.

HEBER D. CURTIS, "On the limits of unaided vision," *Lick Observatory Bulletin*, No. 38, 2901.

A. M. HUNTER, *Introducing the New Testament*, SCM Press, London, 1957.

T. W. MANSON, *The Sayings of Jesus*, London, 1949.

RAYMOND E. BROWN, *The Birth of the Messiah: A commentary on the infancy narratives in Matthew and Luke*, Doubleday, New York, and Geoffrey Chapman, London, 1977.

Chapter 2: The great light

E. HENNECKE, *The New Testament Apocrypha*, Vol. 1, Lutterworth, London, 1963.

J. B. LIGHTFOOT, *The Apostolic Fathers* (Revised Texts), Macmillan, London, 1891.

R. M. GRANT, *The Apostolic Fathers*, Vol. 1, Nelson, New York, 1964.

EPHRAEM SYRUS, "The Hymns for the Epiphany," in *The Nicene and Post-Nicene Fathers*, Second Series, Vol.

XIII, The Christian Literature Company, New York, 1898.

HENRY CHADWICK, *Origen: Contra Celsum,* Cambridge University Press, 1953.

Chapter 3: Men from the east

TERTULLIAN, *Adversus Marcion,* III, 13, edited and translated by Ernest Evans, Oxford 1972.

HERODOTUS, *Histories* I, III, LXIII, LXXIII, LXXIX.

STRABO, Book XI, IX, 3.

PHILO, *The Special Laws,* Book III, XVIII.

TACITUS, *Annals,* II, 27-33.

SUETONIUS, *Tiberius,* 36.

JOSEPHUS, *Antiquities,* XX, vii, 2; 142.

CALVIN'S Commentaries, *A Harmony of the Gospels Matthew, Mark and Luke,* The Saint Andrew Press, Edinburgh.

J. C. MARSH-EDWARDS, "The Magi in Tradition and Art," *Irish Ecclesiastical Record,* 85, 1-19, 1956.

C. S. MANN, "Epiphany—Wise Men or Charlatans?" *Theology* 61, 495-500, (1958).

W. K. LOWTHER CLARKE, *Divine Humanity,* SPCK London, 1936.

JUSTIN, *Dialogues,* LXXVIII, 9.

W. D. DAVIES, *The Setting of the Sermon on the Mount,* Cambridge University Press, 1964, pp. 72-82.

J. B. LIGHTFOOT, *The Apostolic Fathers,* Part II, St. Ignatius, St. Polycarp, Macmillan, London, 1889.

H. CHADWICK *Origen: Contra Celsum,* Cambridge University Press 1953.

JOSEPHUS, *War,* VI, v4; 312.

TACITUS, *Histories,* V, 13.

SUETONIUS, *Vespasian,* 4.

Sibylline Oracles, III, lines 784-794.

LACTANTIUS, *Divinae Institiones,* VII, 24.

CONSTANTINE, *Oratio ad Sanctorum coetum,* 19-21.

JEROME, *Epistola,* LIII.

F. W. FARRAR, *The Life of Christ,* Cassell, London, 1896.

CLEMENT OF ALEXANDRIA, *Stromata* I, XV.

EPHRAEM SYRUS, *"Hymn for the feast of the Epiphany,"* *The Nicene and Post-Nicene Fathers*, Second Series, Vol. XIII, Christian Literature Co., New York, 1898.

B. W. BACON, *Studies in Matthew*, Constable, London, 1930.

JACK FINEGAN, *Handbook of Biblical Chronology*, Princeton University Press, New Jersey, 1964.

JUSTIN, *Dialogue with Trypho*, LXXVII, LXXVIII, CII, CIII, CVI.

EPIPHANIUS *Expositio Fidei*, VIII.

DAVID W. HUGHES, "The Star of Bethlehem" *Nature*, 264, 513-517, 1976.

JOSEPHUS, *Antiquities*, XVI, vl, 136-41.

DIO CASSIUS, *Roman History*, LXIII, 1-7.

SUETONIUS, *Nero*, 13.

PLINY, *Natural History*, XXX, VI, 16-17.

CICERO, *De divinatione*, I, 47.

DIOGENES LAERTIUS, II, 45.

SENECA *Epistles*, 58.

Chapter 4: The birthday star

F. GODET, *A Commentary on the Gospel of St. Luke*, Vol. 1, T. T. Clark, Edinburgh, 1870.

ALFRED PLUMMER, *The Gospel according to Luke*, T. T. Clark, Edinburgh, 1913.

JOHN SEYMOUR and MICHAEL W. SEYMOUR, private correspondence and "The Historicity of the Gospels and astronomical events concerning the Birth of Christ," *Quarterly Journal of the Royal Astronomical Society*, 19, 194-197, 1978.

TACITUS, *Annals*, I, II

TERTULLIAN, *Adv. Marc.*, 19.

EMIL SHÜRER, *A History of the Jewish People in the Time of Jesus Christ*, 5 vols, 1896.

F. F. BRUCE, *New Testament History*, Nelson, London, 1969.

E. V. HULSE, *Nature*, 268, 566, 1977.

N. TURNER, *Grammatical Insights into the New Testament*, T. T. Clark, Edinburgh, 1963.

JACK FINEGAN, *Light from the Ancient Past: The Archeological Background of Judaism and Christianity*, 2nd ed., 1959.

OPPOLZER, "Canon of eclipses," 1887.

F. K. GINZEL, *Handbuch der mathematischen und technischen Chronologie*, Vol. II, p. 541.

S. PEROWNE, *The Life and Times of Herod the Great*, Hodder and Stoughton, London, 1956.

ORMOND EDWARDS, *A New Chronology of the Gospels*, Floris Books, London, 1972.

W. E. FILMER, "The Chronology of the reign of Herod the Great," *Journal of Theological Studies*, 17, 283-298, 1966.

TIMOTHY D. BARNES, "The date of Herod's Death," *Journal of Theological Studies*, 19, 204-209, 1968.

BRYANT TUCKERMAN, "Planetary, Lunar and Solar Positions," 601 BC-AD 1, *Memoirs of the American Philosophical Society*, vol. 62, 1962.

JUSTIN MARTYR, *Dialogues*, 78.

ALFRED EDERSHEIM, *The Life and Times of Jesus the Messiah*, Longman Green, London, 1884.

JUSTIN MARTYR, *Dialogue with Trypho*, 88.

ORIGEN, Commentary on Matthew, Frag. 23, in *Die griechischen christlichen Schrifsteller der ersten Jahrhunderte*, vol. 41, p. 25, ed. Erich Klastermann.

EUSEBIUS, *Quaestiones ad Stephanum* XVI, 2, in Patrologiae cursus completus, Series graeca, ed. Migne, vol. 22, column 934.

A. WALKER, *Apocryphal Gospels, Acts and Revelations*, T. T. Clark, Edinburgh, 1890.

JAMES MACKINNON, *The Historic Jesus*, Longman Green, London, 1931.

JELLINEK, *Beth ha-Midrash*, 6 vols. Leipzig and Vienna, 1853-1878.

Holy Quran, translated by Abdulla Yusuf Ali, published by the Muslim World League, 1965.

Babylonian Talmud, Sanhedrin 25 b.

CLEMENT OF ALEXANDRIA, *Stromata,* I, 21, 145-146.

EPIPHANIUS, *Panarion,* LI.

JOHN ADDEY, "The Astrology of the Birth of Christ," *The Astrological Journal,* 1959.

G. MACKINLAY, *The Magi, How they recognised Christ's Star,* Hodder and Stoughton, London, 1897.

Chapter 5: The feast of the star

W. WARDE FOWLER, *The Roman Festivals,* Macmillan, London, 1908.

JOSEF A. JUNGMANN, SJ, *The Early Liturgy to the Time of Gregory the Great,* University of Notre Dame Press, Indiana, and Darton, Longman and Todd, London, 1959.

Chapter 6: Star or planet?

R. R. NEWTON, *Mediaeval Chronicles and the Rotation of the Earth,* Johns Hopkins University Press, Baltimore and London, 1972, p. 691.

BRYANT TUCKERMAN, "Planetary, Lunar and Solar Positions, AD 2 to AD 1649 at five and ten day intervals," *Memoirs of the American Philosophical Society,* vol. 59, 1964.

WERNER KELLER, *The Bible as History,* Hodder and Stoughton, London, 1956.

JOHANNES KEPLER, *De Anno Natali Christi,* 1614, reprinted in *Johannes Kepler, Gesammelt Werke,* vol. V, pp. 5-126, Munich, 1953.

C. PRITCHARD, *Memoirs of the Royal Astronomical Society,* Vol. 25, pp. 119-124, 1856.

RONALD A. ORITI, "The Star of Bethlehem," *Griffith Observer,* December 1975, vol. 39, p. 99

ROBERT RODMAN, "A Linguistic Note on the Christmas Star," *Griffith Observer,* December 1976, vol. 40, p. 8.

FRANZ BÖLL, *Aus der Offenbarung Johannis,* 1914.

OSWALD GERHARDT, "Der Stern des Messias," 1922.

P. I. SCHAUMBERGER, "Textus cuneiformis de stella Magorum?" *Biblica,* vol. 6, pp. 444-449, 1925.

M. TESTUZ, *Papyrus Bodmer V*, Bibliotheca Bodmeriana, Cologny-Genève, 1958.

Chapter 7: Comets and novae

RALPH S. BATES, "Second Astronomer Royal, Edmund Halley," *Sky and Telescope*, March 1942.

HO PENG YOKE, "Ancient and Medieval Observations of Comets and Novae in Chinese Sources," *Vistas in Astronomy*, 5, 127-225, 1962.

JOHN WILLIAMS, *Observations of Comets from 611 BC to AD 1640 Extracted from the Chinese Annals*, 1871, London.

NIKOLAUS B. RICHTER, *The Nature of Comets*, Methuen, London, 1963, p. 130.

ORIGEN, *Contra Celsum*, I, 58, translated and edited by Henry Chadwick, Cambridge University Press, 1953.

PAUL and LESLEY MURDIN, *The New Astronomy*, Reference International, London, 1978.

HSI TSÊ-TSUNG, "A New Catalog of Ancient Novae," *Smithsonian Contributions to Astrophysics*, 3, 109-130, 1958.

K. LUNDMARK, *Publications of the Astronomical Society of the Pacific*, 33, 225, 1921.

DAVID H. CLARK, JOHN H. PARKINSON and F. RICHARD STEPHENSON, "An Astronomical Re-Appraisal of the Star of Bethlehem—A Nova in 5 BC" *Quarterly Journal of the Royal Astronomical Society*, 18, 443, 1977.

DAVID H. CLARK and F. RICHARD STEPHENSON, *The Historical Supernovae*, Pergamon Press, Oxford, 1977.

CHRISTOPHER CULLEN, "The Star of Bethlehem: some confusion in a recent discussion of Biblical and Far Eastern evidence," *Quarterly Journal of the Royal Astronomical Society*, 20, 153, 1979.

HO PENG YOKE, *The Astronomical Chapters of the Chin Shu*, Moulton, Paris, 1966.

HAN-SHU, collated and punctuated edition, Chung-hua Schu-chii, Peking, 1962.

C. PAYNE-GAPOSCHKIN, *Galactic Novae*, John Wiley, New York, 1957.

GRANVILLE, *Sceptsis Scientific*, ed. J. Owen, 1885, chapter XX, p. 150.

J. F. FOUCQUET, *Tabula Chronologica Historiae Sinicae*, Rome, 1729.

H. SLOANE, "On Foucquet 1729," *Philosophical Transcriptions of the Royal Society*, 36, 397-424, 1736.

F. MUNTER, *Der Stern der Weisen*, Copenhagen, 1827.

K. LUNDMARK, "The Messianic Ideas and their astronomical background," *Actes du VIIIe Congrès International des Sciences*, Jerusalem, 436-439, 1953.

H. W. MONTEFIORE, "Josephus and the New Testament," *Novum Testamentum*, 4, 130-160, 1960.

DAVID W. HUGHES, "The Star of Bethlehem," *Nature*, 264, 513-517, 1976.

A. J. MOREHOUSE, "The Christmas Star as a supernova in Aquila," *Journal of the Royal Astronomical Society of Canada*, 72, 65, 1978.

B. V. KUKARKIN, P. N. KHOLOPOV, Yu. P. PSKOVSKY, Yu. N. EFREMOV, N. P. KUHARKINA, N. E. KUROCHKIN, B G. I. MEDVEDEVA, N. B. PEROVA, V. P. FEDOROVICH, M. S. FROLOV, *General Catalogue of Variable Stars* (third edition), Astron. Council of the Academy of Sciences of the USSR, Moscow, 1969-71.

T. KIANG, *Nature*, 223, 599, 1969.

G. MICHANOWSKY, quoted in *Scientific American*, 235, 66, 1976.

Chapter 8: Celestial phenomena

MONTAGUE B. RICHARDSON, *The Star of Biet Lahm*, 1978.

C. ST. J. H. DANIEL, "The Star of Bethlehem," *Planitarium*, 1, 38-41, 1967.

SUSUMU IMOTO and ICHIRO HASEGAWA, "Historical Records of Meteor Showers in China, Korea and Japan, *Smithsonian Contributions to Astrophysics*, 2, 131-144, 1958.

MICHAEL KAMIENSKI, *Stella Magorum*, Cracow, 1946.

ST. MARIA DE AGREDA, *The Holy Town, or the life of the Blessed Virgin Mary in connection with the Life of Our*

Savior Jesus Christ, written according to the revelation received by Maria de Agreda, Abbess of the Order of St. Francis, Anno 1655.

Chapter 9: The sign in the sky

JOHN ADDEY, "The Astrology of the Birth of Christ," *The Astrological Journal,* 1959.

The Urantia Book, Urantia Foundation, Chicago, 1957.

ROY A. ROSENBERG, "The star of the Messiah reconsidered," *Biblica,* 53, 105-109, 1972.

H. LEWY, "The Babylonian Background of the Kay Kaus Legend," *Archiv Orientalni,* 17, pt 2, 62, 1949.

F. M. CROSS, "Yahweh and the God of the Patriarchs," *Harvard Theological Review,* 55, 250, 1960.

Chapter 10: Planets in conjunction

K. FERRARI D'OCCHIEPPO, *Der Stern der Weisen-Geschichte oder Legende,* Wien, 2nd ed., 1977.

K. FERRARI D'OCCHIEPPO, "The Star of Bethlehem," *Quarterly Journal of the Royal Astronomical Society,* 19, 517, 1978.

A. J. SACHS, *Late Babylonian Astronomical and Related Texts,* Providence R. I., 1955.

Chapter 11: Miracle, myth or fact?

H. J. RICHARDS, "The three Kings," *Scripture,* 8, 23-38, 1956.

J. C. MARSH-EDWARDS, "The Magi in Tradition and Art," *Irish Ecclesiastical Record,* 85, 1-19, 1956.

VIRGIL, *Aeneid,* II, 692-694.

JOSEPHUS, *Jewish War,* VI, 288.

TACITUS, *Histories,* V, 13.

SUETONIUS, *Nero,* XXXVI.

TACITUS, Annals, XIV, 22.

E. NESTLE, *Zeitschrift für die Neutestamentliche Wissenschaft,* VIII, pp. 73 and 241, 1907.

PLINY, *Natural History,* II, IV, 28.

Epilogue

R. M. GRANT, *Miracle and Natural Law in Graeco-Roman and Early Christian Thought,* North Holland Pub. Co., 1952.

Glossary

Acronychal rising An outer planet rises acronychally when it is at opposition, on the opposite side of the Earth to the Sun. It rises in the east as the Sun sets in the west and remains in the sky all night, being due south about midnight.

Altitude In astronomy this is defined as being the angle that the direction of a celestial object makes with the horizontal (horizon) plane.

Angular measure A complete circle is divided into 360 degrees (°). The degree contains 60 minutes (′) each of which contains 60 seconds (″).

Aphelion The point at which a body orbiting the Sun in an elliptical orbit is at its greatest distance from the Sun.

Astronomical Unit A unit of distance defined to be the average distance between the Earth and the Sun. It is equal to 149,600,000 km/92,960,000 miles.

Brightness The energy received from a celestial object (at, for example, the Earth's surface) per unit area of the detector, per unit time.

Celestial sphere An imaginary sphere of large radius centered on the Earth and on which the stars are considered to be fixed for the purposes of position measurement. This sphere appears to rotate around the Earth once a day (in actuality the sphere is stationary and it is the Earth that rotates).

It spins from east to west at a rate of 15 degrees per hour about an axis joining north and south celestial poles. These are the points at which the projected spin axis of the Earth intersects the sphere. The celestial equator is the circle around the sphere obtained by allowing the plane of the Earth's equator to intersect the sphere.

Colure A colure is a longitude circle on the celestial sphere. These are perpendicular to the ecliptic.

Conjunction A coming together of planets on the celestial sphere. It can be defined as the time when the planets have the same celestial longitude.

Constellation A grouping of stars and the area of the celestial sphere associated with it.

Declination (dec) The angle between the direction of a star and the plane of the celestial equator. It is positive when the body is north of the equator and negative when it is south. Declination is equivalent to latitude on the Earth's globe.

Direct motion When the apparent motion of a planet in the sky as seen from Earth is from west to east it is said to be direct.

Ecliptic The path on the celestial sphere which the Sun traces out among the stars. It is also defined as the plane of the Earth's orbit. The orbits of the planets are only slightly inclined to this plane so they will always be found in the sky not far away from the ecliptic path.

Elongation The angle between the line joining a planet to the Earth and the line joining the Earth to the Sun.

Evening star When a planet is located to the east of the Sun in the sky it has an eastern elongation and, since it sets after the Sun, it is referred to as an evening star.

First point of Aries This is the point on the celestial sphere at which the Sun moves from south to north of the celestial equator. It is also known as the vernal equinox and is one of the intersection points between the ecliptic and the celestial equator.

Heliacal rising The planet has just passed superior conjunction. The planet is thus on the right hand side (west) of the Sun, rises just before the Sun and its light soon becomes swamped in the light of the dawn sky.

Inferior conjunction This can only apply to the planets Mercury and Venus, which are closer to the Sun than Earth is. They are at inferior conjunction when they are aligned with the Earth-Sun line and are between the Earth and Sun. At this point the planet is closest to the Earth.

Light year The distance that light travels in one year: 9,460,000,000,000 km.

Local time The time system for an observer in which the Sun is due south at noon.

Magnitude A measure of the brightness of a celestial body. Hipparchus in the second century BC classified the one thousand brightest stars according to their "importance." There were six classes, the brightest stars being of first importance (or first magnitude), while the faintest star normally visible to the unaided eye on a clear dark night was of sixth importance (sixth magnitude). Nowadays a difference of five magnitude is defined as being equivalent to a change in brightness by a factor of one hundred (a difference of one magnitude is equivalent to a brightness ratio of 2.512). The magnitude of an object decreases in value as that object gets brighter. For example, the bright stars at night are about + 1 in magnitude, Jupiter at its brightest is about −4, while the full Moon is −12.

Massing A planetary massing occurs when three or more planets appear to come close together on the celestial sphere.

Morning star When a planet or star is on the west (right hand) side of the Sun it has a western elongation and it rises before the Sun and is referred to as a morning star.

Opposition The point on the orbit of an outer planet at which it is in line with the Earth-Sun line and is on the same side of the Sun as the Earth. The planet is usually at its brightest at this point and crosses the southern meridian around midnight.

Perihelion The point at which a body orbiting the Sun in an elliptical orbit is nearest to the Sun.

Retrograde motion The apparent motion of a planet is retrograde when it appears from Earth to move from east to west in the sky.

Right Ascension (RA) The celestial sphere may be divided up into a coordinate system similar to that of the Earth's. In this system the right ascension is the angle, measured eastward, between the plane containing the celestial poles and the First point of Aries and the plane containing the celestial poles and the object in question. Right ascension is equivalent to longitude on the Earth's globe.

Superior conjunction This occurs when a planet is aligned with the Sun and the Earth and is on the opposite side of the Sun to the Earth, from which it appears to be behind the Sun.

Zenith The point on the celestial sphere which is directly above the observer.

Zodiac A circular band on the celestial sphere centered on the ecliptic and extending to about 9 degrees on either side. The motions of the visible planets, the Sun and the Moon take place in this band. It is divided into 12 constellation zones each 30 degrees long. Moving eastward from the first point of Aries the signs are Aries the Ram, Taurus the Bull, Gemini the Twins, Cancer the Crab, Leo the Lion, Virgo the Virgin, Libra the Scales, Scorpio the Scorpion, Sagittarius the Archer, Capricorn the Goat, Aquarius the Water Bearer and Pisces the Fishes.

Index

Pocket Bibles and
inspirational writing to carry
with you always—comforting you
through troubled times,
bringing you

JOY and STRENGTH.

_____82385	ART OF CHRISTIAN MEDITATION, David Ray	$1.95
_____81624	BIBLE THERAPY, E. C. Wittman & C. R. Bollman	$2.50
_____83597	GOOD NEWS FOR MODERN MAN: The New Testament in Today's English Version. American Bible Society	$2.95
_____41653	GO OUT IN JOY!, Nina Herrmann	$2.50
_____81636	HE WALKS WITH ME, David Graham	$1.75
_____81048	I'M OUT TO CHANGE MY WORLD, Ann Kiemel	$1.50
_____82626	LET THE HAMMER DOWN, Jerry Clower	$1.95
_____41016	PLEASE LOVE ME, Keith Miller	$2.75
_____48784	POCKET AQUINAS, V. Bourke, Ed.	$1.95
_____41889	SACRED SHROUD, Thomas Humber	$2.50